Praise for
THE END OF SANITY

"Martin Gross's talent for diagnosing what ails us
has never been put to better use than in *The End of Sanity*.
An incredibly readable account of the incredible
with superb documentation from a seasoned, careful author."
—*Washington Times*

"Gross goes beyond stringing together anecdotes
and tries to assemble a systematic theory
about what the New Establishment is and what it wants.
Its power, he says, 'is the central cause of our unease.'"
—*Orange County Register*

"In his fine new book, Mr. Gross worries about national cohesion...
A New Establishment, he tells us—journalists, college
administrators, bureaucrats, clergy, judges, artists, etc.—
seeks to remake American culture in its own image.
The End of Sanity is part of a larger backlash.
The New Establishment has got to go."
—*Dallas Morning News*

"We're in this goofy fix because of the prescriptive intolerances
of the New Establishment...with good sense being replaced
by experimental dogmas. Sounds as if the book
would make a good Christmas present."
—*Chicago Sun-Times*

"Martin Gross is a writer of exceptional insight."
—Nelson DeMille, bestselling author of *The Gold Coast*

"One of the best [books] I have ever read,
and the most provocative in the last ten years...
Everything you had hazy notions about
is now made crystal clear...
This book is not for the faint-hearted.
You won't like what this brilliant author has to tell us,
because it might give you a headache.
Thinking usually does."
—*Muskagon* (Mi.) *Chronicle*

THE END OF SANITY

SOCIAL AND CULTURAL MADNESS IN AMERICA

MARTIN L. GROSS

AVON BOOKS ⬥ NEW YORK

AVON BOOKS, INC.
1350 Avenue of the Americas
New York, New York 10019

Copyright © 1997 by Martin L. Gross
Published by arrangement with the author
Visit our website at **http://www.AvonBooks.com**
ISBN: 0-380-78783-0

Library of Congress Cataloging in Publication Data:

Gross, Martin L. (Martin Louis)
   The end of sanity : social and cultural madness in America / Martin L. Gross.
     p.   cm.
   Includes bibliographical references and index.
1. Social problems—United States. 2. United States—Social conditions—1980-
3. United States—Moral conditions. 4. Social values—United States. I. Title.
HN59.2.G75   1997   97-18420
361.1'0973—dc21   CIP

First Avon Books Trade Paperback Printing: December 1998
First Avon Books Hardcover Printing: November 1997

AVON TRADEMARK REG. U.S. PAT. OFF. AND IN OTHER COUNTRIES, MARCA REGISTRADA, HECHO EN U.S.A.

Printed in the U.S.A.

OPM 10 9 8 7 6 5 4 3 2 1

To my wife, Anita

To Thomas Jefferson,
from whom all liberty springs

ACKNOWLEDGMENTS

To my editor, Stephen S. Power; to my publisher, Lou Aronica; and to my agent, John Hawkins, for their help in disseminating this message to the American public.

Those whom the Gods wish to destroy they first make mad.
—Euripides

CONTENTS

PROLOGUE   1

CHAPTER ONE   **THE NEW ESTABLISHMENT**
                   The Spread of Contemporary Madness   **4**

CHAPTER TWO   **GODS OF THE NEW**
                   ESTABLISHMENT
                   The Trinity of Freud, Marx, and a
                   Distortion of Jesus   **39**

CHAPTER THREE   **AMERICAN WOMEN**
                   Darlings of the New Establishment   **68**

CHAPTER FOUR   **COLLEGES IN THE NEW**
                   ESTABLISHMENT
                   Extraordinary Ignorance, PC, and the
                   New McCarthyism   **107**

CHAPTER FIVE   **DIVERSITY, MULTICULTURALISM,**
                   BILINGUALISM, AND OTHER MYTHS
                   The Threat to American Culture   **144**

CHAPTER SIX   **SEXUAL HARASSMENT**
                   Assault, Vulgarity, or Romance?   **174**

CONTENTS

CHAPTER SEVEN   **AFFIRMATIVE ACTION:**
THE NEW RACISM AND SEXISM
Are You One of the Preferred?   212

CHAPTER EIGHT   **THE NEW IMMIGRATION**
The Plot Against the Europeans   258

CHAPTER NINE   **OUR IRRESPONSIBLE,**
IRREPRESSIBLE COURTS
The Enforcement Wing of the
New Establishment   281

CHAPTER TEN   **DOGMA IN THE DOMINANT**
CULTURE
The Selling of the New Society   305

ENDNOTES   315

INDEX   329

ABOUT THE AUTHOR   337

PROLOGUE

SINCE THE PUBLICATION OF *THE GOVERNMENT Racket: Washington Waste from A to Z* in 1992, I have written several books detailing the failure of government, an *external* weakness in the American civilization.

But another phenomenon—a social and cultural madness that distorts virtually everything we do or contemplate—is ravaging us *internally*. It has shaped a potent attack on the nation's mind and morale that is proving even more debilitating than bad government.

This new attack on America is being mounted by hidden forces that seek to undermine the traditional strengths that built this society into the most progressive and open democracy in history.

The attack comes in various forms, but it is united within a single rubric, the New Establishment, which is defined here for the first time and which has woven itself into the very fiber of the nation, weakening it as never before. The threat of Orwellian societal totalitarianism, which failed to fully materialize in 1984, is now coming to fruition, just a dozen or so years off the prophet's mark.

1

The most disturbing aspect of this new force is that it exploits America's desire to conform, an insidious way in which our culture suffers damage. In 1835, the French seer Alexis de Tocqueville, who was an admirer of American democracy, warned us of the danger of fashionable crusades that may not be rational, adding that most civilizations that die are eroded from within.

Today, we are living through such a form of collective insanity that daily gains in power despite its punishing effect on everything it touches, including the national psyche.

In our history, we have suffered several such onslaughts of irrationality—the thought control of the early Massachusetts Bay Colony, the Alien and Sedition Acts of the 1790s, the Know-Nothing crusades of the nineteenth century, the Prohibition folly of the 1920s, the McCarthy smear campaigns of the 1950s.

We now face still another anti-intellectual movement, one that threatens grave danger to our society. Worse yet, it masquerades, as do most destructive forces, from the Spanish Inquisition onward, as a positive development.

It is reminiscent of Communist China's Cultural Revolution, with its brainwashing and sensitivity training for nonconformists. In America today, a similar movement—a form of *secular theocracy*—is in full swing.

Not only is its influence destructive, but it has taken control of virtually all our major institutions, whether schools and colleges, churches, the courts, the military, law and government, the arts, foundations, and even relations between the races and sexes, which it has shockingly inflamed.

Like many tyrannies, it seeks to impose its supposed "beneficence" (more likely, vainglory) through intimidation and false dogmas that harm the majority of the citizens. Not the least of these is the Machiavellian "political correctness," which has invaded our educational and cultural worlds.

Rather than advance "fairness" and "equality" as claimed, these new forces have set back that goal a generation by producing a divided and divisive nation, a rare failure of onetime American civic genius.

By conforming to someone else's definition of proper speech, attitudes, thought, and behavior, we are both losing our freedom and violating common justice, attributes that had distinguished America from the once-dogmatic states of Europe and Asia. We gave these blessings to the world, only now to find ourselves losing them at home.

The first casualty has been truth; the second may well be Western civilization itself. Thus this book is intended as a wake-up call to Americans and all those inevitably involved.

My goal is to investigate social and cultural madness in virtually every field and to provide rational remedies. Only then can we be free of the aggressive movement that has transformed the traditional institutions designed for our stability into the very instruments that threaten us.

To that task, in the hope of restoring reason to our injured public lives, this book is dedicated.

CHAPTER ONE

THE NEW ESTABLISHMENT

The Spread of Contemporary Madness

THE MUSEUM SHOW WAS EXTRAORDINARY. AS YOU paid the $6 entrance fee at the door, you received a pin that you were expected to wear. Like fortune cookies, there were several different messages, but all applied to the "art" spread out before you.

One of these pins read: I CAN'T IMAGINE EVER WANTING TO BE WHITE.

Many of the exhibits were just as combative, seemingly designed to put the majority of Americans in their place. The catalogue, which costs an impressive $40, explains: "Whiteness is a signifier of power."

By wearing the button, the museum philosophized, white people, especially men, could "absolve themselves of some of the privileges of cultural imperialism."

There were jars filled with jigsaw puzzle pieces, each with the face of a nonwhite, demonstrating subjugation. Another exhibit of videotapes of movies had messages disparaging you-know-who. One had this label: "Have you ever noticed that the villain is always a Puerto Rican?"

The exhibit tried to be all-inclusive. One female artist's work was labeled: "The art world can suck my proverbial . . ." This, the catalog insists, "wrenches painting away from its white male domain." In one room devoted to male greed, giant letters ran around the walls, declaiming: "In the rich man's house, the only place to spit is in his face."

Of course, this exhibit must have been housed way-off Midtown Manhattan, perhaps near old Hell's Kitchen on Eleventh Avenue, in the uncharted areas where civilization had not fully deposited its artistic balm.

Guess again. The exhibit was ensconced in the heart of the Establishment—at the prestigious Whitney Museum of American Art on Madison Avenue at Seventy-fifth Street. It was, in fact, one of its much-publicized "Biennial" displays of what Americans are creating. Showcased every two years in the Marcel Breuer modern stone monument, it was paid for by a foundation endowed by the wealthy—whose visages are now to be spat upon by those they had subsidized.

Surely, a singular aberration in traditional America.

Hardly. In every precinct of life circa the closing years of the twentieth century, institutions once considered the pillars of our society are now metamorphosing into something quite different, and apparently designed to commit mayhem—on us.

But this is "art" and therefore unique and excusable, one might say. Surely, other distinguished institutions in America avoid such swampy goals. Take the *military,* for instance. It must be exempt from contemporary madness. No?

Don't be naïve. The rush to adopt fashionable thought is as irresistible in the Pentagon as on Madison Avenue.

The result is that the newest military behavior in the mixing of the sexes is almost as hair-raising as combat, whether in basic training, the military academies, or below the decks of aircraft carriers. This behavior has led to almost weekly scandals of sexual harassment involving everyone from male drill sergeants to female trainees to the highest echelons of generals and admirals.

Much of the Pentagon's new reasoning is not racial or ethnic, but based on the simple concept that men and women are not only the same, but *interchangeable.*

When the USS *Eisenhower,* a nuclear aircraft carrier, left on combat duty in the Adriatic to patrol the no-fly zone over Bosnia, its complement of 4,919 sailors included 367 females ready for action, an unprecedented situation in American naval history.

Fraternization was *verboten,* but nature has a way of outwitting bureaucrats. To quiet the fears of spouses who hoped their mates would husband their libidos until they came home, the Navy held special "support" seminars.

But just to be sure, a gynecologist was sent aboard for the six-month tour. It turned out he was needed. Twenty-four sailors were found to be pregnant just before the *Ike* sailed, and fifteen more with child were removed from the ship during the cruise. Two women claimed they had been sexually harassed aboard the carrier. Despite the no-fraternizing rules, half a dozen couples told the captain they had found time to rub more than noses and were in love.

A male and female sailor, each married to someone else on shore, had their acrobatic fornications in the ship's hold videotaped, then proudly showed it to fellow sailors, most of whom were frustrated that they had been left out of the naval camaraderie.

The official word from intimidated top Navy officers was that the voyage was a success. But one candid lieutenant leaked the real dirt: "We have taken the focus away from being a potent fighting ship and made the *Ike* a showboat."

Another ship, carrying Army personnel back to the States after Desert Storm, was dubbed "The Love Boat" as one-tenth of all female personnel were returning pregnant.

The Army, too, has a new eccentric sexual code. While attention has been focused on attempts to integrate homosexuals with heterosexuals, the Army had moved quietly toward integrating men and women—under the very same roof, or tent. Adopting that same strange theory that the sexes are quite alike, they first used Haiti as the setting for a large-scale experiment that threatens to be permanent.

Of 6,000 American troops who had been stationed in that nation, there were 400 women who *did not* sleep in separate barracks, but mixed freely all night with the men, often in small, intimate tents with no privacy. Major Cindy Sito, a female Army spokesman in Port-au-Prince, explained the revolutionary new bedding-down principle, which is euphemistically called "unit integrity," by stating: "In my opinion, it's easier to run a unit if you're able to reach out and touch everybody." One would think so. In Desert Storm, a woman Army sergeant told a Presidential Commission that male and female soldiers on guard duty necked and cuddled to keep each other warm, and officers of both sexes had affairs with enlisted personnel, once a Pentagon no-no.

As we shall see, the over-cozy fraternization between male and female soldiers and sailors right in their quarters has been facilitated by the Pentagon, putting a contemporary twist on an old admonishment to "make love, not war."

(It would be cruel in wartime for male combat troops to see *others* with a sex partner while they are left out in the proverbial cold. Fairness insists there should be one combat female for each male soldier to carry the current policy to its logical *ad absurdum*.)

The Pentagon's frustration that men and women are not *exactly* the same has even led to a scientific attempt to repair God's mistake. A new program has been developed to make women as strong as men. Hiring an Olympic decathlete, the Army has funded what they call "Effects of a Specifically Designed Physical Conditioning Program on the Load Carriage and Lifting Performance of Female Soldiers."

The goal? To enhance the upper body strength of women,

perhaps so that they can engage in hand-to-hand combat against male North Koreans or other enemy regulars, freeing men for less masculine duties.

Blatantly irrational behavior is rapidly being established as the norm in almost every area of human endeavor, from the military to the kindergarten class to the university to our churches to office settings. Disorder is becoming omnipresent as tradition and good sense are assigned to the ideological dump heap while new theories and practices, some more ludicrous than others, plague our public life.

"The country is going crazy" is the curt, angry phrase heard in supermarkets, barber shops, and living rooms from Bangor to Burbank.

People are confused and distressed, often feeling uncomfortable in their own nation. Indigenous American optimism has been dampened, and it's fair to state that we are in the midst of a national cultural instability much greater than that we experienced during the Cold War. If Alexis de Tocqueville were to return today, he might not repeat his prophecy of a magnificent American tomorrow.

"What the hell is going on?" perturbed Americans ask.

On the *surface,* life in America seems much the same as always. We go to work, love and argue in our families, struggle to pay our bills and taxes. It may not be the halcyon days of the 1950s, but we're not in a Depression and we are at peace.

So what's wrong?

What's wrong is that *underneath* the nation is roiling. There seem to be new customs, new rules, new anti-intellectual theories regularly foisted on us from every direction, creating little we agree with or even understand. Supposedly designed to solve problems, they have instead exacerbated the situation in every area from education to the law.

Americans are not sure what, but they know that *something* without a name is undermining the nation, turning the mind

8

mushy when it comes to separating truth from falsehood and right from wrong. And they don't like it.

From out of the media blue come daily flashes of absurd and outrageous stories. Some are ludicrous, others disturbing, still others tragically humorous. But all are threatening to our collective sanity. No segment of American life is spared as the good sense of the nation seems to have gone topsy-turvy, with reality turned upside down.

• At Antioch College in Ohio, a "progressive" institution that enjoys nude intergender showers, young men having sex with coeds must not only receive a passionate grunt from their partners, but clearly enunciated verbal permission at each step of the process, from kissing, to petting, to final fornication. (All clearly spelled out in a printed college directive!) Pious promiscuity? Despite the rules, one senior commented: "They're still doing it like rabbits."

• A mugger who attacked an elderly man in a New York subway was shot by a policeman when the criminal tried to escape. Recovered from his wound, the mugger took the city to court for using "excessive force" against him, and received a sizable cash judgment.

• In Massachusetts, the Legal Services Corporation, which is federally funded with tax money, distributed a brochure to welfare recipients explaining how to quickly spend an inheritance, lottery winnings, or an insurance award—and still stay on welfare.

• A psychological therapist dredged up an "old memory" from a mentally disturbed adult woman that she had been sexually abused by her father in childhood. The therapist, who helped his patient sue the father, appeared on PBS television to explain that in memory that is repressed, then recovered, it made no difference if the act really happened. It was only important, he told the television audience, that his patient *thought* that it had happened.

• In New Jersey—despite the death of several patients throughout the nation who had been infected by dentists who secretly had AIDS—the state commissioner has announced that health providers who are HIV-positive *need not* tell their patients that they are infected.

• At the College of William and Mary (Jefferson's Alma Mater), students tried to change the name of the school team, "The Tribe," because it was supposedly insulting to local Indians, only to learn that the authentic Virginia chiefs truly liked the name.

• At the University of Pennsylvania, in a state where thousands died at Gettysburg to eliminate the scourge of slavery, the president of that college has officially set up segregated dormitory space for African-American students.

• At another Pennsylvania institution, a copy of Goya's famous painting *The Naked Maja* was ejected from a classroom where it had hung for ten years. The charge from a female faculty member? "Sexual harassment."

• In San Francisco, city fathers have passed an ordinance protecting the right of transvestites to "cross dress" on the job, and for transexuals to have separate toilet facilities while undergoing surgical sex changes.

• At Harvard University, curriculum has been so weakened and "grade inflation" has so taken hold that 84 percent of a recent class graduated with honors.

• In New York City, children who don't speak a word of Spanish have been placed in bilingual classes to learn their three Rs in Spanish *solely* because their surnames are Hispanic-sounding.

• In California, parents of a disruptive child who had threatened to kill fellow students sued when the child was suspended. They won an award from the U.S. Circuit Court of Appeals for $20,000 for private school tuition and $360,000 in legal fees.

• And who could forget the six-year-old boy who obliged a

young lady in his class with a buss on the cheek, only to be charged with "sexual harassment" and the loss of an ice-cream party?

On every societal front, nonsense is replacing good sense in our once-pragmatic nation. It is accompanied by a distortion of thought that weakens our ability to distinguish truth from falsity, the basic skill of a civilized society.

Are these examples of bad sense just isolated and unconnected anecdotes? It would be nice to answer "yes," but the reality is that social and cultural madness is part of a distinct nationwide pattern. It has burgeoned so in the last decade that the phenomenon must be thoroughly examined and understood if our civilization is to survive.

Is it all part of some nefarious conspiracy? Either Communist or Fascist? Hardly. But neither is it accidental.

Americans are accustomed to the madness of individuals, whether serial killers or graffiti masters. But this newest mayhem is not the work of sociopaths or crazies. *Instead, it is the deliberate product of much of the leadership of the nation, in almost every area of responsibility.*

It comes from the will and voice of what I call the "New Establishment," the official America of school administrators and teachers, deans and faculties of colleges, judges and lawyers, politicians, journalists, social workers, teachers, military leaders, law enforcement people, church clergy, many in the arts, bureaucrats, ad infinitum.

It is not responsibility denied, but leadership run amok, with many of its programs totally outside the bounds of Western civilization.

We tend to think of the Establishment as staid, gray, stable, and old-fashioned. Collectively, it reflected our institutions, which were the rocks on which we built our extraordinary civilization. But that's a time long gone, a reflection of the 1950s and 1960s, when the Establishment was tied to the Anglo-American tradition of family, good schools, and expected behavior.

It was somewhat starchy, even creaky, yet it worked effectively in maintaining American values. But it came under heavy attack as a larger-than-life Skull and Bones. Unless pressed (as it was) it admitted few immigrants and women, and almost no nonwhites to its sacred enclaves. At the pinnacle of its power, the Old Establishment was caricatured in countless volumes of critical analysis that weakened its hold.

The New Establishment that has taken its place is quite different in makeup and motivation, representing more an attack on the American polity and its traditions than it is their protector.

Over the past thirty years it has quietly, almost stealthily, replaced the Old Establishment with a new "experimental" society whose unproven, destabilizing concepts are not fully understood and are raising confusion among most Americans.

The Old Establishment was quite recognizable and therefore instantly vulnerable. Its geographic ground zero was New York, Boston, and Washington, with only a few hinterland chapters in such metropolitan areas as Chicago, Philadelphia, Atlanta, and San Francisco. Most of its leaders were Ivy Leaguers, and it only reluctantly accepted outlanders from such institutions as the University of Chicago, Stanford, and Berkeley.

Its lineage was deep, going back before the Civil War, with many members tracing their ancestry to Colonial days, even to the Mayflower. It was mainly Anglo in composition, with only a handful of members from such early immigrant groups as German Jews, and other German and Irish citizens.

The New Establishment, on the other hand, is not nearly as recognizable, at least at first sight. Thus it has successfully evaded description, dissection, and criticism. But it can be made quite visible if one is familiar with its inner configuration.

This new institution has no geographic ground zero, with "chapters" everywhere, including the most unlikely nooks of influence. Its membership is more likely to include a psychologist or politician or professor or bureaucrat than the industrialist who was central to the Old Establishment. The leadership of the New Establishment still includes many Ivy Leaguers, but its power and membership also extend into the least known and unheralded centers of academe.

Its lineage is shallow in years and its leaders and adherents are of all races, genders, and ethnic groups, even white males, the object of much current calumny. Despite rumors to the contrary, it is not a formal conspiracy. It does not hold meetings or collect dues, except of the immaterial kind.

But there is a collective feeling of "sensitivity" among its ranks. What connects it is a *belief system,* which grows each day in context and tapestry, and may yet evolve into a "bible" that will guide its adherents in what is correct, and incorrect, thought in human relations and practical activity. Though there are no formal meetings of the New Establishment, members do recognize each other through a few key words and phrases, much as a secret handshake once announced Masons to one another.

Like its Old Establishment counterpart, the New Establishment is not monolithic. Within such a broad umbrella, there is obviously discord and disagreement. Most of its members accept the majority of its tenets while eschewing some others. At least one institution, the military, has entered it through intimidation (pressure from female members of Congress), but for political survival now cooperates enthusiastically, especially where women are involved.

Some college professors fight doggedly against PC on campus, while schoolteachers, even some federal judges, strive to preserve the old, fairer, more rational systems. But the resistance and exceptions are not sufficient to hold back the New Establishment's extraordinary advance into near-total power. The result? Its overall belief system is in rapid ascension.

Because it is such a fashionable organization, it includes many members of the rising new elite, especially those who clutter up the fashion and society pages. It can be all things to all people, presenting itself as an amorphous, flexible organization when it wants to be seen that way.

Yet at other times, it shows its true self—a rigorous, aggressive, dogmatic New Establishment that demands conformity to its beliefs from both its followers and its many victims.

For those who belong and accept its tenets with little reservation, it can be highly beneficial, financially and socially, much as membership in the Kiwanis or Rotary once was. But to those who refuse to accept its tenets, ostracism from the increasingly powerful institution can result, with severe penalties to one's career and social acceptance.

Has the New Establishment become truly powerful in the American landscape? Absolutely. In fact, as we shall see, it is the central cause of our unease.

Behind every successful movement there must be a concept that stimulates people to follow its blandishments, no matter how fatuous.

What theory sustains the New Establishment?

Unlike prior revolutionary movements, this one doesn't spring from the dispossessed in the socioeconomic hierarchy. The New Establishment is dominated by the newly privileged (including deserter-converts from the Old Establishment), who for reasons we shall examine, insist that America has not been the kindly force that assimilated millions into her eagle nest of beneficence as we were once taught.

Instead, it sees American society as basically dishonorable, with poor intentions toward everyone except those who occupy its top rungs.

The concept underpinning the New Establishment is its claim of massive exploitation. Once seen as a people elevated by opportunity and freedom, Americans are now portrayed by the New

Establishment as exploited individuals tied to a system of the master and the victimized.

That insensitive master is supposedly the white male—alive and dead. From Socrates to Jefferson, from Archimedes to Pasteur, from Homer to Shakespeare, he had once been credited with creating the arts, science, and government that shaped Western civilization, the pinnacle of human existence.

Nonsense, says the New Establishment.

History, they insist, has been the story of a descending pecking order with dominant white men preventing all others from the Third World poor to American wives from realizing their full potential.

In this scheme, whites exploit blacks, Hispanics, and Native Americans. Men exploit women. Adults exploit children. The developed nations exploit the undeveloped. Teachers exploit students. Administrators exploit teachers. Heterosexuals exploit homosexuals. Employers exploit employees. The judicial system exploits criminals and prisoners. Citizens exploit legal immigrants, and everyone exploits illegal immigrants and their children. Even the thin subjugate the fat and the tall the short.

The New Establishment has divided the nation into dozens of groups, each of which seeks surcease from (even revenge against) the dominant ones. And the New Establishment is ready to help out. It is a clever, Machiavellian, if destructive, idea that divides America into pieces, then pits one piece against the other. Each reaches for greater fulfillment at the expense of someone else—and society itself.

It is a system of *social individualization,* in which the supposed rights of each person (as a member of a "victim" group) are more important than those of the whole. Each group shouts out its grievances, whether Irish gays and lesbians, African-Americans in the ghetto or college, or illegal immigrants, single mothers with children, Hispanics in the barrio, students in voluntarily segregated dorms, criminals in prison, or alcoholics and drug users on government pensions.

Even women in general—sometimes especially women—feel put upon, as we shall examine. (See Chapter Three.)

And if no one is personally responsible, then society at large must be the villain. It's an easy sell, and it's being brilliantly marketed.

To gain and maintain power, the New Establishment has organized various groups of victims into a common voice, using the taxes and charity contributions of everyone to accomplish its goal. It's an unprecedented case of a nation subjecting itself to grave damage, even possible suicide, and being forced to pick up the tab in the process.

The tragic reality is that the powerful New Establishment that increasingly controls our lives is less concerned about the average American than any institutional leadership in our history. Rather than advance the needs and values of the working middle class, it looks down on them as the great unwashed, the "booboisie" of H. L. Mencken—people who couldn't possibly appreciate the sensibilities of the new experimental society.

And if truth be known, for the first time in our history, that typical citizen is more stable, more sensible, and better intentioned than are our institutions.

There is no end to the madness that has invaded us. In the law and the courts, capricious juries are backed by judges with little judgment. Together they have made jurisprudence in America a laughingstock. In this, they are aided by an army of lawyers, among the leading robber barons of the twentieth century. (*The New York Law Journal* boasts that their *average* reader has a $248,000 income!)

The case of the woman who received a giant sum for spilling hot McDonald's coffee while driving is topped by that of the female Navy lieutenant who sued because she had been "groped" by drunken Navy fliers.

16

In the infamous Tailhook incident, Lieutenant Paula Cough-lin of the Navy was awarded $5.1 million—not for rape or as-sault—but for being touched while running a vulgar gauntlet. She did not sue the Navy, or the fliers, or the U.S. Government for this intrusion on her person. Whom did she sue? The Hilton Hotel chain for not protecting her honor, a rather new obligation of commercial enterprises. (Are hotels also responsible for the lost virginity of their young guests?)

The latest affront to legal sanity in the civil court? A victim of a gunshot wound is suing the gun manufacturer as the cause of his injury.

In the criminal courts, few any longer expect justice and are surprised when juries deliver sane decisions. Lorena Bobbitt walked when the jury declared her "temporarily insane" for hav-ing amputated her husband's penis. After Francisco Duran opened fire on the White House, three therapists concluded that he was driven by a "hallucinatory" mist controlled by multicol-ored extraterrestrials who had taken control of the President's mind, who might in turn destroy the world.

(This is a tribute to the unwholesome influence of Dr. Sig-mund Freud in many areas of the American life, something we will look at more carefully in Chapter Two.)

In addition to their often poor performance in regular cases, judges are brazenly entering the ideological arena. Capitalizing on the dignity of the bench, they are injecting their personal biases into the law and exercising political muscle they don't rightfully have.

They're actually *making,* instead of interpreting, law. Increas-ingly, judges at every level are usurping the power of the legisla-ture, which is a blatant violation of the constitutional separation of powers. We've all witnessed a federal judge in California knock down that state's Proposition 187 (which cuts off social services for illegal immigrants) even though it was passed by almost sixty percent of the voters under the state's Initiative law.

That was followed by similar action by a federal district judge to stop the implementation of Proposition 209, which prohibited affirmative action in public employment. Only the intervention of the Supreme Court reinstated the will of California voters on that proposition.

Emboldened by the New Establishment, a Kansas City judge actually raised taxes to pay for his personal scheme to build a giant integrated magnet school, which has proven to be a billion-dollar failure. In a bizarre decision, a New York City judge temporarily blocked a subway fare rise. He ruled that since so many riders were black or Hispanic, it was a case of "racial discrimination"!

The Supreme Court is also subject to judicial fashion, strangely vacillating back and forth on such vital Constitutional issues as affirmative action. Meanwhile the original 1789 document sits unchanged in its glass case at the National Archives.

If the New Establishment operates in such a world of enforced, mainly dubious, ideas, why is it gaining so much power? Why does it attract so many adherents, people who in their personal lives are quite sane and sensible?

The answer, simply, is that in this era of great transition it has set itself up as a *secular religion*. The New Establishment fills the spiritual void in millions who no longer truly believe in either Christianity or Judiasm, yet who insist on a faith larger than themselves.

The New Establishment has all the tenets of a religion, or perhaps more accurately, a cult. It preaches a specious "goodness" and asks only that one give up one's mind and reason in exchange for modern salvation—gaining the reputation among one's peers for being "sensitive" or "concerned."

Like all "religions," it has its dogmas. But in this case, its belief system had been tied closely to secular power in government and the courts. Violations of this new "faith" can become matters of civil, or even criminal, liability for those who break the code. In this aspect, it bears a strong resemblance to the theocracies of old Massachusetts or the modern world of Islamic fundamentalism.

But though this faith is earthly, its tenets are usually based on fantasy and unproven, even disproven, theory. Still, it forces its adherents, and eventually will force all of us, to accept speculation in place of truth. In such a circumstance, society loses the ability to distinguish truth from falsehood, theory from reality, in all arenas of life. Surely this would be the most detrimental fallout of the New Establishment in the closing years of the twentieth century.

On the surface, accepting the tenets of the New Establishment may seem like a poor bargain, but it would be foolish to deny the seductiveness of this new faith. By merely mouthing its dogma, whether at school, work, or at a cocktail party, one immediately verifies his or her *self-worth*. Without ever putting a dollar in a church plate or uttering a sincere prayer, an adherent assumes a stance of moral superiority, even easily gained if spurious "sophistication."

Unlike a true religion, the new dogma makes almost no demands on its followers. It's an easy faith. Adherents need not demonstrate any spirituality or improvement in their own lives, or show any greater kindness to individuals. They don't have to examine their true thoughts and ingrained prejudices and hypocrisies.

All they need do is trade on the facile dogmas of the New Establishment. It is a sad commentary, and one that augers poorly for our civilization, but there it is. And we must deal with it.

No one has yet laid out the full context of the New Establishment or codified its unwritten social contract with the nation. Nor has anyone attempted to find solutions to its swamp of distorted policies. That is my goal in this volume.

Why is it important?

Because unseen, even stealthily, one after another of our institu-

tions is falling to its blandishments, threatening the Judeo-Christian ethic and Western civilization itself.

One of the most egregious of the new dogmas is Political Correctness, which was originally developed almost simultaneously by the National Socialist Party of Germany (NAZIS) and the Stalinists of the Soviet Union. In Nazi Germany, PC became official national policy. Not only were books burned, but "liberal" professors were purged at universities. In the Soviet Union, only politically correct Marxist authors could be published and "fascist" academics were driven out of colleges.

PC—if not as governmentally enforced as in those dictatorships—has had a revival in modern America under the aegis of the New Establishment.

Its thesis is simple. PC states that certain political and social ideas are correct and honorable and must be repeated and accepted, while other views—including those held by most Americans—are unacceptable, even prohibited and punishable.

In the last decade, PC has swept to the core of our culture, especially in the University. Once the open debating ground for what Paul Goodman called a "Community of Scholars," the university was designed to be immune to the fashions and pressures of outside society. Instead, the American college has become the ground zero of know-nothingness, a reincarnation of the McCarthy era of intimidation.

(It's ironic that as the anti-intellectual madness of this New McCarthyism infects the American landscape it should find its most fertile soil in the institutions of higher learning, a totalitarian twist that not even Orwell envisioned in *1984*.)

There are several hundred colleges with "speech codes" that spell out what a student can say and think, part of a program of limiting free speech and the First Amendment, ostensibly to protect minority sensibilities. Actually, of course, it is a carefully developed New Establishment scheme to control thought at the crucial university level, then see its theses carried out in the adult world.

At the University of Arizona, a Diversity Action Plan was developed to block students from making negative comments involving "color, ethnicity, gender, religion, and national origin." Not only that, the Arizona campus had even restricted speech about one's "physical and mental ability, Vietnam-era veteran status, socioeconomic background, and individual style."

As the student chairman in charge of "Diversity" explained: they wanted to protect *"everyone."*

Calling a fellow student "stupid," once the mainstay of informal college arguments, or ridiculing someone's abysmal taste in tee-shirts (the "style" thing), are now official violations of that university's Orwellian code.

On campuses nationwide, failure to conform to PC and its thought control is punishable by denunciation, sensitivity training, even expulsion. An English professor at the University of Texas was harassed into resigning because he voted against a freshman requirement to attend race and gender "Sensitivity Training." At some schools, students gather in the gymnasium and assume different roles—men as women, whites as blacks, etc.—as other students shout stereotypical insults at them.

The well-known story of the University of Pennsylvania student, Eden Jacobowitz, who was threatened with expulsion for calling a group of noisy black sorority students "water buffaloes" (a never-explained epithet) leads the parade. But there are many unpublicized cases of students and faculty members who have suffered at the hands of the College Thought Police.

Much of this nonsense stems from the increasing separation of college student bodies into "group identities," whether African-American, Hispanic, Native American, or whatever, a trend that has reached the caricature stage.

At Tufts University in Massachusetts, where it is called "Categorical Representation," the hard-pressed student senate cut

$600 from the budget of an Asian group, the Chinese Cultural Club. Their representative, a young woman, claimed "institutional bias," saying that the money was going to be used for takeout food for a Chinese New Year celebration. Reducing the amount, she protested, was an attack on her racial "legitimacy," a move that "questioned the authenticity of takeout food as part of our (Chinese) culture." Naturally, the $600 was restored.

To make the sophomoric ideas of PC palatable, the college curriculum, which is heavily under the control of the New Establishment, has been nearly destroyed to accommodate this anti-intellectual thrust. The National Association of Scholars has released a damning report on the poor quality of today's university education, which we will explore in detail. (See Chapter Four.)

One of the most telling PC violations of intellect has taken place at Georgetown University, where the bard Shakespeare, surely the master dramatist-philosopher of any age, has been tried and found guilty of being insensitive to women and other minorities. The school's action? Shakespeare is no longer required for English literature majors.

The chairman of the curriculum committee at Georgetown explained that the reason for downgrading Shakespeare was that "we want to get away from the notion that literature is sacred."

To further carry out their theory, Henry James, Herman Melville, and Nathaniel Hawthorne have been reorganized at Georgetown under Course No. 112, "White Male Writers," the most perjorative insult in the PC netherworld.

As the required college curriculum weakens and ridiculously inflated grades become nearly meaningless (a scandal that we shall investigate), invented PC courses proliferate. Fashionable classes in Women's, African, Chicano, and Native American studies continue strong even as a new "discipline"—lightly labeled "Queer Studies"—is making headway.

Officials at the University of Iowa played host to the Sixth Annual Gay and Lesbian Studies Conference, which proponents hope to develop into a "major academic field." Some of the enlightened courses?: "The Erect Penis: Can We Top It," "Recontextualizing the Meaning of Butch in Lesbian Culture," and the creative chef d'oeuvre—"Anals of History."

PC is also breaking out from its cloistered college halls into every venue of our culture.

The federal government has also fallen under New Establishment mesmerism. Washington has become an active PC center, aggressively intimidating citizens who think independently. An employee of the U.S. Forest Service wrote me, enclosing brochures on "Multiculturalism" in hiring and tolerance, commenting that they spend more energy on that than on their regular work.

One federal agency, the Department of Housing and Urban Affairs (HUD), has even been in the forefront of legal assault on free speech and the First Amendment. In a case in Berkeley, California, HUD officials conducted a seven-month investigation of three homeowners, then threatened them with a $100,000 fine and possible jail for violating Washington PC.

The charge? Protesting against placing a housing project for the homeless in their neighborhood. The HUD said that the "Berkeley Three" had expressed *opinions* that violated "discrimination against disabled" laws. According to PC-Uncle Sam, that speech was ostensibly not protected by the First Amendment.

As this case illustrates, attacks on free speech can come from any quarter—even officially from the government itself. Whether initiated from the left or right, from the Old Establishment or the New, they must be thwarted, rapidly and effectively.

Under pressure from several sources, including an editorial in *The New York Times,* Washington finally backed off in the HUD fiasco. But in other cases of "thought police" action, federal agencies have acted like fascist Star Chambers, harassing those who would defy official PC.

The New Establishment knows that to effectively reconfigure

our society in its image (which is its major goal), and establish a set of taboos that others must follow, it would have to take command of the language. For as George Orwell taught us, words control thought and thought controls all civilization. Thus by manipulating words to its advantage, the New Establishment attempts to rearrange normal thought processes so that irrationality will seem rational. This is especially true of the media and academe, which have become willing transmission belts for the most egregiously fashionable nonsense.

It is doing just that. English is being PCed every day. "Gentleman" may be acceptable (it's PC to insult men), but "lady" is considered a put-down for "woman." Eccentric euphemisms are used to replace conventional descriptions. "Disabled" is being replaced by "differently abled." In a phrase that can only have been invented by a comedian (Jackie Mason, take notice), short people are "vertically challenged," ad nauseum. People are no longer "ignorant"; instead they merely lack "learning skills."

These are not isolated instances. The *Scrabble* game has eliminated one hundred fifty words from its "family" acceptability standard for fear they might offend someone.

"We have an *Official Scrabble Player's Dictionary, Second Edition,*" relates the director of the National Scrabble Association, a group of 10,000 players. "About two years ago—I think as an offshoot of political correctness—we started to get complaints about words used in our game. Since then, we've published a third edition, from which about one hundred fifty words have been deleted because someone or some group claimed that they are offensive."

Examples? *Jesuit* has been taken out because it was once used to describe a scheming person. The same with *Jew*, because it has been used as a pejorative verb. *Fag* is still in because it has another meaning (to be made weary), but *faggy* is out, as is the sometimes British term for homosexual, *poof*. Because Hispanics found *wetback* offensive, that has been taken out as well.

Groups from Wales complained about "welsh," as in a bet, and the Romani people were angry at "gyp," since it is presumed to be derived from "gypsy." But in both cases the complaints came too late for the words to be excised.

"I think this kind of censorship is nonsense and dangerous, but we felt we had to compromise," says the Scrabble spokesman. "The third edition is for families and it has all the curse and scatalogical words out, as well as the words that are offensive to races and groups. We even got letters from people saying the words *gun* and *war* are the most offensive, so there's no end to it. But for tournaments, we use the second edition, which has all the supposedly offensive words still in."

Twisting the English language is a staple of the new dogma. One of its gravest affronts to rational thought is a concept called "Deconstruction," which even tries to deny that words have *specific* meaning. Instead, it seeks to weaken reality and boost destabilizing fantasy by claiming that words, like values, are "relative."

The deconstruction bible, the journal *Social Text,* and the discipline's guru, Professor of English Stanley Fish at Duke University, promote the theory that when language is properly broken down, words, as in *Alice in Wonderland,* mean what you want them to, especially in different social contexts. In such a world, the thinking process is also "deconstructed." (In a recent hoax, a scientist aped the gibberish of deconstruction so well that the editors of *Social Text* published his parody verbatim!)

Though some of this is harmless nonsense, it becomes significant when commonly used words become falsely defined, yet are unchallenged. This is especially true of the media, much of which has easily fallen into the trap.

Words like *multiculturalism* and *diversity* and *racism* and *sexism* are loosely bandied about, and as we shall explore, are advancing the increasingly common habit of anti-thought.

Take the overused linguistic invention, "minority." Its common definition is meaningless, even blatantly false. Are European

Greeks and Jews, who make up a minute part of the American populace, minorities? Of course they are. But not by *official* criteria, which seeks to exclude Americans of European origin. But how about Palestinians and Pakistanis, who are non-European Asians? Their numbers are also very small, so are they true minorities?

No. Again they fail to fit the New Establishment stereotype.

If not they, who? Naturally those who can do the most good for the power of the New Establishment. High among that short list would be a majority of the people masquerading as a minority. Who is that? None other than American women of all ethnicities and races.

In the definition of women as supposed victims of "oppression" by white males, they have been given a legal, if unconstitutional, status as a minority despite the ridiculous mathematics.

Women make up almost 52 percent of the entire population. With African-Americans, Hispanics of all races, East Asians (Chinese, Korean, Filipinos), Native Americans, and Eskimos, we're talking about more than two-thirds of the country. *Only in America could an overwhelming majority be considered a minority.*

So what is the true definition of minority? What is the answer to this conundrum of the 1990s and beyond?

According to the New Establishment, a member of a minority is anyone except a white male, the much-maligned citizen who bore, and still bears, the *major* responsibility for the nation and Western civilization.

Of course, the reality is that the white male is a part of a minority himself, and not an overly large one at that. At its maximum it comprises 35 percent of the populace. Effectively, though, that number is much smaller. Certain white males are themselves categorized as "victims," reducing the ranks. These include the male homeless, the unemployed, the disabled, alcoholics, drug-dependent men, the mentally ill, and the aged, all of whom are eligible for various programs that provide either monetary rewards or protection.

In fact, the true ranks of the white male "oppressors" become even thinner as still others are singled out as victims. Of whom? Naturally, of the remaining white males.

In Pasadena, California, Armenian-American men are a "protected" class. The same is true of Portuguese-American men in Massachusetts; French Arcadians in Louisiana; those of "Appalachian regional origin" in Cincinnati; transsexual white men in Minneapolis, Seattle, San Francisco, and Santa Cruz; Hasidic Jewish-American men in the eyes of the Department of Housing and Urban Development (HUD); and even "economically disadvantaged" white male bankers, a category that defies even New Establishment stereotypes.

To these protected white males, we must add still others, further reducing the ranks of the much-maligned "Ruling Class." They include retired men on Social Security and the working "aged" over forty years who are protected by government statutes against discrimination.

Who does that leave? Less than 20 percent of the population, which constitutes a most peculiar "majority." In fact, it is only one-fourth the size of the privileged "minorities."

It's especially peculiar because despite the enormous handicaps placed upon this small group by granting privilege to others, they still have the primary obligation to run the nation's corporations, its military, and its political structures. Simultaneously, they are expected to do the great mass of our creative and inventive work, from developing the Internet to complex telecommunications devices to heart transplant surgery to building the latest space vehicle, skyscraper, or suspension bridge.

Defining who is and who is not a member of a "minority" is important because gaining that status in America is like winning a lottery. It's the usual entry point into hundreds of social service programs, preferred hiring and college admission, private and public scholarships, protection against insult and "discrimination," including being fired or not being promoted, and a leg up on government contracts, all parts of the catch-all "affirmative action."

The New Establishment is always counting, dividing America up into pigeonholes it can manipulate, punishing some and rewarding others, always for its own gain of greater power. But sometimes its cleverness backfires.

The "minority" theory is based almost completely on the idea that all people other than white males are discriminated against, which supposedly explains their lower performance, whether in income or scores on tests or success in their careers. We are assured that discrimination restricts full potential and explains the failure to achieve.

There are naïve people who believe that. But one of the first chinks in the ridiculous "discrimination cripples performance" theory is the history of American Jewry. Suffering harsh discrimination for over 1,900 years since the Roman war of 70 A.D., and up against anti-Semitism since they reached these shores, mainly at the turn of the century, they began with two strikes against them. So how, others have constantly asked, could they have achieved so much—both materially and in scholarship—in the hostile environment of prejudice?

The usual answer? *Because they were discriminated against and had to work and think harder to get ahead.*

That obviously deflates the theory that discrimination cripples, but the New Establishment counters by insisting that's old history. Today, it ostensibly works the other way around. We are told that discrimination against minorities—racism, sexism, whatever, past and present—is obviously the main cause for inadequate accomplishment. We see it in African-Americans, Hispanics, even white women.

True? Of course not. We now have a perfect *new* case of excellence despite discrimination. (Or perhaps because of it?) The history of bias that propelled the Jews is replicating itself in America in the shape of Asians. One of the newest minorities is the East Asians—the Chinese, Koreans, Vietnamese, Japanese—who make up only 3 percent of the population. They are nonwhite racially, easily identified as "different," and often recent immigrants with little command of the language.

Surely, these oppressed people must be failing if we follow the modern theory of victimization.

But quite the opposite is true. In fact, the most accomplished and fastest rising group in America are these Asian minorities, who easily outperform the supposed Ubermenschen, *the white male!*

At Stuyvesant High in New York, a science and math scholarship school (my alma mater) and winner of an outsize number of Westinghouse and National Merit scholarships, the enrollment is no longer heavily Jewish as it used to be. It is now dominated by Asians, who monopolize the high scores on the competitive tests needed for entry. At the prestigious University of California at Berkeley, the queen of that state's higher education system, the student body is now 43 percent Asian.

That institution estimates that Asians will make up a majority of the students once the Regent's plan to eliminate favoritism is put into effect—if it ever is.

So much for the false New Establishment theory that white male oppression is the cause of failure among minorities. Either discrimination is a stimulus for achievement, as in the case of Asians and Jews, or it is the cause of lower performance, as in the case of blacks, Hispanics, and women. We can hardly have it both ways.

The New Establishment seems to specialize in false social theories.

"Bilingualism" is another of its concepts that fails to hold up. According to dogma, it is "psychologically repressive" to be forced to learn English. Therefore, the New Establishment claims, students should be taught in the language spoken at home as well as in English. They claim that one language is as good as another—whether Spanish or Chinese or "Black English," a poorly-conjugated patois that has severely held back many African-Americans.

But as all studies show, success in upwardly mobile America is not closely tied to one's race or ethnic background or parents' social class. It is more a factor of one's command of English, which, as we shall see, is weakened in bilingual curricula.

(Imagine, if you will, if the eloquent Mario Cuomo, former Governor of New York, had had to submit to bilingual education as a boy in the New York school system, studying public speaking in Italian, the language then spoke at home. The same is equally true of Alan Keyes, the brilliant African-American candidate for the Republican nomination for President in 1996, who speaks no "Black English" and who articulates considerably better than most of his fellow Harvard Ph.D.s.)

We now spend $2.3 billion a year on bilingual education, teaching students in 62 native tongues nationwide, seriously retarding their assimilation, the final arbiter of success. Shockingly, not just ATM machines (which often work in English, Spanish, Chinese, and Vietnamese), but even the Social Security Administration asks for a person's "language preference," as if English were merely one of many choices, and not even *primus unter pares*.

One wonders if the proponents of the New Establishment don't actually prefer failure for their followers.

After all, its leadership—of whatever race or ethnicity—is well-educated, financially comfortable, and fluent in English. They demand full assimilation for themselves because they know it's the route to success. But they still encourage "multiculturalism" and "diversity" among the ranks of their movement. Is it perhaps designed to keep the masses of the faithful in both penury and supine worship of their false doctrines?

Later (Chapter Seven), we'll look at the entire affirmative action program, which has been as badly administered as it is theoretically questionable. Most often it functions best for the socially mobile and relatively well-to-do, offering its benefits to those who either don't need it to get ahead or who have connived to receive it.

The government control of affirmative action is so uncoordinated and unreliable that bureaucratic nonsense often dominates. For example, one anecdote shows the power of the vague phrase "Hispanic" in the New Establishment dogma.

An Italian-American man suddenly remembered that his father, also an Italian, had been born in Brazil. As a newly retrofitted "Hispanic," he applied for affirmative action. Under federal minority guidelines he received an $11 million construction contract at Denver Airport. This is particularly baffling, since Brazil is a Portuguese-language nation and not at all Hispanic—except in bureaucratic America.

The New Establishment thrives on class, ethnic, gender, and racial discord, capitalizing on the ancient dictum of divide and conquer. It has especially interfered in two vital areas—relations between the races and between the sexes. It argues that it has become involved to ease the conflict and mollify the participants. But in reality, relations in both areas have become seriously inflamed, even damaged, as a result of its intervention. In fact, never in recent history has there been as much friction in these areas.

The New Establishment, for example, has become obsessive about African-Americans. It has now transferred that compulsion to the nation as a whole, much to the detriment of both blacks and whites. Even though only one in eight Americans is black, that obsession has made the state of their progress, or lack of it, often seem like the most important aspect of national life.

That exaggerated concern, fed by government, academe, the media, and others in the New Establishment has contributed mightily to the sense of national unease and has held back the progress of the African-American and Hispanic communities.

Years ago, Senator Daniel Patrick Moynihan of New York suggested that America treat the black minority with "benign neglect," the very same treatment accorded to Italians, Greeks, Irish, Jews, Slovaks, and other minorities at the turn of the century. They were left alone to sort out their problems, then enter the mainstream when ready, as they did so successfully once their assimilation into the Anglo-American culture was near complete.

But African-Americans have received a different, and more destructive, treatment by the New Establishment. They have been counted, probed, analyzed, become the object of enormous guilt, had their progress recorded ad infinitum, and placed under a continuous sociological microscope. The New Establishment has intruded into every aspect of their lives, from child bearing to child raising to housing to schooling, even to sex, accomplishing the maximum possible harm.

The result is that the black population of America has been seriously injured in two ways. First, through patronizing attitudes by the New Establishment that weaken discipline and resolve, especially in education and work. And second, in countenancing, even encouraging, the destruction of families (the basic unit of Western civilization) though scores of government programs, including "welfare," which rewards illegitimacy, nonmarriage and nonresponsibility.

From a manageable 19 percent out-of-wedlock birth rate for African-Americans after World War II, the rate, according to a Bureau of Census report, has now soared to 67 percent, with an attendant increase in crime and drug dependency, especially among teenagers with no father at home. There's ample proof that single-parent homes headed by women, in both the white and black communities, are unable to handle male teenagers and young adults, the major perpetrators of mayhem.

In fact, the migration of African-Americans to the North from the rural South, which began heavily in the 1960s, has unfortunately taken place during the rise in power of the permissive New

Establishment, which has made African-Americans the victims of its know-nothingness.

Affirmative action for African-Americans is seen as "reverse discrimination" against whites. It obviously is, even though not in massive proportions. But despite preference in government, police, and fire department jobs, and in some corporations, it has generally been a failure. It has helped the elite of African-Americans to advance smartly, but it has had little positive effect on most blacks.

Why? Because of the lack of college degrees, statistically the most reliable stepping stone to success and higher incomes. African-American males make up over 6 percent of the population, so after thirty years of easier college admission, has it paid off?

Generally not. Obviously it has helped some, but it has not reached the masses. According to the U.S. Department of Education, of the 1995 college graduating classes, only 3 percent of those receiving baccalaureate degrees were African-American males, which is only half what would be expected based on population figures. Among Master's graduates, only 2 percent were African-American men, with no appreciable record among doctorates.

Who, then, has cashed in on the largesse, materially and psychologically, of the New Establishment?

Naturally, the *majority of Americans*—women of all races and ethnicities. Since they comprise almost 52 percent of the entire population, they have become a top priority for the New Establishment, which has promoted their advance in every walk of American life. The rationale? Supposed past discrimination from their oppressors—the American male. The resulting affirmative action is of such massive proportions that it makes the black-white controversy pale in contrast.

Female affirmative action is often based on false premises, as we shall later document. (See Chapter Three.) But that doesn't diminish its widespread application in every field, from fire and police departments to the military to the corporation, even to medical school admissions, where women expect, and are generally granted, special privileges.

Sometimes, it even assumes comical dimensions. We know of Susan McDougal of Whitewater fame receiving a Small Business Administration–backed $300,000 loan for the "disadvantaged"—read "women"—even when her net worth was over $1 million.

That's easily topped by the case of Alice Walton, daughter of the late Sam Walton of Wal-Mart, and now one of the richest women in the world. But as a "victim" of male bias, she was granted affirmative action in securing a government bond contract, adding large profits to her fortune. So much for modern madness.

The New Establishment has also heavily interfered in the world of male-female relations, escalating the age-old battle of the sexes. Once simply part of life's chancy games—with some proving luckier than others—relations between the sexes are fast becoming a matter of *official* action.

Sexual harassment is a case in point. It originally had a clear meaning: someone in power was legally liable if they threatened an employee or subordinate with dismissal or demotion for refusing to provide sexual favors. That makes infinite sense and normally involved solicitation from men—despite Hollywood's attempts to defend Michael Douglas against female predators.

But in the exaggerated American climate, especially in the mass hysteria stimulated by the New Establishment, sexual harassment now means anything that women want it to mean. In the office environment, men have been punished for telling lewd stories or displaying pin-up pictures, creating a "hostile" environment that offends supposedly innocent women, if any such person still exists. One college professor was dismissed because he "stared" at a coed in a swimming pool. Men have even been charged with "complimenting" a woman's appearance, as in "I like your outfit" or "Your hair looks nice today," a polite way of showing approval.

Unfortunately, as we shall document, this stretching, even perversion, of the law has been supported by fashionable courts, up through the august, if confused, Supreme Court.

The power of the New Establishment extends into every human activity, with resulting distortion. It even reaches into the bowels of America's history and our concept of ourselves. He who controls the past, Greek philosophers remind us, will control the future.

The answer? Rewrite history as you would like it to have happened, expecting to influence those who were not born at the time. This is called "Revisionist History," and it has become a favorite tool of the New Establishment idea factory. Even the federal government is staunchly behind this type of falsification, as we have recently observed.

One major medium for revisionism has been the Smithsonian Institution in Washington, which secretly seems to have full New Establishment credentials. The museum has been a willing tool in the plan to bend, alter, and change the historical truth of America.

In the past few years, several of its exhibits have been blatant propaganda attempts, with an anti-American bias. (It is particularly surprising since taxpayers spend $350 million a year on the museum complex.) Its most shocking performance was the draft of an exhibit commemorating the fiftieth anniversary of the *Enola Gay,* the B-29 that dropped the first atomic bomb on Japan. That action ended the war and saved upwards of one million American lives, and even more Japanese.

Rather than praise the event as the one that destroyed the brutal Japanese empire, the curator of the exhibit, a federal employee, had plans to rewrite history by making Japan the victim and America the aggressor.

He portrayed the Japanese as involved in a "war to defend their unique culture" and the United States as an "imperialistic" power. In a further distortion of history, the Smithsonian claimed that the atom bomb was unnecessary—that Japan was ready to surrender, a view that virtually all historians (except revisionists) consider totally false.

Veterans' groups protested the Smithsonian exhibit, which was finally stopped short of madness. The exhibit curator resigned, but, as we shall see, it's obvious that the Smithsonian, like a number of federal agencies, is still firmly in the grip of the New Establishment.

Even the Department of Education has been called in to do a revisionist job on America. Academics at UCLA were given a $2 million federal grant to write a new American history curriculum for high schools—the National History Standards. What appeared to be an innocent assignment became one in which New Establishmentarians used taxpayer money to besmirch the nation's past. The result? A fanciful distortion in which America was portrayed as an oppressive nation. To stress the country's racism, for example, the Ku Klux Klan was mentioned seventeen times while dozens of outstanding Americans from Samuel Adams to Edison to the Wright Brothers were totally omitted from the syllabus.

These new history guidelines even compared the American Revolution to the revolts that created Communist Cuba, China, and even the Bolshevik Revolution of 1917!

Not only is the New Establishment often antinationalistic, it also has a clear bias against Western Civilization, which it typically portrays as an unreasonable and oppressive force. It also knows that to replace that power with its own theocracy, the concept of Western greatness must first be eroded in people's minds.

Its first assault on the wave of Western heritage was to redefine it as *Eurocentrism,* a term meant to imply that the West was "repressive" and "exclusionary" of other cultures. (At Stanford, students chanted "Hey, hey, ho, ho, Western Culture's got to go.")

Using fanciful "facts," the New Establishment historians have even glamorized ancient primitive cultures, from the Mayan in Mexico and Central America to that of Mali in Africa. But they conveniently forget that all the world, including Mexico and poverty-stricken Africa, now strive to imitate Western Eurocentric society. Arthur Schlesinger, the famed historian, has exposed one supremely ridiculous Revisionist claim: that America copied its democracy from the Iroquois Indians!

The New Establishment, like Christianity, Capitalism, Marxism, or Freudianism, is internally consistent. Its dogma seeks to encompass all of human endeavor, and it has developed its own carefully delineated responses for every aspect of life.

Fearing that failure to conquer even one division of society might provide an opening for rational dissent, it has thus worked overtime to cover all bases, especially the "idea centers." Quite successfully it has ensnared our universities and public schools, along with much of the media, the arts, the foundations, even the control of honors and prizes.

The New Establishment and its ideas, including that of "multiculturalism," are even potent in the world of multibillion-dollar foundations. The Rockefeller Foundation, for one, has a Humanities Fellowship whose 1996–97 rules reportedly required that the research either be about women or conducted in non-Western cultural areas. In the case of California's Proposition 209, which would prohibit affirmative action for women and minorities in public institutions, the Rockefeller, Ford and other foundations contributed $1.3 million toward its defeat, an effort which proved to be futile.

America stands at a philosophical crossroad. It can acknowledge both its greatness and its faults and move ahead, continually seeking to improve democratic society, as it has always done under the umbrella of the Judeo-Christian culture. Or the nation (and by extrapolation, the world) can yield to the seductive blandishments of the New Establishment and continue to accept its debilitating tenets of "victimization" and "oppression" as the key vectors of American life.

The first choice means victory; the second not only means defeat, but possibly the end of the most productive and free civilization in the history of humankind.

In the chapters to follow, we will further examine the inner workings of the New Establishment and its philosophical underpinnings. And since it seeks to be a modern "religion," we will look closely at the gods it worships and dissect what sustains this new theocracy.

Understanding that, we can start our diagnosis of the end of sanity that is overwhelming us and provide the remedies to the social and cultural mayhem that threaten our commonweal.

CHAPTER TWO

GODS OF THE NEW ESTABLISHMENT

The Trinity of Freud, Marx, and a Distortion of Jesus

EVERY FAITH NEEDS ITS GODS, AND THE NEW ESTAB-
lishment is no exception. Inventing divine beings is not easy in a
world crowded with false gurus, who come and go as rapidly as
the best-seller list of inspirational books.

Instead, the New Establishment has drawn on the familiar for
its spiritual base, creating a trinity of gods whose tenets are known
and who can be blended into a faith that has modern resonance.

Of the three great world religions—Judaism, Christianity, and
Islam—the same parallel holds true. Each drew from the first,
Judaism. Christianity was the offshoot of Hebrew messianic belief,
with Jesus the longed-for savior foreseen by the prophets. But it
was not an entirely new faith, for the Father of that Trinity was
still Jehovah, the strong and vengeful Jewish God.

A similar melding created Islam centuries later. The prophet
Mohammed, though not divine, was the voice of Allah, the original God, who bears a strong resemblance to Jehovah. In the Muslim faith, both Moses and Jesus were adopted as prophets of
truth.

The New Establishment has its own trinity, with two secular gods and one traditionally spiritual. Of the three, two are of foreign origin, but they have found acceptance in fertile American soil.

As religious historians tell us, the establishment of a faith requires at least two criteria: a special insight and a miraculous beginning. Together they can build a structure of faith that explains virtually every human occurrence and gives it meaning and structure.

That was the case in Vienna, Austria, in the closing years of the nineteenth century. There Professor Sigmund Freud, who was to become the first god of the New Establishment, was a practicing medical neurologist with a set of patients common to his time, generally referred to as "hysterics."

Freud was not a full-fledged academic. His title was mainly honorific, and he did not teach formal classes at the University of Vienna. (Some claim he received his professorship by brokering a painting for a patient, the wife of the Minister of Education.) But it did bring him both a respectful tip of the hat from Austrian burghers and the right to use the university facilities for lectures of his own.

But what can the convoluted psychosexual and psychoanalytic theories of Freud have to do with the New Establishment?

A great deal. In fact, they represent a good part of the underpinnings of this secular new faith.

From his home and office at Bergasse 19 in an unfashionable section of Vienna, Freud probed the unconscious of his patients, and was involved when the first "miracle" of psychoanalysis took place. Actually, the case was in the hands of his mentor, Dr. Josef Breuer. Anna O. (her real name was Bertha Pappenheim), an attractive twenty-one-year-old puritanical Jewish girl, was suffering what Freud called "conversion hysteria."

In Vienna, that fashionable illness struck a number of upper middle class Victorian ladies, some of whom had developed such symptoms as loss of memory, paralysis of limbs, and even temporary blindness and deafness. The illness had been considered by medieval philosophers, and by many peers of Freud, to be a womb disorder, and the offending organ was then removed. Thus the term, *hysterectomy*.

Anna O. reported paralysis in her neck and in part of her limbs, and could not speak for two weeks. Breuer would hypnotize her and Anna would talk out what Freud later called "repressed memories" of traumatic experiences. Once that secret memory was retrieved and bought out into the open through the "talking cure"—as Freud and Breuer termed it—the analysis was complete. "To our great surprise at first," they assured the world, "each individual symptom immediately and permanently disappeared."

This was the "miracle" of the new faith of psychoanalysis. Of course, despite Freud's claim, no cure actually took place and Anna O. remained mentally disturbed all her life. But word of "miracles," false or otherwise, travels quickly. As years went by, that "cure" and others that ostensibly followed became cherished folklore to millions, especially in America, where unlike Europe, Freud's fanciful theories took hold.

Fortunately for Freud's career, Anna O. fell in love with Dr. Breuer, and his wife insisted he drop her as a patient. When Breuer found his "cured" patient in the throes of a false "hysterical pregnancy," he stopped using the method.

Freud inherited the work, transforming the repressed aspect of the "hysteria" to matters of *sex*, a most captivating, if upsetting, idea for the prim world of Vienna. In the *Studies of Hysteria*, published in 1895, in four cases he personally handled, Freud described sex as the unruly cause of the illness, generally the result of a father or relative sexually abusing a younger person.

Freud was obsessive about sex and was determined to prove that it was the villain in all cases of mental disturbance. "Factors arising in the sexual life represent the nearest and practically the most momentous causes of every single case of nervous illness," he claimed.

At first, on the basis of stories told to him by his patients, Freud believed that their common secret was that they had been seduced as children. In females, Freud claimed, the culprit was generally the father or older brother. In boys, it was typically female nursemaids, servants, or teachers. The seductions were "coituslike," Freud insisted, involving manipulation of the genitals or use of the anus or mouth, and in some cases, actual intercourse. "You can see that I am in the full swing of discovery," he exuberantly wrote his confidant, Dr. Wilhelm Fliess, a nose specialist in Berlin.

Freud's theory soon came crashing down. His patients confessed that they had lied to him, sometimes led on by Herr Doctor himself. Freud wrote Fliess that he was depressed and would have to settle for a "modest" life and give up his dreams of fame, travel, and financial independence.

Suddenly, in a maneuver that was to inject irrationality into the very core of his work (and by extrapolation into the modern New Establishment), Freud decided to turn his error to success. Though his patients had not really been seduced, they thought they had been. Eureka! In a sharp reversal of theory, he now concluded that the *fantasy* was more important than the reality. Those childhood fantasies of early sex with a parent or elder, he was sure, were at the heart of all neuroses.

From that agile twist, Freud developed the concept of infantile sexuality. The parent was the one who stifled the childhood impulses—the raw, untamed, uncivilized, unconscious instinct— that were constantly seeking gratification, sexual and otherwise. But in order to civilize the child, the impulses were rebuffed by elders and society, and were thus *repressed,* a key word in the new discipline (actually a mystical faith) that he was creating.

Freud then set out to give his insight a structure. He divided the mind into three compartments: the Ego, the conscious self;

the Superego, the influence of society, parents, and conscience; and the Id, the little unconscious devil within us all that demands gratification, the sooner and fuller the better.

Ostensibly, the Id has no conscience. It is not rational. It wants fun, love, power, sex and happiness—if only the Ego and Superego would allow it. It will lie, steal, perhaps even kill, to achieve its goal of satisfaction.

Before Freud, parents were considered not only the protectors of children, but the conduit through which they were civilized. Elders transmitted knowledge and tradition from generation to generation. The young might be charming, even delightful, but they were seen as little savages who had to be tamed and taught, not only for their sake, but for that of society.

The result of Freud's work and its subsequent popularization was that this traditional idea was turned on its head. *He created the new concept of the young as victims of the old.* It was revolutionary, and though it did not come directly from him in simple prose, it evolved from his work into a supposed truism.

The young were pure; the elders corrupted them. The young had intuition and instinct. Their Ids needed outlet and expression. The older generation—using the Ego and the Superego as weapons against the uncivilized inner drive—were bottling up and injuring the Id, forcing it to come out in aberrant ways. Thus psychoneurosis in the innocent child.

It was a tale of monumental impact. Children were thus turned into first victims in the Freudian dogma, an idea readily absorbed into New Establishment theory. And the older generation, in every era, automatically became the *villains* in what was to become a dramatic paradigm of the struggle between the oppressed and their oppressors.

Among these supposed victims are adolescent boys and girls. Once they were thought of as individuals living through a period of furies, even a form of minor mental disturbance designed to help them break away from a secure home to shape a new generation. But to the older generation, those furies had to be tamed to keep them on a level keel until it was time for them to leave.

This concept had been traditional for thousands of years, until Freud stimulated a change in perception. Suddenly, by the middle of the twentieth century, youth were seen as noble and bold, courageously fighting off the repression of parents and a society determined to stifle them.

Youth might be irrational, the theory went, but they were pure. And in some unknown way, they were wise even if ignorant. Youth became a symbol of both independence and victimization, the idea of a beneficent reaction against tradition that was to find ready acceptance among the young everywhere—and surely among the curators of the New Establishment.

It was a reversal of historical attitudes, based on an unscientific, even paranoid, theory of one man whose own mental stability is now debated. But it worked. It was, of course, the idea that fathered what we later termed "the generation gap" and all that it implied.

Most important, Freud made victimization seem scientific. There was now a supposedly "objective" basis for rebellion and radical change. Science was the key, even trumped-up science.

Vienna was the birthplace of Freudian theory, but it was nurtured in America, beginning in 1909. Rejected by academics in Europe, who considered his strange theories to be medical charlatanism, Freud accepted an offer to speak at Clark University in Worcester, Massachusetts. Founded by industrialist Jonas Clark to provide inexpensive education "without any religious, political, or social tests," it welcomed new ideas.

Simultaneously, the once-dominant Congregational Church of New England, the descendant of the strict Puritan Church that had been the nucleus of Yankee discipline and excellence, was running out of fire and brimstone. Becoming more permissive and secular, it was moving toward its present post-Calvanist form. That, along with the undeniable sexual titillation of Freud's theories in a Puritan nation, made the Viennese doctor-philosopher welcome in Massachusetts as a harbinger of "new thought."

Freud came and went, leaving with a poor opinion of America, especially of its "aggressive women" and bad food. But he left behind a huge imprint, one so large that it has overwhelmed much of the traditional American sensibility, helping immeasurably to destroy the Old Establishment in favor of the new one.

The power of Freud grew exponentially in the 1930s after his work was translated by Abraham Brill, a New York analyst. Like Freud, Brill was a brilliant writer: Freud in German, Brill in English. In fact, the only important prize that Freud ever won was the Goethe Prize for German Literature.

The world was turned on its emotional ear when Freud's simply titled work, *Das Es und Das Ich* (The It and the I), became *The Id and the Ego* in the English-language version. The glamorous Latin translation caught on with the literary community and with the intelligentsia, setting up a sense of mysticism that has continued to this day. It is one in which the uncharted "unconscious" has become as real, and sometimes more so, than conscious reality itself.

Thousands of the elite flocked to the analyst's office, where on the couch they tried to unlock their inner minds to find psychological peace. Through the influence of prominent analysands, Freud's ideas spread—from the cocktail party into the media—to the general public, who became entranced with the Unconscious.

The repression of the Id, infantile sexuality, and the supposed neuroses and psychoses created by parents, along with the "cure," became storied in print, film, and the theater.

Soon the theory had totally invaded the educated American psyche. (I recall Id, Ego and Superego being taught in public school in the ninth grade!) Onstage, Katherine Cornell in *Lady in the Dark* brought the mystical world of Freud to the Broadway stage. Then Hollywood was inundated with films like *Spellbound,* starring Gregory Peck and Ingrid Bergman, in which the great unconscious trauma was suddenly recalled and became conscious, producing a cure.

None of what was depicted was true, or in any way scientific. But it entranced the movie-going audiences of the 1940s and 1950s and injected Freudian theory into the minds of millions.

Freud was an imaginative literary genius whose work was developed and marketed at a time when there was little scientific knowledge of the mind, and poetry was called upon to fill the gap. The theories of Freud, who was once known as "the Father of Modern Psychiatry and Psychology," dominated American psychology and the departments of psychiatry at the majority of medical colleges from the decades of the 1930s up through the middle of the 1980s.

But in the last twenty-five years, his clinical influence has declined greatly. Almost all of Freud's theories have been proven false by new scientific knowledge of the mind and the discovery of the biological base of mental illness.

Among the ones that have been discredited by newer research are his ideas on dream interpretation, early sexuality, and the Oedipus Complex—an idea borrowed from Greek tragedy in which the boy-child loves the mother and desires to kill the father.

It now appears that Freud himself suffered from the Oedipus complex and saw himself as typical, falsely projecting the drive as universal among all young males. But beginning in the 1950s, at New York University School of Medicine, the child psychiatrist, Dr. Stella Chess, over the objections of her Freudian colleagues, studied the Oedipus complex by watching boys develop from the nursery to late adolescence. She found that only a handful were subject to the complex and that these, probably like Freud, generally turned out to be emotionally disturbed young adults.

Scientifically, Freud is no longer taken seriously in most medical circles. But that was only after he had done immeasurable damage to the mentally ill and their relatives, especially grieving parents. Accusing fingers were pointed at the parents of those suffering from schizophrenia. They were said to be to blame for having shaped the illness in the child, generally in infancy.

James Wechsler, the late *New York Post* editor-in-chief, was one of those innocent, but accused, parents. When his twenty-seven-year-old son, Michael, committed suicide, he felt the whiplash of the Freudian psychiatric community. While institutionalized, Michael snapped at his father: "You know, Dad, I wasn't *born* this way."

Wechsler heard it everywhere. "The accusation against me required no elaboration," he wrote. "He (Michael) was saying what he—and others—were later to say in one way or another in many family therapy sessions we attended: that their illness could be traced to some parental illness or neglect."

Science now knows better.

But while Freud has been downgraded in the clinical world, his influence in societal power has paradoxically grown enormously. In fact, Freud's ideas have taken over much of the thought processes of two generations.

That takeover has been gradual, sometimes even unseen, but Freud now casts a long shadow over American society. It is especially true within the New Establishment, much of which has been shaped in his godlike image.

What have Americans (and others throughout the world) extracted from Sigmund Freud?

Mainly that there are psychological villains lurking everywhere, determined to repress the Id, or the "Child," as an American Freudian backwater, Transactional Analysis, calls it.

That Id has now been transposed into New Establishment dogma in the form of various social and cultural institutions that financially and morally support the supposed victims of traditional Western society. Like the Id itself, these victims are seen as desperately striving to express their inner selves over the objection of those who would dominate them.

Beyond the clichés, most people are ignorant of Freud's complex doctrines. But despite the inaccuracy of the theories, they do intuitively know his popular thrust: That society is divided into two distinct groups—the psychologically repressed and their oppressors.

How was that idea implanted in the American mind? Simple: *Freud made personal self-indulgence, self-pity, and weakness scientific, and therefore eminently acceptable.*

(Reverence for Freud is not total in the New Establishment. Freud has his opponents in the new order. Feminists, for one, hate Freud and his concept of "Penis Envy." But it should also be noted that in terms of *victimization,* which has flourished on Freudian terms, they include themselves as among the psychologically oppressed. By whom? By men, naturally.)

Freudian folklore also reminds us that the Id is impressionable and fragile. Too much pressure from parents, schools, employers, or society is ostensibly transformed into a "neurotic stimuli," which can make it crack wide open. But by cherishing the Id, and nurturing and feeding it, you will supposedly save the child, and eventually the adult as well.

During the American Cultural Revolution of the 1960s (coming not long after China's own rebellion) we saw the Id elevated to near-godhood. Across the nation, the movement to "Do Your Own Thing," and "Let It All Hang Out," and the directive, "Don't Trust Anyone Over Thirty" (now "Fifty"), headed by such countercultural gurus as Abbie Hoffman, Jerry Rubin and Fritz Perls in Big Sur became a calling for perennial youth.

This movement was, and is, the reason why maturity and rational thinking are so delayed, even crippled, in our adolescent (read "Id") culture. It is why drugs are such a welcome alternative to reality. It is why our arts are puerile, why individual personalities are so arid, and why violent teenage crime is so rampant.

The lazy, the corrupt, the criminal, the addict, are never truly responsible for their failure, the faithful believe. They are merely victims of the strong. In this Freudian drama, the lack of discipline and accomplishment is not only permissible, but actually a badge of honorific victimhood. It has become a saintly virtue in the new dogma. Or if you will, the New Religion.

The theory is false but, unfortunately, it can be infinitely seductive. It's doubly successful because it focuses on SELF, which has now become a scientific quest. Never before has a philosophical system been so preoccupied with self-focusing, self-interest, and self-indulgence and so little interested in the collective health of society.

The inner self of each person has become the center of existence. The major mystery is "finding one's self," which generally results in exploring nothing deeper than gastrointestinal distress.

The New Establishment capitalizes on this *scientific selfishness* by making each person, and each group (no matter how small), the nucleus of the Universe. It focuses on the emotional, political, and legal rights of each person, and each subgroup, all of which supercedes the needs of a decent society.

We've heard of the "me" generation of the 1970s and 1980s, but this phenomenon is not just a reflection of one period. It cuts across all age groups, genders, races, and ethnic backgrounds, and swears its allegiance to Freud as a central god of the New Establishment. But never before has the SELF commanded such immediate attention, enabling anyone who gives obeisance to the New Establishment to shout: "I AM ENTITLED."

The second law of the Freudian dogma inevitably follows. It is the denial of personal responsibility. If "I" am a psychological victim, then *something* or *someone* must be the cause of my problems. This frees the individual from blame and places it everywhere else. Irresponsibility—personal or that of a group—has now become not just an "excuse" but the scientific reason for failure.

Who then is the Great Satan? Who is to blame?

Naturally, the white male—alive or dead. This major force in the creation and maintenance of Western society is now the villain of the piece and the supposed oppressor of virtually everyone else.

What the New Establishment states as dogma is that the victims are unable to self-actualize because male-dominated Protestant American society has repressed them, making them feel inferior and thus less able to work, study, think, and succeed.

That dogmatic litany is blatant nonsense, but, surprisingly, it is bought by otherwise intelligent people. But just because it is false doesn't mean that its popularity and power should be underestimated.

It can be very attractive within a society that is worn and tired (like ours?) and in which people feel rejected, frustrated or superfluous. It also has instant appeal to those who would cop out of the stern requirements of Western culture. It has, in fact, taken over the minds of millions within American society, and made blaming others one of the underlying props of the New Establishment.

With that sanctification of failure and irresponsibility comes still another message: that observable reality is a lie. Instead, *social salvation,* at whatever cost, is the true goal of mankind. In that new faith, truth has no currency except when its followers believe that it advances their basic argument—that traditional Western Judeo-Christian civilization and its concentration on reason is the enemy.

Free will, they maintain, is a myth fostered by the oppressors. The theory that "someone made me do it," or "kept me from doing it," is patently false. In reality, almost all victimization is produced by individuals and groups *themselves.* People, genders, races, ethnics, subcultures—unless they are in legalized slavery—are fully responsible for their actions, and will always achieve according to their ability and willpower, regardless of obstacles.

But the New Establishment has turned its back on this truism. The result is that we have schools without physical or mental discipline; racial pandering and strife; welfare with checks but without hope; antinationalism as a matter of faith; children who fail to appreciate the sacrifice of parents; illegitimacy as an epidemic; crime that is forgiven because it ostensibly springs from poverty; lies masquerading as social truths; individuals without gifts or discipline seeking rewards due to others; the end of shame; illegal immigrants demanding their "rights" in a foreign nation; art that denigrates the nobility of life; widespread drug usage; false worship of youth; people without hope who claim they have lost it to their oppressors.

While the elite members of the New Establishment have created this mayhem, they cleverly strive to isolate themselves from its harmful effects.

They may preach one dictum, but they live by another. They may dabble in therapy, even in recreational drugs, extoll the fragile Id, and champion the weak, but underneath, they eschew the blandishments of their own faith. They do not tolerate lack of accomplishment in their own lives, where they prefer the tougher Protestant Ethic, its discipline, and especially its material rewards.

The result is a massive hypocrisy that is becoming evident to even the most superficial student of the era. Scientific forgiveness and permissiveness may be all right for the poor, the racial minorities, the failures, and the dysfunctional, even for many women— the "great unwashed" who can be manipulated and provide the elite with charitable points—but it's not for New Establishmentarians, who *secretly* know how destructive their ideas really are. Hypocrisy has always been the hallmark, or the Achilles heel, of the supposedly religious, but it has now been elevated to an art form.

Since the New Establishment has helped push millions of innocents into a dysfunctional life—intellectually, economically, and spiritually—what better strategy than to create a giant industry to take care of those they have injured? And at the same time to enroll still more adherents while receiving plaudits for good works.

That is exactly what has happened. It is called the "Therapeutic Society." Its corps of workers now numbers several million, a vast army of college graduates in vague disciplines who would otherwise be working in lower-paid, less prestigious jobs.

These "healing professionals" have flourished in the sympathetic ethos of the New Establishment, which took them over as one of its first conquests. Their ranks include psychotherapists of varied nature (including New Age adherents), social workers, probation officers, school guidance counselors, criminologists, poverty workers, even teachers and administrators, ad infinitum.

What is known as "psychiatric social work," for example, has expertly blended Freud with what used to be the province of what Thorstein Veblen called "leisure class" ladies with charitable instincts. Today, an army of pseudoprofessionals trained in neo-Freudian ideas administers to the poor and supposedly dysfunctional, many of whom were weakened in the first place by the dogma of the New Establishment.

The public school system was also one of the first institutions absorbed into the New Establishment. Instead of training teachers for traditional schooling, education colleges now lean heavily on the developmental psychology of the child—a thin, amorphous study that has become more important to educators than knowledge. Adopting this esoteric post-Freudian stance, they have fashioned themselves as "experts" who pretend to know more about teaching than laymen—a claim that has regularly proven to be false.

The New Establishment has developed a strong vested interest in poverty, failure, and dysfunctional behavior. It needs large ranks of the downtrodden in order to put its dogma into play. If all Americans were to become middle-class property owners and self-sufficient (a goal we started to achieve in the 1950s and 1960s) who would then be the subjects for its psychologically based charity?

The older Judeo-Christian culture would rejoice at such an accomplishment. But the New Establishment would be confounded. Could there be an unconscious (one for Freud!) need to *increase* rather than decrease the number of victims just to sustain the New Religion?

For the Therapeutic Society, the growing dysfunctional behavior in all subcultures is like manna from heaven. The New Establishment not only grants healing workers prestige and affluence, and billions to spend from federal, state, and local governments, but it indoctrinates the public in the false idea that individual failure is most often the result of oppression and persecution. American society, it insists, is actually a conspiracy against the less fortunate.

In reality, the blame belongs to the accuser. The army of New Establishment healers appears to be in collusion with its clients in sustaining illegitimacy, welfare, illegal immigration, school failure, joblessness, drug dependency, and even crime.

We regularly see that these "healers" fail to set decent standards and stronger discipline (the secret of the successful Protestant ethic) that would improve their clients' lives and perhaps even remove them from the ranks of the poor and the dysfunctional. Instead, they use contemporary New Establishment excuses to explain away failure.

Why? *Perhaps because if too many of their clients succeed in shaking dependency, it could eliminate the giant "poverty-sickness" industry and thus damage the healer's own emotional stability.*

The second god in the New Establishment firmament is another non-American, Karl Marx, whose philosophy dovetails nicely with that of Freud. He too has failed as a practitioner of truth, but his legacy has assumed enormous inner power in the New Establishment—even if it outwardly denies it.

Born in Trier, Germany, the son of a lawyer, Marx lived in Berlin, Paris, and Brussels, where in 1848 he wrote the *Communist Manifesto*. Expelled from Belgium, he settled in London, where he lived in obscurity and relative poverty, supported by the English socialist textile manufacturer Friedrich Engels. It was in the British Museum that he wrote his magnum opus, *Das Kapital,* and changed man's view of society.

Written in 1867, *Das Kapital* helped launch the Socialist-Communist movement throughout the world, from the democratic Socialist parties of Western Europe to the ultimate Communist state of the Soviet Union. That revolution took place fifty years after the publication of Marx's bible, then lasted seventy years until its disintegration.

Despite formal failure (as with Freud), the residual legacy of Marx is enormous. One doesn't have to accept the concept of state ownership or even read a word of his works to absorb the basic tenet of the Marxism dogma—that the rich oppress the poor. If wealth were better distributed, the dogma states, the poor would become richer.

Though history has demonstrated that the theory is false, it is still held by many millions of adherents throughout the world, even in America.

If the theory were true, poverty could be easily solved by such forced redistribution. It's been tried everywhere, including the U.S.A., but it hasn't worked. One reason is that wealth is not a zero sum game. Most important, redistribution doesn't teach its recipients the secrets of work and education, the twin pillars of self-sufficiency.

Taking some impetus from Marx, European welfare states have developed effective, if prohibitively expensive, safety nets for their populations, including substantial retirement pensions at an early age (in France, it can begin as early as 55), sizable employment insurance checks, virtually free medical and university systems, etc.

Some even went heavily into the business of government-owned industries, especially in the 1960s and 1970s, when the Marxist theory was fashionable. But they have since realized their failure and are privatizing, just as Russia is now doing. The once-socialist British Labor Party has even renounced its goal of nationalized industry.

Though Marxism has had some structure in Europe, that hasn't been true in America, where most citizens dislike strong government control. So one would think that Marxism would find no home in the New World.

But it has. Not as a formal idea, as in the former Soviet Union, or even as in Europe. Instead it has infiltrated the American psyche as a kind of emotional mythology, somewhat tied to its first cousin, Freudianism. That is, a large number of Americans influenced by the New Establishment give credence to the idea that if too many people are successful and rich, then it must follow, as the night the day, that many others will become poor because of exploitation.

Following that thesis, U.S. governments at all levels highly tax the successful and the mildly successful and *supposedly* give the money to the poor in order to narrow the gap between the rich and the less successful.

Sounds good, and seems to make perfect sense. It even follows exactly the victim-oppressor theories of the New Establishment. The only problem is that it doesn't work, as we are now witnessing in America.

As more people succeed each year, and more become millionaires, and more wealth is redistributed through excessive taxes, the gap between the rich and the poor has *increased*, not *decreased* as forecast by Marxist theory.

In fact, never before has America had so many heavily taxed rich. And never before has so much money been redistributed to the poor through eighty inefficient, overlapping, poorly designed, and bureaucratic federal welfare programs. Yet despite $3 trillion expended to date, poverty has reached an all-time high and the rich are richer and the poor have become poorer.

According to the Congressional Research Service, which publishes the catalogue, *Cash and Non-Cash Benefits for People of Lim-*

ited Income, the amount of welfare has now passed $400 billion a year (more than $300 billion federal and over $100 billion from the states) to feed, house, clothe, heal, and educate the poor, the largest category of government expenditure by far. (This does *not* include Medicare or Social Security.)

Despite the publication of false statistics in the press, all forms of welfare are collectively the largest category of government spending, exceeding by far the second largest, the defense budget.

So why hasn't this Marxist-inspired program lifted people out of poverty? Because the supposed redistribution of income (much of which is used up by the bureaucracy) is like Christmas turkeys from a reborn Scrooge. It is a palliative that does take from the comfortable, or once-comfortable, but does not increase the earning power of the poor.

The true battleground is education, experience in business, personal initiative, and the collective economic striving of any group's subculture—whether Asian or African-American. Unfortunately, these are concepts that the Freudian-Marxist dogma actively discourages.

In the Great Depression, Franklin Roosevelt, determined to fight Marxism, closed most welfare programs and instituted the WPA, the Works Progress Administration, which, over its eight year span, gave work to eight and a half million Americans— equal to seventeen million today—in a variety of activities, from painting murals to repaving streets, all of which maintained the work ethic until the economy improved.

But this doesn't satisfy New Establishment criteria. That requires *victims,* especially those mired in poverty from generation to generation, in order to have sufficient charity cases to advertise the munificent workings of their false gods.

In actuality, the New Establishment and its diluted Marxist influence is the major cause of the rising gap between the economic classes. It may heavily tax the rich and the upper middle class, but its welfare is based on illegitimacy and the dysfunctional behavior it stimulates.

Perhaps most damaging is its insistence that racial and ethnic bias, which mainly affects blacks and Hispanics, is the *central* reason for poverty. This is not only false, as those who rise into the middle class soon realize, but it isolates the poor, mentally and physically, from the working and business mainstream where the real money, not welfare handouts, abounds.

American Marxism, in the form of welfare and supposed redistribution of wealth, has been the greatest curse for the poor in the modern era, keeping the underclass down to provide a constant case study for New Establishment professionals.

Not only is American Marxism destroying the poor, but it is destroying the middle class as well. Its siren song of "soaking the rich" sounds appealing to most at first blush. But they forget that in the New Establishment system, millions of citizens are paying taxes *as if* they were rich!

When the Constitutional prohibition against income taxes (the major reason for the rapid growth of the middle class) was repealed in 1913 by the Sixteenth Amendment, it was sold by Presidents Taft and Wilson as a system to tax the robber barons and never disturb the middle class. The rates were only 1 to 7 percent and the $4,000 exemption freed all but the relatively wealthy at a time when the average annual income was below $1,500.

But as time went on and government costs rose, it became evident that the rich could not support the massive redistribution of income by themselves. Today, for example, the wealthy—defined as the top 1 percent of earners who make $185,000 or more—pay for 28 percent of the federal budget. The poor contribute only a few percentage points of the whole.

One need not be a statistician to realize that the great majority of the vast $1.7 trillion federal monies (plus another $1 trillion-plus for state and local governments) had to come from somewhere else. And that was the great cash cow—the hard-working, often struggling American middle class.

The real victim of the New Establishment is that typical working American. His income tax rates rose regularly, as did his property taxes, while his deductions decreased in every so-called "reform," making him more the oppressed than the oppressor in the New Establishment lexicon. The theme of "soak the rich" became "soak the middle class" under the Marxist influence of the New Establishment. So squeezed is he that, after taxes, the American working man, a *real* victim of redistribution, now earns less in real dollars after taxes than he did in 1973.

In this topsy-turvy world, the family of four that paid only $66 in federal income taxes in 1950, out of a typical income of $3,300, or just 2 percent, now—courtesy of the Great God Marx, through Uncle Sam—pays 1,000 percent more, plus an enormous local and state burden that has risen 350 percent in *real* dollars since 1960. Today, that same family spends more on some thirty basic taxes, from school taxes to bridge tolls, than it spends on food, housing, and clothing combined.

Overall, government—federal, state, and local—spends almost 40 percent of the Gross Domestic Product, as compared with only 17 percent in the supposed big government of FDR and only 22 percent under Harry Truman when we fought the Korean War and had the Marshall Plan and the GI Bill to support.

To see the effects of the Marxian concept of soak-the-middle-class we have only to look at the oppression of the self-employed, from carpenters to musicians, who must pay almost double social security taxes. When they reach the extraordinary wealth of a $42,000 annual taxable income, they are pushed into the 41.3 percent federal bracket, plus state and local taxes, punishing them more than we once did J. P. Morgan.

Marxism in America, as expressed through the New Establishment, is not a serious attempt to take the poor out of poverty. If that ever was its goal, which one doubts, it has been an abysmal failure. Instead,

Marx, as one god of the secular trinity, serves mainly as a threat to the stability of the middle class and a false sop to the frustrations of the poor.

The growing gap between the rich and the poor, which is expanding, is used as a tool not to help the poor, but to punish the successful, a key factor in maintaining its control of the underclass. The constant drum beating of the New Establishment, that poverty is a result of "bias" and "exploitation" and "sexism" and "racism," rather than the absence of education and good-paying work, makes it an agent of the failure.

Both Freud and Marx are foreign gods. Were they the only "religious" pillars of the New Establishment, it might be seen as a radical movement outside the American framework and collapse.

But the New Establishment is no fool. It knew it also had to draw on the Old Establishment God, Jesus, for leavening and softening, and to gain public acceptance.

Jesus is a god whose personality is more familiar to Americans than that of either Freud or Marx. But the New Establishment has not called on the mystical God Jesus, whose sacrifice on the cross represents salvation for believers. Rather, it has made use of the prophet Jesus who preached love and compassion and thus became the third god of the New Establishment Trinity. But their Jesus is not the true Jesus, just a distortion that they have used and misused.

The New Establishment knows the generosity of the American soul and how to manipulate it for its own ends. The key word is *compassion*, which is seldom used today as a phrase of praise. Instead, it is employed as a bludgeon to silence its critics. Whenever the New Establishment is accused of stupidity, irrationality, or irresponsibility, it counters by charging its naysayers as lacking in compassion.

Does the ploy work?

Exceptionally well. Americans insist on being good people,

and the charge that they lack compassion shakes them thoroughly. So much so that the shock empties their minds. Quickly, they yield to the intimidation and are silenced.

By *posing* as Christians, the New Establishment dogmatists turn the true teachings of Christianity against the people. It is a clever, devious, but unfortunately quite effective ploy.

Why does the charge of not having compassion work so well?

Because it plays off another easily triggered American emotion: Guilt.

America has always had a vein of guilt running through its national psyche. The Puritan fathers preached success in this world and glory in heaven. But that came at the price of guilt, an emotion that was much less prevalent in the Old World, where shame was the operating force of societal control.

That trait of guilt has been exploited by the New Establishment, which constantly seeks to use it for its own purposes. One prime method is to exacerbate black-white relations by stimulating guilt among whites about slavery, which mainly existed in the Southern states up until 1865. (The Emancipation Proclamation was issued by Lincoln in 1863, but could not be enforced until victory.)

Most Americans have innocently fallen into that guilt trap without realizing that the great majority of them had nothing whatsoever to do with it, and that there should be no collective indictment.

The reason? Most of our ancestors were not even in America at the time of slavery. They were in Europe and elsewhere and had no contact with that atrocious situation, and therefore deserve no blame. The descendants of immigrants who came to our shores *after* the Civil War now make up a majority of the population. Just the progeny of those who came through Ellis Island, from its opening in 1894 until its closing in 1924, now number over 100 million.

The immigration since 1865 has shaped a population that is

mainly post–Civil War, when there were only 33 million Americans, one-eighth the present count.

Besides, of Americans living then, more than two-thirds were in the North. If one wants to ascribe "group blame," which makes no moral sense today, it would rest on a small minority of Americans who are the descendants of those who lived in the Confederate states. But those in the North were not only not slaveholders, or defenders of slavery, but fought a bloody war started by the South's insistence on maintaining blacks in bondage.

Unlike Germany, where the government sponsored genocide with little public opposition, the U.S. Government—the same federal government as today—attacked the slaveholders and their supporters with an army of whites and blacks and lost 225,000 lives, and suffered even more wounded in the process. It was a carnage that, proportionately, exceeded that of World War I and II combined.

For the overwhelming majority of Americans living today, there is no ancestral blame, a fact Americans should absorb and use to redirect the race conflict, where it exists, into more wholesome understandings that can result in solution, not guilt.

The whole question of guilt has arisen because American Christians were taught concern for each other, which established a charitable streak that is unrivaled anywhere in the world. Last year, aside from the trillions spent on government, Americans gave $128 billion to charity, a form of religious atonement—not for their sins, but for their success.

Today, the New Establishment capitalizes on that generosity. It welds together the joint concepts of *guilt and compassion* and wields it as a double-edged sword to enforce its painful hold on our society.

When did the new dogma begin to affect our social and intellectual sanity? When did the traditional Old Establishment start to lose its power to the interlopers?

By the early 1950s and into the 1960s, the American ethic

had achieved a *Good Society*, actually the most successful in the history of mankind. But as in any culture, there were still blemishes. Many said it was not enough to just be "good." How, for example, could a suburbanite enjoy his barbeque and blessings while others were not sharing equally?

Beginning then, and accelerating into the late 1960s and 1970s, and even into the 1980s, we sought to transform the *Good Society* into the *Perfect Society*. America was the ideal setting, religiously and philosophically, for such a drive. Hadn't Jefferson said that "all men are created equal?" And wasn't egalitarianism the basis of the great American dream?

So why not a Perfect Society?

It was a noble goal, and its first victory was the Civil Rights revolution that gave blacks, especially those in the segregated South, freedom for the first time. It was a base, many believed, to build on, and raised hopes of greater equality and equanimity.

Instead, the crusade was taken away from the people, both from the African-Americans and the whites. Rather than continue the American style of extending more freedom and opportunity to all through *assimilation* under the great American umbrella (or in the huge Melting Pot), the New Establishment sought another route.

First, it sought to destroy the old institutions and build new ones based on *separating* America into special groups, each with its own complaints, and each with a label of "victim."

The nation was being redefined. It was not in terms of expanding the freedom that had just been won, but in terms of a civilization that could only work if each violated group—from women to blacks—was recognized as being oppressed. Only then could all receive their just, and previously denied, rewards.

We've begun to sow the bitter harvest of that new direction. But from the New Establishment's viewpoint, it was a clever maneuver that would sharply divide the nation. Every facet of society—the media, the arts, the government, the foundations, the courts, the schools, and even sympathetic religious pulpits—was called into action. It spoke (and speaks) of hatred, of oppression, instead of freedom and opportunity. And its goal of divisiveness is being achieved, sometimes silently, other times vocally.

The result? Not only have we not achieved the *Perfect Society* as hoped, but the *Good Society* of yesteryear has been lost in the process. With it has gone much of American unity and its attendant happiness.

So defeated have the premises of our society become that even if a widespread new affluence, as in the 1950s, were suddenly granted to us, few would know how to recapture the spirit of the once-Good Society. Most of us fear that it is a thing of the past, even though we yearn for its return.

How, we might ask, does the New Establishment accomplish its daily magical destruction? What themes does it play on to eventually *play down* the American experience? What sophistry is employed in its armamentarium against social harmony?

There are several themes that it uses and distorts. One of them, of course, is *Egalitarianism,* a powerful and traditional concept that should always receive enthusiastic approval. It is part and parcel of our history. Jefferson's phrase, "All Men Are Created Equal," heralded that thought and surely meant that all *people*—men and women of all races everywhere—had inborn natural rights that could never be taken away.

But Jefferson the philosopher was also an expert scientist. He did not mean that all individuals had equal intellectual capability or talent, or were equally dedicated, ambitious, or hard-working. By anyone's definition, Jefferson himself was surely more than equal in brains and industry. The egalitarianism that Jefferson preached, and which good Americans have eagerly adopted, was for equal rights under the law and for equal opportunity. No less. No more.

The initial failing of the Constitution in not granting equal legal rights to blacks or women has, as democracy evolved, been corrected. In the American experience since then it has been up to the individual to achieve at his or her own level of success. No groups are exempt from the rule, no groups are excluded, and no groups should be favored.

But the New Establishment thinks otherwise. To it, *Egalitarianism* means *Equal Achievement,* a highly unlikely goal that no religion, no government, no god, can order up. All groups, they say, must attain the same level of success, or ipso facto, it is proof that discrimination and bias have raised their ugly snouts. Reduced *performance* by any group, whether African-Americans or women, is supposedly automatic confirmation of oppression.

This, of course, is a ridiculous concept no matter how many times the New Establishment asserts it.

However, the government, other institutions, and often the pliable press, go along with this irrational idea and regularly regale us with *counting.* Women earn less than men by X dollars a year; blacks represent a higher percentage of those in jail; the Hispanic unemployment rate is higher than that of whites; disabled people have a tougher time in life; African-Americans score less well on the SATs; fat people are less well-liked than thin people.

It's a constant litany, and rising in volume. What are we to infer from this all? The New Establishment says that it's proof that America is unfair, that the disparity between group performance represents an evil of bias that must be attacked.

The latest affront to reason is the New Establishment notion of what they call "Under-representation." It states that all professions and activities must show equal representation of all groups in relation to the overall population. If not, we are supposedly witnessing discrimination at work.

Of all the New Establishment theories, this makes the least sense. Naturally, some groups will always be proportionately "underrepresented" in certain activities, businesses, and professions, either as a measure of choice or differing abilities or varied interests. And conversely, other groups will be overrepresented.

Let's look at some of the grievously "underrepresented" groups. Whites are gravely underrepresented in special schools of science and math where Asians excel. Gentiles are heavily underrepresented in psychiatry, accounting, law, and most professions in relation to Jews; conversely, Jews are underrepresented in farming, where white Gentiles are dominant.

Whites are underrepresented in pop music and sports in relation to blacks. In fact, "discrimination" is so rampant in pro basketball that whites are virtually absent—particularly short whites.

Irish are overrepresented in the upper echelons of police and fire departments in most cities. Caucasians are underrepresented in the fruit and vegetable field, where Koreans dominate, as do Indians (from India) in the newsstand business.

Greeks seem to have victimized other European-Americans in controlling the "diner" industry, while the Chinese have a hammerlock on Chinese restaurants and hand laundries. Italians are overwhelmingly present in the asphalt, concrete, sand-and-gravel, and masonry businesses, surely at the expense of the Irish and Anglos, for instance. Portuguese-Americans are overrepresented in the fishing business.

One of the most unfair cases of group domination involves women, who have not only hogged the raising of children, but are increasingly top-heavy in the ranks of failing public school education, where they are pushing male teachers out of the classroom. The National Library of Education reports that 84 percent of all elementary-school teachers are women, and that, for the first time, women now make up a *majority* of high school teachers!

(Where does the New Establishment stand on that obvious case of bias?)

"Victims" can be found everywhere if you look at group statistics, which have nothing to do with democracy or America or Western civilization or free choice. Though the New Establishment concept of affirmative action—what I call "Achievement

Charity"—is nonsensical, it is at the heart of the raging cultural and social insanity in America, a condition that will continue until we stop counting.

The lie that inferior performance is related to bias has been exposed, as we have seen, by the record of two small minorities, the Jews and Asians. Together, they make up only 5 percent of the population, yet considerably more of those with superior achievement.

One answer to the question of the New Establishment's obsession with unequal achievement, and the angst that seems to accompany it, is found in the commentary of the French sage Alexis de Tocqueville, whose impressions of America still ring true today: *"Aristocractic nations are liable to narrow the scope of human perfectability; democratic nations to expand it beyond reason."*

The failure to achieve the unlikely visions of the New Establishment—that Egalitarianism means Equal Achievement—is, quite literally, driving the nation mad.

One of the New Establishment's favorite thought techniques is the fantasy game of "What if?" That's a luxury not usually entertained in the pragmatic Protestant Ethic, where the normal query is either "What?" or "How?"

But "What if?" has become a keystone of today's experimental society. It enables the New Establishment to imagine whatever it wants, and then present the conjured idea in place of reality and seek its enforcement through the government, the law, or the pressures of conformity. The "What if?" may be true only because it says it is, but that clever technique has been instrumental in upsetting the national stability.

What if women are made into combat troops even if they're physically weaker than men? *What if* we prefer to teach children to read with pictures instead of phonics, the proven superior method, as several studies indicate? *What if* it's better to bring immigrants with AIDs into this country from the Third World while healthy people from Europe are excluded? *What if* we pretend that it benefits Hispanics never to learn to speak English well in school because we honor their native Spanish as much as our native English? *What if* we segregate already segregated Native Americans on the college campus?

None of the "What ifs" has to be true, or even reasonable, to become rigid dogma. The new faith can theorize about virtually anything, no matter how bizarre, and use its enormous power in the schools, in government, in the judiciary, and elsewhere to put its unproven theory into action.

Perhaps a "What if" turns out to be true only one in ten times. The New Establishment seldom scores even that well, but it is the great mass of society—not the New Establishment—that ends up paying for the failure, both in money and in still more national instability.

In the Great Guilt Game, the New Establishment confounds and upsets society by constantly proposing irrational "What ifs." It then screams bloody murder when society doesn't measure up to its goals, none of which are as honest or effective as the American Old Establishment's tradition of assimilation and opportunity.

We will look at one of the great "What ifs" of our time, the status of women in the dogma. The proponents of the New Establishment say the subject is taboo, but nothing could be more important or better exemplify the national madness.

Join with me in this most intriguing of examinations.

CHAPTER THREE

AMERICAN WOMEN

Darlings of the
New Establishment

DESPITE THE NEW ESTABLISHMENT AND RAPID change whirling around us, many Americans believe there will always be old standbys in the culture that are reassuring touchstones with the past.

One is the family doctor, who has been portrayed in movies and television as a symbol of sympathy and stability. In the 1930s and 1940s, there was the white-haired film thespian Lewis Stone, sitting patiently beside the sickbed waiting for the "crisis" to pass. In the 1960s, there was handsome young Dr. Kildare, gowned in green, followed by that landmark family physician in suit and tie, Marcus Welby, M.D., so warmly played by Robert Young.

In every case, of course, the doctor was a man. But isn't that still the case?

Hardly. If we examine the first-year class of medical colleges today to see who will be checking our heartbeat tomorrow, we'll find the stethoscope increasingly resting on the bosom of a woman, that special friend of the New Establishment. More than likely, the physician to whom you'll soon entrust your life will be *Marsha* Welby, M.D.

Having taken over America's campuses (see Chapter Four), the New Establishment has now moved into a commanding position in professional schools, especially medicine and law, where it is aggressively enrolling women through the modern vehicle of "affirmative action." So successful has that push been that it makes the black-white controversy pale by comparison.

Its rationale? Since women seeking to become doctors were once supposedly discriminated against (a masterful lie we shall soon examine), society is now obligated to correct the error. But this is not just a matter of gender hierarchy and power. Since it involved medical care, the stakes are much higher—a matter of life and death.

The change in medical colleges has been so dramatic that women now outnumber men in the entering class at eighteen schools, especially in the most prestigious ones.

In the 1995–1996 first year class at the University of California, San Francisco, medical school, for instance, there were seventy-two women and sixty-nine men, the same female majority as in the Yale class of 1994–1995. The Harvard Medical School, class of 1995–1996 had a similar breakdown: eighty-five women and only eighty-one men.

Are these just a handful of medical schools experimenting with the "What if" theory that women are as scientifically inclined as men and will be just as skilled at diagnosis, surgery, research, or doctoring in general?

Absolutely not. This is an authentic national gender revolution. According to the Association of American Medical Colleges, (AAMC), the entering class at medical schools nationwide is already over 42 percent female, radically changing the complexion of the profession. In 1970, says the AMA, only 7 percent of doctors were women. Today, the number has reached 24 percent, and more significant, over 35 percent of doctors 35 years of age or younger are women.

With 42 percent females in the first year classes, in the next fifteen years, the ranks of women doctors will increase *nine* times as rapidly as men.

It takes less than a Ph.D. in statistics to visualize what the profession will soon look like. Unless there's an abrupt reversal, half (or more) of the nation's doctors will eventually be women.

And why not? Women make up a majority of the population. Aren't they just as competent in science as men? Aren't any claims to the contrary just another case of blatant gender prejudice?

To find the answer we must first look briefly at the history of medical care in America. Prior to 1910, medicine wasn't a true profession. The Flexner Report, commissioned by the Carnegie Foundation and authored by Abraham Flexner, the son of a German-Jewish immigrant, exposed medical education of the day as a near-primitive discipline.

Often untutored physicians in makeshift schools taught what little they knew, passing on such ignorant techniques as leeching, cupping, even bleeding (which killed George Washington) from generation to generation. There were exceptions such as Johns Hopkins in Baltimore, but most of the 150 medical schools of 1910 were diploma mills with little academic overview.

As a result of the report, two-thirds of the schools were closed by the states and the remainder were forced to affiliate with universities. It was the beginning of medical education as we know it today, an excellent postgraduate training program.

The Flexner reforms were of great value, but medicine was still not the scientific enterprise it had to be to fulfill the patient's expectations. The recently deceased Dr. Arthur K. Shapiro of Mount Sinai Hospital in New York, a noted medical historian, explained that up until World War II medicine was not scientific enough to correctly claim that it had saved lives overall.

The net value to the patient was mainly the result of hope and the placebo effect, not science. But even that small gain was wiped out by the deleterious effects of iatrogenic, or doctor-caused, illness.

Only in the last fifty years has medicine become a true scientific discipline, moving ahead more dramatically than anyone had imagined. The result is that millions of lives have been saved and lengthened.

The improvement has been continuous. In 1966, I authored *The Doctors,* a nonfiction study which laid out the clinical liabilities of American physicians, especially in relation to superior university medicine. I was supported by many academic physicians but attacked by the American Medical Association (AMA) because of my recommendations, almost all of which have since been adopted. Today, clinical medicine in America, with its expertise in many specialties, is the best in the world, even if too often uneven in quality and selfish in its economics.

Is the New Establishment's push to recruit more women into medicine designed to enhance that excellence? Is it motivated by a desire to train more creative stars, especially in the subspecialties of oncology, neurosurgery, organ transplant, kidney dialysis, brain and cancer research, or complex heart bypass surgery?

No, it has nothing to do with superior science or medicine. The New Establishment campaign to bring more women into medicine is a matter of simply balancing the genders.

Which returns us to the prime question: "Are women in general as qualified to become doctors as men?"

The New Establishment loudly proclaims "Yes." And why not? Women are its greatest boosters and most enthusiastic clients. But judging from available evidence, the answer in too many cases is "No." It may be an unfashionable response but the information supplied by the profession and by outside measurement sources sustains that negative opinion.

In building a scientific profession, the medical schools once chose only those with the *verifiable* brightest talent. But that goal seems to have dramatically changed. Instead of science as the prime criterion, social justice for women (and minorities) is now the clear goal of the New Establishment. Women are being enrolled in medical colleges in overwhelming numbers even though all indices show that, in general, female applicants possess less scientific aptitude than men.

Women have lower scientific skills? Why bring up that old chestnut, a case of male stereotypical thinking that should have gone out with universal suffrage? Why would medical colleges accept students who are less qualified than others? And who's spreading this anti-female calumny, anyway?

Good question. Surprisingly, the villain is the profession itself, which admits that in objective measures of scientific aptitude, women candidates for slots in medical school fail on average to measure up to the men.

"For the last three years, equivalent proportions of women and men have been accepted [into medical schools] despite the tendency of women to score lower than men on most parts of the Medical College Admission Test (MCAT) and to have a slightly lower science GPA (Grade Point Average.)"

Who penned that seemingly biased evaluation? It is none other than the official organization, the Association of American Medical Colleges, as reported in their bulletin, "Women in U.S. Academic Medicine, Statistics, 1995."

Not only students, but women medical faculty members are rapidly moving ahead through affirmative action. In 1995, the number of female full professors grew 9 percent, as against only 3 percent for men. While the older faculty is still heavily men, some 44 percent of the younger instructors are already women.

Again, one need not be a statistician to see that absent a radical shift, women will soon share equally with men, as both physicians and faculty members, totally changing the face of American medicine.

For the better? The answer to that is still another question: "If merit were the only criterion would women in medicine be enrolled and move ahead at the present rate?"

Probably not. The profession is frank about its affirmative action goals. The dean of admissions at Harvard Medical School, Mohan D. Boodram, stated when interviewed that affirmative action at Harvard has been in place there for almost a quarter of a century.

The AAMC is also frank about it. Says that organization: "AAMC recognizes that medicine needs more women in top administrative positions and has launched a new initiative with multiple strategies to increase the number of women leaders."

Should these official views draw applause for seeking social justice for women? Or should their political initiative engender fear among the public—all of whom are, or will be, patients of the doctors they train?

Is the AAMC admission that women do not score as well as men on certain sections of the MCAT significant? It is referring to the two science sections of that test, the *only standardized instruments* that admissions officers have to go by. Even though men score slightly higher on college undergraduate grades, those measures are becoming less meaningful because of widespread "grade inflation," a new academic phenomenon.

MCAT scores are more significant because they are the only *objective* measure we have to gauge scientific aptitude.

How much better than women do men score on the MCAT?

The 5¾-hour examination, which is given each April and August, comes in four sections: verbal, writing skills, biological sciences, and physical sciences. The top score in each of the three (other than writing) is fifteen points, for a total of forty-five.

Of the four tests, the writing skill test is considered the least important. On the verbal and writing, the two sexes score about the same, with the men only a touch ahead. *But of the remaining two tests, both in science, women score significantly lower than the men, even dramatically so.*

The AAMC figures are rather startling for a profession based on science. In the physical sciences, the male mean score is 8.58, while the female tally is only 7.54. In percentage points, it means that the men score 14 percent higher than the women, a giant leap in academic terms. For patients, it is even a greater leap of faith. Translated in terms of everyday school grades, it is the difference between a *B*+ for men and a *C* for women.

On the biological sciences, a slightly less "hard" discipline, the women hoping to become doctors also score considerably lower, a matter of 10 percent less. That represents the spread between a 75 and an 83 grade, which any schoolchild knows (or used to know) cannot be easily overlooked.

Fewer women score in the upper reaches of the MCAT, from whose ranks we would expect the most brilliant and inventive doctors to emerge. In the physical science test, for example, men reach the "exemplary" grade of 10 at the sixty-third percentile, which means 37 percent of male applicants scored higher. But the women don't reach that level until the eightieth percentile, which means that only 20 percent scored higher.

What does this mean? Surely, that on a national level, places for future doctors are being taken away from talented men and given to less qualified women.

Critics might answer that standardized tests such as the MCAT are not necessarily good predictors of talent, and that grades, interviews and subjective opinions might be as valuable. All evidence indicates the opposite. The experience of New York's science scholarship schools—Stuyvesant High School and the Bronx High School of Science—is excellent corroboration of the value of using *only* standardized tests in selecting superior candidates.

To gain admission to either school, students take a standardized test, and do not reveal their race or ethnic background. There is no interview and their previous grades are not taken into account. The applicants are never seen and therefore there is no subjective judgment of them by school officials.

Has it worked out? Have these test-selected students done better than others?

Absolutely. Though the Stuyvesant and Bronx High students make up less than one-twentieth of one percent of all American secondary school students, in 1996–97, they won over 10 percent (32) of all three hundred Westinghouse Science Talent Search semifinalist slots in 1996—*two hundred* times more than the average student.

What then would the makeup of the 1997–1998 medical school class look like if there were no affirmative action for women and the standardized MCAT science tests were the criteria for admission as they generally used to be?

It requires complex statistical work, but the answer appears to be that the class would be as high as 80 percent male, and even higher if slots were not set aside for minorities. That is quite different from the present ratio, and more like the admission standards of old.

In trying to satisfy this New Establishment "What if" about women are we risking the excellence of an entire profession? Should we put the initials "A.A.P." after the M.D. of many of our female doctors—"Affirmative Action Physicians"?

Medical college admissions officers counter with an extraordinary theory: that there are things more important than skill in science when choosing doctors. The admission deans at both Harvard and Yale medical schools stress the importance of the interview, the personality and attitude of the applicant, the student's extracurricular work, and the *subjective* opinion of medical interviewers on how the student views the doctor-patient relationship.

"Women seem to communicate better in the interview," Gerald Foster, Harvard's associate dean for admissions, has been quoted as stating. He added that women "bring some life experiences and maturity that add to the class." Measuring 'life experiences" that put women ahead of men seems to be a new discipline invented by Harvard and other New Establishment psychometricians.

The prejudice in favor of women is evident in this new environment. "I have seen men with a perfect 4.0 Grade Point Average and top MCAT scores who I would consider near psychotic," an admissions officer at Yale told me. "I wouldn't admit them to our medical school."

A reasonable attitude? Perhaps, or perhaps not. He might be screening out a brilliant "mad" male genius who would cure cancer in favor of a female who "interviews well."

The implied thought in this new feminization of medicine is that women might be better at the doctor-patient relationship than men, which is a highly doubtful premise. Unlike the MCAT, there's no objective proof of either sex having better skill in that area. Even if it were true, which it probably is not, are we turning back the clock to the prescientific days when physicians made consoling house calls—which became even more humane as the patient was about to die? The early twentieth-century doctor was noted for his concern, but surely not for his command of medical science.

From among the vast pool of the *best* young scientists—who appear to be overwhelmingly male—the medical colleges can surely find candidates with the right attitude toward patients without accepting scientifically inferior students.

When the doctor's knife slips during a heart bypass operation or the physician is dumbfounded trying to diagnose an atypical cancer, does the patient care that the doctor was the president of the high school class or played the tuba in the band? Or even that the physician loves humanity, or "interviewed well," as admissions people like to say to rationalize their obvious gender bias?

In any case, man or woman, won't all inferior candidates flunk out of medical school anyway?

Absolutely not. The best answer comes from Dr. Thomas Lentz, Assistant Dean for Admissions at the Yale School of Medicine. When interviewed at New Haven, he responded, "Almost no one flunks out for academic failure. We carefully select our people so that they will succeed."

That, of course, is the self-protective response designed to uphold the professional myth that everyone who is chosen is eminently qualified—part of the old boy (now old girl) network of common defensiveness. Statistics show that the profession sticks to its mythology. Only a handful of entering students fail for academic reasons. Of the 16,289 medical students in the fourth year graduating class, only *fifty-one* were dismissed for academic reasons—or one-third of 1 percent, the lowest failure rate of any academic institution, from high school upwards. Another study conducted by the AMA, showed that of 67,000 medical students in all four years, only 207 were dismissed for academic reasons, the same ridiculous one-third of one percent.

But surely, the incompetents will be caught by the medical licensing exam, as in the case of the bar exam, which flunks about one in three would-be lawyers.

No. Future doctors are *not* strictly screened by the United States Medical Licensing Examination (USMLE), an easy obstacle that permits those who pass to practice in any of the fifty states. Unlike the bar exam, the threshold for passing it is low. Ninety-six percent pass the final test the first time, and two-thirds of the remainder pass the next time.

Lawyers generally have only three tries at the bar exam, but to accommodate affirmative action students, minorities as well as women, medical licensing exam standards have been lowered. Applicants can take the test an unlimited number of times. Naturally, virtually 100 percent of all medical school students are eventually licensed as M.D.s.

77

Dr. Philip A. Korzeniowski of the UCLA School of Medicine decries the new permissive medical licensing exam standards, which no longer have a point score, but are merely graded as "pass" or "fail." Previously, many hospitals would not take residents who scored under 450, when the passing grade was 380. Now that the USMLE has no scores, there is no reliable way to distinguish one graduate from another, he says. "Medicine," laments Dr. Korzeniowski, "is not a pass-fail career."

But let's take a moment and return to the old saw that women are finally being admitted to medical school today "to make up for past discrimination."

That conjures up a simple image of male venality. In the old days, say almost forty years ago, women applicants to medical school were supposedly turned down en masse because of gender bias. Medicine was an old boy's network and they just weren't going to let women in no matter how many applied, or how talented they were.

It's a consoling image for the New Establishmentarians who now control our medical school application process. *But the reality is that it is a bald-faced lie.* In 1960, 1,044 women applied to medical school, some 7 percent of the total. And 600 were accepted—7 percent of the total. They were accepted in exactly the same ratio as the men. There was *no discrimination,* just an absence of female applicants.

In 1996, there were 19,779 female applicants, or 42.5 percent of the whole, with the same percentage of admissions.

There was absolutely no prejudice against women in medical school admission back in 1960. But there is an enormous bias today. However, it is against men, most of whom score higher than women but are turned away from medicine by the thousands because of female affirmative action.

How seriously will this affect medicine? Will the quality of medical care suffer? Most assuredly it will, a conclusion backed by statistics supplied by the profession itself.

One major reason for the damage is the eccentric, even distorted, view of the field held by most new women doctors. Do female physicians follow the same path as men, one that has produced the finest clinical medicine in the world?

Absolutely not. An AAMC study of all 32,694 women residents in specialty training shows that they cluster in a handful of fields, taking the easy route by entering the "soft specialties."

According to those statistics, most women doctors enter one of five fields: psychiatry, pediatrics, family practice, internal medicine, and obstetrics and gynecology. In both obstetrics and pediatrics, women now comprise a *majority* of trainees.

The New Establishment's feminization of medicine will dramatically change medical care in America—for the worse. It will shape a field with less attention to the forty specialties that now characterize American excellence and attract patients from around the world. In a gender-equal profession, that emphasis will be enormously diminished as the older men die.

The female switch in direction is obvious, and rather frightening. According to the AAMC, almost two-thirds of all female doctors (62.7 percent) are training for just those five specialties, while ignoring most of the others, especially the more complex ones.

But the male doctors cover all the spots quite well, with only 39 percent going into those same five basic specialties. The rest enter the more demanding ones, especially the surgical subspecialties. Unlike the women, men cover all the specialties quite well, at least until the female revolution overwhelms them numerically.

So what will American medicine look like in that not-so-distant future?

It will be skewed toward feminine wishes, not medical necessity. What will the "Achievement Charity" granted women (and minorities as we shall see in Chapter Seven) do to American excellence? Obviously, it will tend to destroy it, if only because of female nonparticipation in needed fields, to say nothing of the

79

quality of female doctors in general, which is still an unknown factor.

Surgery is a case in point. Most women doctors avoid the physically and mentally demanding work that surgical training and practice require. In the AAMC survey, only one in twenty-two recent graduates are going into this field. That will mean a weakening of cardiac surgery, orthopedics, urology, breast surgery, and colon and rectal surgery. Of the latter, only *seven* women residents are now training in all of America.

The same deficiency is demonstrated in an AMA tally, which showed that there wasn't a single woman training in adult reconstructure orthopedics or in general hand surgery. Though a majority (61 percent) of pediatric residents are women, they avoid pediatric surgery, where only eight females are training in the entire nation.

Take heart surgery. Today, 501,000 heart bypass operations are performed each year, with the number expected to rise to 1 million. This procedure has granted new health with a survival rate approaching 99 percent.

But what will the future of this field look like when the women doctors are equal numerically? Bleak. Why? Because there are now 2,293 male cardiovascular surgeons. And women? A total of 45. But surely there are many more in training. Not really. A study of all six years of surgical residency shows that only *fourteen* women are in training as cardiac surgeons. Who will do the million operations when the time comes? (Perhaps one shouldn't wait too long to get that triple bypass.)

The same dilemma exists in the newest and most promising of surgical fields, the organ transplant of hearts, kidneys, and livers. New women doctors are not picking up the slack created by men retiring from that difficult, but life-saving, field.

Extrapolating the heart surgeon figures to other complex fields, we can easily see a return to the prosaic, even inferior, American medicine that we had before the full specialty revolution that began in the 1960s. In the future—unless male doctors are willing to work twice as hard and twice as long—we can anticipate that American patients will go to Europe for their complex medical care, instead of vice versa.

Is the relative failure in science and math demonstrated by women in the medical school admissions test just a factor of the MCAT, or does it show up in other standardized tests as well?

Apparently the difference is evident everywhere.

The Scholastic Assessment Test (SAT) already taken by millions of high school youngsters to buttress their college applications shows the same differences between boys and girls aged seventeen, and ostensibly men and women as well.

From 1972 to 1995, both sexes scored virtually the same on the verbal part of the SATs (both dropped 25 points over those years!), though men now outscore women by a modest few points on that scale. But the SAT math scores, which correlate strongly with science and technical ability, have consistently shown a *very large spread* between boys and girls, with males far ahead.

In 1972, on average, boys scored 505 on the math SATs and females 461, or a difference of 44 points. In 1995, the difference has held up: 503 to 463, a spread of 40 points, with no statistically significant change over the last twenty-three years. Equally disappointing, in the new "recentered" scale of the SATs, women have consistently scored a substantial 38 points less on the math exam in recent years, a figure generally equal to the over-40 spread on the old scale.

This difference is actually greater than it seems. The bottom score on the SATs—which students get just for signing their names—is 200. So a 40-point spread is really over a 263, not 463, base, an enormous disparity in demonstrated ability.

Why?

Proponents of the "interchangeable" theory of men and women loudly proclaim that "cultural values" are to blame. They contend that in our society women are less exposed to math and less encouraged to study the subject and therefore score less well on it. However, the spread in math and science aptitude scores between men and women is universal, occurring in Europe and Asia as well.

To test such "cultural" theories and eliminate so-called "gender bias," the Educational Testing Service, which runs the SATs, continually tries to create questions that are gender-neutral. Each year, they give youngsters a battery of "experimental questions," which are not counted in the applicant's scores. But the responses to these questions enable the SAT people to eliminate any question in which one group scores lower than the norm.

"For example, if Hispanic girls don't do as well on a question as members of other groups, we just eliminate the question," says an ETS spokesman in Princeton, New Jersey. "Eventually, we hope the test will be gender-, race-, and ethnic-bias free."

(The ETS has also learned that when the SAT tests are speeded up, girls do not do as well as boys. The result? The tests are not speeded up.)

Have the bias-test changes had any positive effect on SAT scores? In the case of race, they have. The difference in SAT scores between white and black students, for example, has been cut down. But the point spread between men and women on the math test seems immune to any efforts to eliminate what is falsely called "gender" bias. It is still large and virtually constant year to year.

Why? Because the difference in performance on the MCAT science and the SAT math tests by boys and girls, as well as on other such tests, is probably not a cultural effect. Rather, it seems to be a biosocial (biology interacting with society) phenomenon.

Men seem to be hormonally stimulated in the direction of both math and science aptitude while women, *in general,* are not. It seems that girls do almost as well in math in the early years, but that boys move rapidly ahead in both math and science with the onset of puberty, and continue onward.

This failure of females in general to do as well as males in mathematics has frustrated the New Establishment. That frustration only increased when it was learned that the lack of math aptitude was keeping young women from becoming National Merit Scholars, a respected award for superior high school students.

That honor is based on scores on the Preliminary SATs (or PSATs), taken in the eleventh grade. The test, which is similar to but shorter than the SAT, also has two parts, math and verbal. Instead of being graded from 200 to 800, it is scored from 20 to 80. The comparative results between boys and girls? Virtually the same as on the SATs. This test also shows the inability of girls to keep up with boys in mathematics, and by extrapolation, science.

As a result, the National Merit Scholarship awards were not gender balanced. The honors were given to the 15,000 semifinalists in the ratio of 60 percent for boys and only 40 percent for girls.

Actually, this female ratio is already generous, for the selection includes a touch of affirmative action on behalf of girls in the way the test is scored. Unlike the SATs, the verbal score is *doubled* in the National Merit test, then added to only a single math score. This helps the girls, some of whom can excel in the verbal test as boys do in math. On a simple basis, using the SAT single-weighted scores, for example, the boys would probably have considerably more than 60 percent of the scholarships, which brings winners $2,000 and a leg up on good college admission.

This disparity between the boys and girls troubles some people, who are convinced that the genders are interchangeable academically and that any difference in test scores is the fault of the test rather than the students. It is a difficult argument, since the math disparity is uniform and consistent.

But powerful lobbies have actually helped to transform that pro-female bias into *law*. In 1993, Congress passed the "Gender Equity Act," whose spirit is that anyone involved in education or testing could be suspect of breaking the law if girls did not do as well as boys! The inference is that such disparity is not normal but evidence of discrimination against females, which is illegal, with penalties to pay.

Legislating intellectual equality may sound ridiculous (because it is), but the Gender Equity Act of 1993 became the basis of a legal complaint against the Educational Testing Service and the College Board, the organizations that run the National Merit Scholarship exam.

(The National Merit group itself could not be sued under the act because it does not accept federal funds. That system of cash-for-control by the federal government is one of the prime pillars of the New Establishment.)

The offended group was FairTest, a nonprofit group out of Cambridge, Massachusetts, that is absolutely convinced that boys do better on math only because the tests are biased.

"I don't believe that women have any intrinsic liability when it comes to math or science ability. I think what we're seeing in the difference in scores is the greater male ability at test taking," says the director of FairTest.

I was confused. Why would one sex do better on tests than another? Where would they learn that valuable trick?

"To what," I asked, "do you attribute that peculiar masculine skill?"

"Since it's mainly on multiple-choice questions," he responded, "I would say it is just 'strategic guessing.' "

Just? He may have inadvertently landed on the elusive definition of creativity, even genius. Was not Newton's apple a piece of strategic guessing? Or Einstein's $E=MC^2$, Napoleon's battle strategy, the Wright Brothers' experiment at flying, or perhaps even Shakespeare's dramatic philosophy as applied to life?

In his defense of relative female weakness at math scores, the FairTest director may have actually defined the intellectual difference between the sexes. "Strategic Guessing" may well be a synonym for "mastery of the unknown" and the tendency for risk-taking, the basic drives behind creativity and invention. Otherwise, why wouldn't women "guess" as well?

But FairTest is adamant that there are no basic sexual differences that can explain lower standardized test scores by females. With the help of the American Civil Liberties Union, FairTest filed a complaint with the Civil Rights Division of the federal Department of Education under Title IX of the Education Act, which prohibits sexual discrimination in education and monitors any complaints.

Rather than fight and aggravate Washington (which helps support the ETS with grants) the testing group succumbed. They have promised to revise their National Merit test, and in effect, add more female scholars, a task once considered solely within the province of the Creator.

How? Since the math disparity seems unchangeable and the verbal in already counted twice, what could be done to correct the oversight—either man's or nature's? The answer was to jigger the results.

The ETS has come up with a brilliant, sex-defying, trick. Years ago, they gave a "writing test," actually a multiple-choice exam based on sentence structure, grammar, etc. From past knowledge, ETS knew that girls scored *higher* on that than boys. The compromise with the federal government was simple. They would add the writing test beginning in 1997, hoping to even out the gender gap.

This entire gambit, one must admit, is an outstanding example of not only the cultural madness of the New Establishment, but its incorrigible slipperiness.

Despite research, there is no credible evidence that the races show any differences in the science of their brain function. But there is substantial evidence to indicate that men and women have different brain systems and think quite differently, if not necessarily in a superior or inferior manner when compared to each other.

It would be sophistry to deny the great intelligence of millions of women, particularly with increased education and their successes in business and even in the professions. Women now make up 46 percent of the labor market, and hold 43 percent of the middle management jobs, if not well represented in the top echelons. Only two of the top Fortune 500 jobs are held by women. In certain areas, such as publishing, fashion, and small business, they often excel.

These examples of success should not be taken to mean there are no substantial differences in the operation of male and female brains. On standard IQ tests such as the Stanford-Binet and the Wechsler, men and women score almost exactly the same. Why? Because those tests are designed to produce that *a priori* result— that there will be no difference in IQ scores by gender, only by individuals.

In the test development of the new Stanford-Binet, No. 5, for instance, a spokesman indicates that if one sex does better on any trial question, that question is discarded.

But despite that apparent, if manufactured, equality, each gender tends to score differently in the subsections of IQ tests. Women do as well or better on verbal items such as vocabulary, but not on "verbal comprehension." Men do better on arithmetic, and most observers report, score better in those areas where three-dimensional thinking is involved.

This is called "spatial skill" or "visio-spatial ability," and many researchers believe it is that faculty of the male mind that involves abstract thinking, along with a disposition to math, science, and inventiveness. (Judging by *New York Times* weekly coverage of significant new inventions, men totally dominate in the number and quality of those filed with the Patent Office, just as they do in the computer field.)

Research seems to confirm the strong suspicion that male and female brains are quite different biologically. At the Yale University School of Medicine, a husband-and-wife research team, Drs. Sally and Bennett Shaywitz, have examined the operation of male and female brains and found many differences, including the handling of language. In males, that function is isolated in one hemisphere (the left) while it is present in both hemispheres of the female brain.

Such differences also include the apparent ability of males to rotate a theoretical three-dimensional figure in their minds, something that is more difficult for women. This ties in with the visio-spatial test results of several researchers and with the increasing consensus that such a phenomenon—being able to mentally manipulate structures that are not really there—is tied to abstract thinking and mathematics, both consistent with science ability.

In IQ testing, one important aspect of the scores is interesting in comparing the sexes. Surprisingly, more women than men show normal intelligence. That is, their typical IQ range—say from 90 to 110—is clustered more around the norm than men's. Male scores are more likely to be scattered all over the IQ projection, from very high to very low.

The result is that there are more men than women *below normal.* At the same time, there are more men than women who score *considerably higher than normal.* As in the MCAT science and SAT math test, the upper percentiles of the intelligence quotient are richer in males than in females. Hence, one might presume, the normative region belongs to woman, while in both the brilliant and abnormally low regions men tend to dominate. (These assumptions are also suggested by Nobel prizes at the top, and the larger presence of boys in remedial reading classes at the bottom.)

Be that as it may, the American woman, whatever her skills or lack of them, is the darling of the New Establishment, which is blindly pushing her claims in the battle of the sexes. In fact, the American woman is so beloved by the New Establishment that it will go to the ends of the earth—even to the ends of reason—to protect and nourish her.

And why not? Without women, of all races and ethnicities, what is the New Establishment's emphasis on preferences but a crusade for racial and ethnic minorities? And not all Americans are universally sympathetic with the cost, financial and social, of the current remedies for minorities, from welfare to affirmative action. If the New Establishment has to rely solely on the backing of other "oppressed" groups, the public might well lose interest.

But Woman. She's a different story. She outnumbers men on the planet and is no minority in any sense of the word. She is omnipresent and totally necessary to society. No one can lose interest in her and she cannot be ignored, either by the general public or her male "oppressor."

She's not just the darling of the New Establishment, as both rooter and client. She's also the perfect foil to outflank the villain of the piece, the Great White Male. (Or is it the "Great White Whale," the Moby Dick of American civilization?) Her secondary position in relation to men, for whatever reason, also keeps up the continual pressure for her to reach her "rightful" place of absolute equality.

This is no easy victim. Aside from supposedly being oppressed by men (though women are eventually wealthier through inheritances and live longer than their oppressors), they also have a special hold on their adversary. Women are men's loved ones— wife, mother, sister, daughter, and sex partner. So it is hard for men to reject any of their demands—personal, political, commercial, and legal—out of hand.

And surely, the sexual and family bond between the genders is hard to break, though the New Establishment is doing everything in its Machiavellian power to accomplish that fracture.

Women are pressing everywhere, seeking full equality in the previously male-dominated world. As we've seen it's not just equal opportunity—which must exist for everyone in a true democracy—but *equal achievement,* which is the New Establishment goal. That, of course, is more difficult to come by.

And on this point, the nation is strongly divided. Even though men are willing to grant that many women are quite intelligent and competent, many men do not feel that women in general (with exceptions) have the imagination or boldness to lead the nation, either its professions or corporations or sciences or politics.

Surprisingly, many women share this so-called "male chauvinist" point of view to some extent. In the marketplace they seem to prefer male lawyers, doctors, CEOs, politicians, or what have you. That tussle of the sexes, confused as it is by mixed support by the genders, is important. Naturally, it will continue with little resolution except over a long time. What is needed is some reasoned examination.

The field of law is the perfect case in point. It's evident that women are moving swiftly ahead in the legal profession. In 1963, the practice of law was overwhelmingly male. Of 21,000 beginning law students that year, less than 900, or under 5 percent, were women.

And today? Of 43,000 beginning law students in 1995–96, over 19,000, or 45 percent, were women. As in medicine, entering female students make up a majority in many schools. Soon it will show itself in the ranks of the American Bar Association, where 26 percent of the membership is already female. At the present rate of law school education, that roster could eventually show a female majority.

We are now seeing women rise rapidly in law, with men yielding—reluctantly—each day. In 1995–96, for instance, a woman, Roberta Cooper Ramo, was named President of the American Bar Association.

Are women as qualified as men in the law?

That's a difficult question. In the only *objective test,* the Law School Admission Test (LSAT), men do score better than women, especially in the upper regions, an indication of the presence of affirmative action in admissions. According to figures supplied by the Law School Admission Council on the LSAT (120–180 scale), there are some 40 percent more men among the brightest students, those with scores of 170 to 180.

But recent experience shows that the greatest differences between the genders in law is *style,* how differently they study and work. There is also evidence that the still male-dominated profession is hesitant to promote woman lawyers as readily as it does men.

Is it prejudice? Naturally, the always aggressive New Establishment believes so.

One of the strongest complaints of women lawyers is that they are not being promoted as partners in private firms. Although women make up over a fourth of all lawyers, they angrily point out that only 13 percent, or proportionately half as many as men, according to the National Association for Law Placement, have become partners. And in those firms where they do, they are less likely to have "equity" and share fully in the profits.

Why is this? One can suppose that male lawyers do not fully respect their female colleagues. This is supported by a bar association report by the Commission on Women in the Profession on the relationship between the sexes. Many male law students said they did not believe their women colleagues were as able as they were.

This does not stop some female lawyers from calling on the law to rectify what they see as simple bias. One of the first suits was brought by attorney Elizabeth Hishon against her former employer, the prestigious Atlanta firm of King and Spalding, which had denied her a partnership. The case went to the Supreme Court, which unanimously ruled that she had the right to bring suit for sexual discrimination, the ultimate remedy. The law firm made an out-of-court settlement.

Rebuffed by some partnerships intent on the bottom line,

many women lawyers have instead gravitated toward corporate and bank work, which is less competitive. Many are doing nicely in the corporation hierarchy, and some have even risen to the rank of Chief Counsel.

The male criticism of women lawyers seems to be based not so much on intelligence as on personality and style. Women are seen as being more pedantic, and less bold, flexible, or imaginative than men.

Some of these naysayers point out that the way the two sexes handle the law was clearly demonstrated in the O. J. Simpson trial. The prosecutor, Marcia Clark, has become the nation's most celebrated female attorney. Even though she lost what many thought was an open-and-shut case, she received a $4.5 million book contract and unstoppable publicity. Clark presented her case in a quiet, reasoned, deliberate, unimaginative way, which to her detractors was much like that of a schoolteacher. She carefully and accurately laid out the facts in order, and went down to a smoking defeat.

Her adversary, famed defense attorney Johnny Cochran was, by contrast, flamboyant, spellbinding, imaginative, even if much of what he said was nonsense. Capturing the jury, he won.

The defense attorney business—following the argument that boldness and imagination are the strong points of adversarial law—is dominated by men: Robert Shapiro, Johnny Cochran, F. Lee Bailey, Gerry Spence, Jack Litman, and many others.

Is there something in the female makeup that prevents women from using the full power of argument on behalf of their clients, and themselves?

Some women lawyers seem to think so. They complain that they are handicapped by a method of teaching that favors the more aggressive male personality. Increasingly women are blaming the Socratic method of instruction at law school, which was dramatized in the film and television series, *The Paper Chase,* for their problems.

A group of women at New York University Law School, for example, is protesting the use of that Socratic method, which is described by the *New York Times* as follows:

"In the law school setting, students are called on by their professor and required to analyze cases in front of 100 peers. Professors grill the students to force them to think more deeply, sometimes embarrassing them if they do not answer correctly. Although professors call on students at random at the beginning of class, they often take volunteers for follow-up questions. Many women, like Ms. Aste, refuse to volunteer."

Ms. Aste is a leader of the NYU law student group trying to change the system. She was stimulated by an article in the University of Pennsylvania *Law Review* by Professor Lani Guinier, whose nomination to be U.S. Assistant Attorney General for Civil Rights was withdrawn. Ms. Guinier's report indicated that women did not do as well as men at law school, especially near the top.

The number of women in the top 10 percent of the class, or those who were chosen for law review, prizes, or prestigious clerkships, was considerably less than that of men, Professor Guinier complained.

Ms. Aste blames that failure on the Socratic method, stating that she found the large classes and confrontational atmosphere in law school intimidating. Says one of her female colleagues at NYU, "I'm uncomfortable when a professor takes my ideas and subjects me to some sort of public humiliation. A man who's more used to competition maybe can take that kind of intense scrutiny."

Another complaint of the female law students is that the men are quicker on their feet. Males raise their hands immediately, and open their mouths rapidly, they complain, while women are more deliberate and slower in responding.

"Why is speed better than depth?" Professor Guinier responds. "Why is it better to be quick-witted rather than thoughtful?" (Of course Ms. Guinier is assuming that slow response is the sign of depth, and vice versa.)

The differences between male and female law students was also detailed by Professor Lucinda Finley at SUNY Buffalo law school, who interviewed a number of law students at random.

"The men generally felt reinforced by law school in their ways of thinking—taking an argumentative cut at things, for example," stated Professor Finley. "They would say, 'It's given me a more powerful vocabulary and tools to refine my thinking.' From women we got tears, agitation, staring at the floor and twisting of Kleenex."

As a supposed reform to help women, the University of Pennsylvania has cut the size of its first-year law lectures down from 120 to 75. New York University has appointed a committee to look into its teaching methods, and the ad hoc female student group is asking for smaller classes, a different method of grading, and more emphasis on social issues.

But at New York University, Law School Professor Larry Kramer strenuously defends the Socratic method as the best replication of real law practice, and suitable for all lawyers, male or female. "I pick a student and have exactly the same discussion I would have with a group of lawyers in a firm to discuss a case."

Is the selection and training of lawyers significant to the nation?

One would think so. For better or worse, those who choose to enter the law often assume leadership positions in American life. So much so, in fact, that 40 percent of the members of the House of Representatives and a *majority* of U.S. Senators are attorneys, as are almost all judges up to the Supreme Court.

The complaints by women in law school, and lower SAT and MCAT scores, keep raising the usually *unspoken* question: "Are women in general as inventive and creative as men?"

The New Establishment answer is an emphatic "Yes."

Otherwise, the affirmative action and legal insistence on

equality would have less of an objective base. But for most of Western history, it was *assumed* that men were more creative and inventive, a piece of conventional wisdom that has been hotly contested in the last thirty years.

What do we really know about that touchy subject?

First, *all* evidence points to male superiority in science and math, and thus in the development of modern technology, from lasers to computers. In verbal skills, it appears that the sexes are relatively even. Men do seem to be more "quick-witted," as Ms. Guinier points out. They are surely more competitive and have a greater ego drive and aggressiveness, which increases their willingness to speak up and be boldly opinionated. That might enhance their intelligence, or at least give such an appearance in contrast to more common female passivity, especially in public.

In terms of the professions chosen by the sexes, women tend to pick the less technical, somewhat easier, academic disciplines, especially those with a more intimate, human touch. A study by the Graduate Record Examination organization, which gives a series of tests in sixteen fields taken by college seniors with at least a "B" average intending to go on for graduate degrees, shows the disparity between the sexes to be enormous.

In engineering, 80 percent of the slots were chosen by men, with 70 percent in the fields of physical sciences, math, and computers. Conversely, in education, 75 percent of the education slots were chosen by women, as were 80 percent in the health services field.

The scores on the GRE also reflect the same male-female spread as the SAT, PSAT, MCAT, etc. In areas where men predominate in number, such as in engineering, science and math, the typical combined math and verbal scores are close to 1200 (on a 1600 scale), while in female-dominant career areas such as education and health services, the scores tend to be in the mid 900s. In fact, men in engineering and science scored higher in the *verbal* tests than women did in the two favored female professions.

On IQ tests, as we've seen, men and women score much the same overall, which is meaningless since the tests are designed to be gender neutral. The great argument revolves around creativity and originality, at which men historically seem to excel. Even with the controlled IQ test environment, men do better on spatial matters, which many believe enhances the ability to think inventively. Thus the da Vincis, the Newtons, the Einsteins, the Jeffersons, the Shakespeares.

In the areas of careful preparation, organization, and work consistency (men are often diverted), women seem to do as well as men, or better. But in an advanced society such as ours, that type of thinking is more associated with routine, rather than extraordinary performance. Consistency is not the trait one needs to conceive of the "quark" or to win a Nobel Prize for economics.

If such an evaluation makes sense, it certainly jibes with nature's plan. Women would be given a broad spectrum of normal and above normal intelligence and good verbal skills in order to nurture children (and even big boys, their husbands). Yet they would not usually be so extraordinary as to divert them from what has been their prime job for millennia—birthing and raising children. To change the goals of nature's plan is obviously not as easy as self-confident moderns would think.

It would be sophist to deny the enormous strides that women have made in the last thirty years, but it would be equally sophist to deny that historically, and currently, men outpace women in creativity and boldness, with perhaps one of those traits feeding the other.

This has triggered sparks as well as extraordinary defensiveness, including convoluted arguments excusing the lack of certain female achievements. It has spawned the most peculiar ideas from women, even from the most brilliant of the gender.

Germaine Greer, a Ph.D. and noted scholar, for instance, decided to tackle one important area: the question of women and men artists and their relative skills. She reported back in her book *The Obstacle Race: The Fortunes of Women Painters and Their Work.*

After years of research, Ms. Greer concluded that men are actually better painters than women. But why? Again, there was an excuse for women.

"There is then no female Leonardo, no female Titian, no female Poussin," she writes, "but the reason does not lie in the fact that women have wombs, that they can have babies, that their brains are smaller, that they lack vigor, that they are not sensual. The reason is that you cannot make great artists out of egos that are damaged . . ."

Who has been doing the damaging? The villain is not hard to imagine: the much-insulted male.

This old saw of an excuse has great appeal to the elite of the New Establishment and their followers, both men and women. The reality, of course, is quite different. More than likely, the male superiority that Ms. Greer found in art is best explained not by the repressed ego of women, but by the research that shows that males are better at three-dimensional "visio-spatial" thought than are women—a necessity for superior art.

I sympathize with the emotions of women as bright as Dr. Greer and the disappointment she shows in her unwelcome discovery. But after years of scholarly research, for her to come up with such a puerile excuse for female failure at artistic creativity does her gender little credit.

That type of frustration can even turn women scientists into betrayers, albeit irrational ones, of their own discipline. It can push them into inventing such fanciful ideas as that science somehow has a gender. "Science is too macho and excludes the feminine," says the director of science education at Beloit College in Wisconsin.

These observers see science as either "masculine" or "feminine," which must be a grand revelation to the atoms and enzymes involved.

This genre of women scientists complains about an aggressive male motivation that supposedly makes their discoveries impure. Sandra Harding, a professor of philosophy at the University of Delaware, even sees a masculine bias in Sir Issac Newton's *Principia Mathematica,* in which he demonstrates the theory of gravity. It is, says Harding, a "rape manual" because of Newton's aggressive language.

Biochemist Linda Jean Shepherd believes that "male science" inevitably leads to such crises as atomic violence and air pollution, while female science would be more earth-friendly, a highly debatable supposition.

Is there a clever propaganda ploy in the seeming madness of these otherwise normal scientists?

Perhaps. Another woman scholar, Noretta Koertge, professor of the philosophy of science at Indiana University, sees a touch of envy of men by women in the concept of "female" science. It is, she believes, an attempt to "dumb down" science to make it more accessible to women. Is that, Koertge asks, just "a rationalization of women's failure" to achieve as much as men in their appointed field?

Whatever the method, the so-called Second Sex, goaded by the New Establishment, will surely continue to act as if there is no difference between the genders, except perhaps in style. It will continue to press the male animal, perhaps until he no longer has the prime place in society. In such a feminized civilization, which we are beginning to experience, no one can truly predict the result: either *total equality* or *societal disaster.*

Many educated women seem torn by this dilemma. Either they can reject the male history of success or become drawn mystically toward it—as if the world of men is the real universe where all the secrets of the Western culture are hidden and have been purposely kept from women all these years.

The result? Women are continually trying to break down the

doors of the male world to seek entrance, as if to view the Gods of Success closer up, even while denigrating them.

One of the first bastions of maleness to fall were the all-men university clubs, followed by such enclaves as the Century Club in New York, and even that formidable symbol of masculinity, the New York Athletic Club, which under court order reluctantly opened its doors to women.

The assault on all-male colleges was equally successful, probably to the intellectual detriment of both sexes. The once-prestigious City College of New York (CCNY) was all male until after World War II. Today, there are only three all-male colleges left. Harvard was integrated with Radcliffe, and Columbia with Barnard. Princeton went coed in 1969, and Yale—"Old Eli"—in the 1969–70 academic year.

Since men are *not* crashing down the doors of female establishments, the famed Seven Sister schools have survived better than their male counterparts, and there are still over eighty all-women colleges. Radcliffe and Barnard are gone, and Vassar has become coed. But Mount Holyoke, Bryn Mawr, Smith, and Wellesley are still single-sex women's colleges.

Women are entering everywhere where men once pursued masculine rituals, even in the most hallowed retreat of all, the military. West Point, Annapolis, and the Air Force Academy—under New Establishment and Congressional pressure—have all gone coed, something old military men still curse about in silence. Women in the armed services began with the all-volunteer force in 1973, and started entering West Point in 1976.

The mixing of the sexes at West Point sometimes has the makings of a National Lampoon skit—if one whose reality is largely unknown to Americans.

One would assume that the Point would have a no fraternization policy between the male and female cadets. Not true. Instead, as a full colonel spokesman at the Point explained, dating between cadets is actually encouraged, a sort of re-creation of normal boy-girl relationships in civilian life, an impossible concept from the onset. There are only two restrictions: plebes (first year cadets) cannot date upperclassmen, but can cavort with other plebes. And cadets may not date those in their own unit, but can ogle a likely prospect in the next squad.

"The men and women date together and can go to Eisenhower hall for a soda or they might go for a run around the track. They're not supposed to kiss on the grounds, but that's hard to police," the colonel stated. "But sexual intercourse—on the grounds—is not permitted. They would be expelled. But what they do off the premises is their business."

The military is becoming one of America's most efficient dating and mating services. In the old days, GIs had to frequent the USOs, or worse. Today, a military base, including West Point, is one of the easiest places for men to pick up and get to know women, up close. At the Point, men and women cadets are bedded down together in coed barracks. The women are in separate rooms, but close by and conveniently right off the same corridor. Since all the military units at the Point are sexually mixed, the squads can fall out easily, what the Army calls "unit integrity."

The amount of hanky-panky at West Point is, of course, officially unknown. But dating is commonplace, as are love affairs, and even marriages between cadets soon after graduation.

No wonder there has been an excess number of "sexual harassment" charges against male cadets. In that type of environment, failed male flirting can easily be labeled "harassment" by a haughty female cadet.

How did such a sexually charged atmosphere and the intrusion of women in the training ground of life and death become official policy at the once-hidebound military academy on the Hudson? The same way all the military has had to silently submit to the New Establishment.

The facilitators were several female Congresswomen, especially Pat Schroeder, veteran Democrat from Colorado, who has recently retired from the House. As a senior member of the House Armed Services Committee (now the National Security Committee) for years, Schroeder constantly pushed—successfully—for the interchangeability of men and women in the armed forces, including women in combat.

When it came to mixing homosexual and heterosexual soldiers, the Pentagon balked. But it did not stand up against Schroeder in the mixing of the sexes. Nor did her House colleagues fight her. After all, the once "fair sex" is not, as we have said, a small aggressive clique, but rather the majority of the voting population.

When queried about Congresswoman Schroeder's part in shaping a new kind of West Point, the colonel spokesman turned the question around. She has, he said in a model of military submission to civilian power, merely cut out the "restrictions" that were keeping women from fulfilling their total military aspirations.

What about military skills? Are women cadets really interchangeable with the men at West Point?

Hardly. Neither physically nor, it seems, academically.

In the old days, every cadet at West Point studied for a degree in engineering, a tough curriculum and good preparation for military thinking. But that has been watered down to accommodate the women.

There are now several academic options, and as in medicine, women generally choose the easier ones. Sixty percent of the male cadets take a degree in math, science, or engineering. But among women, seventy percent opt to major in such relatively soft subjects as public affairs, language, or humanities.

What about brawn? Since they're becoming Army officers with increasing field duties, even combat, can women handle the rough training gaff? Obviously not. Once again, West Point makes special dispensation for the women soldiers.

In the semiannual physical fitness test, which cadets *must* pass, men are required to do forty-two push-ups, fifty-two sit-ups, then immediately run two miles, all in fifteen minutes, fifty-four seconds. What about the women cadets? There the Point yields to the ladies despite the supposed unisex environment. The women are not required to truly compete. They need do only eighteen push-ups, fifty sit-ups, and take almost nineteen minutes to complete the test.

Even more polite, gentlemanly dispensation is given the women on the rigorous Obstacle Course Test, which is held in the gym, and requires cadets to run, crawl, go through tires, climb walls in as short a time as possible. The men are given a maximum of three minutes and twenty seconds to complete the course.

And the women? Again the protocol of helping a lady across a puddle comes into play. They are given so much time—5½ minutes—that in World War II they would have been sushi for Japanese troops. The same is true of any future wars.

West Point was created as a place to train military leaders, including hopefully those few geniuses at fighting and winning wars—the Pattons, the MacArthurs, the U.S. Grants, the Shermans, the Schwarzkopfs. It was not designed as an elaborate social laboratory where boys and girls could cuddle, and women could pretend to be men, an integral part of the New Establishment theorizing of "What if."

The feminization of the armed forces is already showing debilitating results. But the future holds even greater damage—enough to threaten the ability of the services to defend us and our interests at home and abroad properly.

One recent incident at West Point illustrates that ongoing damage. New graduates of the Army academy were being less than well-received by some field commanders, who noticed that many lacked leadership ability. The aggressive military edge that the venerable institution used to instill in men like Norman Schwarzkopf was missing. The field commanders complained that young officers ostensibly being trained to fight brutal wars were too often "weenies."

"In the last thirty years, West Point has had an intellectual crisis as to whether it's a military academy or an Ivy League college," retired Lieutenant General Richard Trefry, former Inspector General of the Army, was quoted as saying. In that culture war, the coed nature of the school has materially helped break the traditional, successful self-image of the Point.

To rectify the situation, a combat veteran, Colonel James Hallums, was brought in to beef up the leadership training. A graduate of the class of 1966, Hallums was the veteran of two wars, was twice decorated for valor, and had become a company commander of the elite 101st Airborne at age twenty-four. After tours in six countries, he attended Harvard and Vanderbilt, earned a Ph.D. in sociology, and was on his way to a generalship.

But he soon learned that trying to fix the new West Point was hopeless from the start. Injecting the concept of real soldiering into the newly feminized Point proved futile. Among the faculty, mainly composed of lieutenant colonels, Hallums encountered what he called "a visceral anti-military feeling," hardly the right attitude for a business dedicated to killing the enemy.

Quickly, he started a campaign to shape up the outfit. He demanded that officers wear their Class A uniforms when on duty instead of the usual sweaters and slacks. Some, like a former battalion commander from the 82nd Airborne, liked his approach, seeing it as an antidote to what he called the "touchy, feely" faculty. Hallums chewed out a few people and even raised his voice to some female officers.

He soon found he was the subject of a revolt by the lieutenant colonels, who saw him as too abrasive and "macho" for the new coed Army. After only nine months, Hallums was forced out of West Point, and without a recommendation for promotion to general, out of the Army—another victory for political correctness and the New Establishment dogma. But surely another defeat for America.

The New Establishment has worked overtime to change the military environment and not just at West Point, but in every possible way. Without the public being told, for example, women are being pushed closer to combat roles for which most are not equipped.

Over the last decade, female power in the military has been continually expanded. In 1991, the Air Force—despite the opposition of former Air Force Chief of Staff Merill McPeak—permitted women to fly combat planes. At present, the Air Force is training women fighter pilots to fly F-15s and F-16s of the Top Gun variety in combat.

The Navy now permits *all* women sailors to go on combat duty, and they are being deployed on numerous ships (except submarines) despite the proven sexual problems of adultery and pregnancy, and the lack of physical strength that a combat emergency aboard ship might require.

Most startling is that the Navy now permits women to fly fighter planes off the navy carrier decks in combat duty. The first women to be so assigned, Lieutenant Kara Hulgreen, was killed when she made a poor landing on a carrier on October 25, 1994. Since then another female Navy pilot was grounded for her inability to land the big fighter on a small carrier deck. Despite that, the Navy is training another group for the same hazardous duty.

The new directives established in 1994 permit women to go into combat everywhere in all three services, with only the exception of the infantry, the tank corps, and the field artillery. But in addition to full flight combat missions, including bombers, they can also go into combat with Army and Marine ground support troops including signal corp, antiaircraft, engineers, transportation, etc.

The military is afraid to openly complain—theirs is to do and/ or die—but some retired personnel do speak out. Retired Army

Lieutenant Colonel William J. Gregor testified before a presidential commission that to have an effective unisex military, women would need the same physical stamina and upper body strength as men, which they don't have. Readiness and unit strength, he pointed out, depend on the ability to carry heavy survival gear in all terrains and weather.

Desert Storm gave Americans—and women soldiers—a false picture of warfare, says Lieutenant General J. H. Binford Peay III, the commander who followed Schwarzkopf. It was an atypical technological war played out on a smooth, open desert. Real combat in venues not as favorable is still a bloody, brutal activity, he reminds us. (Imagine, if you will, women in combat on the beaches and hedgerows of Normandy, in the jungles of Vietnam, or on the frozen Yalu in Korea, and how they, and the nation, would react.)

Elaine Donnelly, President of the Center for Military Readiness, and also a member of the president's commission on women in the military, is another strong critic of the present situation. The new combat policy for women, she says "opens up air cavalry units and some engineer, bridge crew, and Marine explosive ordnance officer positions to women—specialties that involve extraordinary physical strength or a high risk of injury or capture." Many of these women, she points out, "will be single and dual-service mothers separated from very young children."

Donnelly reveals that Desert Storm showed that women are not as easily deployable as men, which can make their presence in a battle zone a liability. The nondeployable rate (meaning they weren't ready for duty) was, she says, "three to four times higher among women, not counting higher rates of voluntary and involuntary discharges because of pregnancy or child-care concerns."

The pregnancy problem is not small, especially considering the increased sexual contact between men and women soldiers, sailors, and airmen, married or unmarried. As we've noted, of the 360 women who returned from Desert Storm aboard the USS

Acadia (the "Love Boat"), thirty-six, or 10 percent of all, were pregnant, evidence of considerable sexual activity in the ranks. Cozy combat.

One argument for allowing women to go into combat has been the supposed experience of Israel, where women *once* served in certain combat capacities. But Israel has since changed its mind. Women are drafted into the Israeli Army (for twenty-one months versus thirty-six for men) but only to support the male soldiers. They are prohibited from serving in combat roles.

Women, of course, can be of great *supplemental* value to the American armed forces. A logical presence for them, as it is in most nations, is not in the service academies or in possible combat roles, as they are today. Instead, women should serve in an auxiliary, not primary, capacity much like the excellent service of WACs and WAVES in World War II. Obviously, the women should be housed in separate barracks to avoid both sexual intercourse and sexual harassment.

The whole question of the interchangeability of men and women in every arena of modern life has endless ramifications.

The female participation discussed here—in medicine, law, and the military—does not usually involve the courts, where much of the gender tussle is adjudicated. That battle revolves about matters of sexual bias and discrimination in the workplace, sexual harassment, so-called "sexism," and other newly minted matters of law. (We will look at the legal and affirmative action questions of women and minorities in later chapters.)

Men and women share a great deal in our society and carry enormous burdens in making it all work. In fact, it is only because of the balance between the two sexes that modern civilization emerged and is maintained. A distortion of that relationship can, and is, seriously threatening what had been achieved.

People of wholesome spirit want the absolute end to prejudice and the opportunity for *everyone* to succeed according to his or her ability and determination. It was this spirit that assimilated the hundreds of millions of immigrant descendants who had to fight to achieve equal opportunity, not equal results.

Gender should be absolutely no barrier to achievement, at any level, up through the chance to produce great scientific work or even gain the position of President of the United States.

But violating good sense and decency in granting women *special advantage* in test scores, admission to professional schools, and assorted "Achievement Charity," ranging from false designation as National Merit Scholars, or having to do fewer push-ups in the military, to weaker academic requirements to misdirected medical specialties to changes in the teaching of law, is not in the best interests of either women or society.

Unfortunately, much of the New Establishment's excessive push in favor of women is not only to the detriment of men, but is also upsetting the balance to *everyone's* disadvantage. That's especially true of women, who in the long run may be much more dependent on the social health of men, economically and emotionally, than many now believe.

For the New Establishment to unfairly push women forward and limit men through modern sex bias may be a social experiment of great titillation and fashionability. But it is also one that toys too frivolously, and dangerously, with the destiny of Western society.

CHAPTER FOUR

COLLEGES IN THE NEW ESTABLISHMENT

Extraordinary Ignorance, PC, and the New McCarthyism

AMERICA HAS ALWAYS HAD TWO STRAINS OF THE mind: intellect and anti-intellect, existing side by side and tangling in the marketplace of ideas.

Intellect had its American origin in the settling of Boston in 1630. As A. L. Rowse, the late history scholar at Oxford, reminded us, among the first 2,000 families that landed in Massachusetts there were 138 graduates of Oxford and Cambridge, the largest concentration of brains in one place in the history of mankind. Their progeny, Alexis de Tocqueville assures us, became "the beacon" that lit up the rest of America.

But the second strain, that of anti-intellect, was just as strong. That came with the flood of later immigrants from England and elsewhere who populated the rough frontier and where "book larnin' " was scarce and not particularly elevated, either in content or as a source of local admiration.

As Americans moved westward, the two strains moved with them, generally creating a mild compromise in which basic learning was considered essential for life and work, but where true intellect carried little currency.

The university, of whatever origin, stood out as an island of the mind in the countryside, a reminder of our greater New England origins. So for hundreds of years, the possession of a college degree was considered the hallmark of the educated man or woman.

And today?

The National Association of Scholars (NAS) has just completed a study of the curriculum of fifty leading American colleges entitled: "The Dissolution of General Education: 1914–1993." It has come away convinced that in the arena of higher education, the anti-intellectual movement has won out. Its overview shows that in America's colleges today, academic *rigor* is better identified with *mortis* than with true mental activity.

It is, once more, a debilitating by-product of the New Establishment, which has established almost total control of America's universities, especially its most prestigious ones.

Though we resist the conclusion, the reality is that our colleges are now the ground zero of anti-intellectualism, the contemporary nucleus of a movement that has always cast a dark shadow over the American mind.

Not only has the university become the center of anti-thought, but it is the major incubator of our accelerating social and cultural madness.

Is this just more "It Used to Be Better" propaganda?

Propaganda, no. Nostalgia? No. The decay of former excellence, yes.

Let's look at the first aspect of the problem: the college curriculum, what the schools do and do not teach. In what kind of academic environment could an honors graduate of an Ivy League school never have heard of Andrew Johnson, the President who succeeded Lincoln and who avoided impeachment by a single vote?

The NAS study, which covers the Bachelor of Arts degree, replicates the college curriculum at four points in our history,

1914, 1939, 1964, and 1993, showing a steady and continuous decline in quality. First, the report outlines what is generally considered the basis of a well-rounded college education: English composition, foreign language, history, literature, philosophy, mathematics, and social and physical sciences.

Those essential "required" subjects are no longer so required, they learned. In 1914, 65 percent of the subjects were mandatory for graduation. The number slipped gradually to 51 percent in 1939, then a bit more to 47 percent in 1964—apparently the borderline year when the college environment turned from fostering true education to indulging irrational student and faculty demands.

And today? By the latest count in 1993, only 21 percent—one in five—were required.

The villain is the New Establishment, which beginning in the 1960s, started the takeover of the nation's campuses.

It has now virtually completed its conquest, much to the distress of those who remember the colleges—when. The result is that the parchment given to several million youngsters each June may be a passport to work, but it is often merely printed proof of the failure of higher education.

(As the number of required courses decreased, the electives—many lightweight innovations—grew enormously. In 1939, the typical school offered 537 courses. And today? Over 1,400.)

Each of the required subjects itself has weakened dramatically. While 96 percent of all schools in 1939 required a composition course within the English department, in 1993 that percentage had dropped to just 36 percent.

History has also been a prime victim of the New Establishment–controlled campus. To quote the study:

"In 1914, almost 90 percent of the institutions accorded some sort of special curricular status in their general education programs to introductory history courses. In both 1939 and 1964, more than 50 percent did. As of 1993, however, only one school did." (The mystery of Andrew Johnson has been solved!)

The same decline is seen in literature, where the percentage of colleges with requirements dropped from 57 percent in 1914 to 38 percent in 1964 way down to 14 percent in 1993. Philosophy has been another academic victim, declining from 43 percent to a mere 10 percent today.

One of the greatest injuries to student knowledge has been in science, whose precipitous decline began in 1964, when the New Establishment instituted its takeover. That year, 90 percent of the top fifty colleges had natural science requirements. And today? Only 34 percent include science in the core curriculum.

Is there any screening before a B.A. is handed out by the colleges? Does the college insist on proof that the student is worthy of a sheepskin?

In 1964, the *majority* of schools required either a thesis or a comprehensive examination before they issued their imprimatur that the student had truly earned his degree.

And today? *Only one in eight colleges has such a requirement for graduation.*

In the pyramid of better and worse prestigious undergraduate schools, Brown and Yale take the award as perhaps the most permissive and weakest of all.

Brown has no required General Education or "Core" courses at all. Outside their specialization, students invent their own curriculum, a task that most eighteen-year-olds cannot accomplish well without professional oversight. Otherwise, the student might well avoid the complex and challenging courses, or be unable to distinguish the titillating from the substandard courses. Despite that, in the modern world of academic deception, Brown has an undeservedly fashionable reputation, particularly among those who fail to gain admission to Harvard.

Brown's disregard for a basic core curriculum was highlighted by a statement made by a university dean of that school that "the world is changing so rapidly that nobody's sure what knowledge is important anymore."

Yale is a more important case study than Brown since "Yale and Harvard" are mouthed almost simultaneously when speaking of the greatness of American higher education. But that accolade no longer has much meaning. Yale has also enthusiastically swung over to the New Establishment concept of education: low on general knowledge and high on Political Correctness.

If so, how has Yale sustained its magical reputation? There are two reasons: (1) Its select student body scores an average of 1450 in the SATs, which places them near the top; (2) parents and employers are ignorant of what students are actually learning at Yale.

Like Brown, Yale College, the undergraduate school, no longer has a core curriculum. *That means that not a single specific course in General Education is required for graduation.*

Instead, Yale permits students to peruse the catalogue of 1,800 courses and take a total of twelve credits from several categories (science, history, literature, etc.) outside their major. Over four years, this is a transparently weak system, especially when one views the minutiae in the abundant catalogue, as we shall soon see.

The theory? That eighteen-year-olds are experienced academics.

Says the Yale brochure, with no hint of irony:

"One of the distinguishing features of a liberal education is that it has no single definition. Yale consequently does not prescribe any specific course to be taken by a student, but instead urges each undergraduate to design a program of study suited to his or her own particular needs and interests from the multitude of courses available to college students in the university."

This is a nicely worded confession of abdication by the college. It includes the understanding that many of the courses students choose may be insignificant, esoteric, and worse. Because students design their own education, no one can any longer be sure that a Yale degree is the sign of an educated person.

As the Director of Admissions at Yale pointed out to me:

"This is a democracy and students should have freedom of choice."

Democracy in education? That's a peculiar concept, as if faculty and students are equals. Are eighteen-year-olds capable of determining what they should learn? If one yields to immature minds, can a system pass on the accumulated knowledge of Western civilization to the next generation, which is the basic obligation of our colleges?

Hardly.

Because they are chosen for their native intelligence, Yalies have an excellent chance to achieve in life regardless of their education. If the school fails them, who is to know? And as they succeed, they will cast further honor on their Alma Mater, which is the essence of the modern college scam: Smart students and poor education. Only society will eventually pay the price in weakened and distorted leadership.

How poor an education? In the Yale "democracy," how shallow a course of study can a student take and still graduate?

Apparently quite shallow. A satirical—but quite true—look at Yale's permissive system was explained by *Light and Truth* (translation of the school's motto, *Lux et Veritas*), a highly critical student publication.

The cynical young journalists scoured the Yale catalogue, then invented a curriculum that could qualify someone for a Bachelor of Arts degree. It was a shallow, almost mindless, academic regimen without any courses of value. Almost none of the subjects would have even been recognizable to a 1964 alumnus of the school.

The fictional major was in Women's Studies, and the four-year curriculum they chose was hilarious, if tragically so. The academic sleight of hand was concocted from the 38 courses required for graduation, selected from the 1,800 available.

What do the courses look like? They appear both contentless and anti-intellectual, to say the least, as if culled from today's supermarket tabloids. The following list of courses for the full

112

sophomore year leading to the B.A. degree from Yale is a fair representation of one whole four-year course at Yale. Believe it or not:

- Redesigning the Family: Challenges from Lesbians/Gay Men
- Photography and Images of the Body
- Love Books in the Middle Ages
- Intermediate Yoruba
- Women's History: Methodical and Comparative Inquiry
- AIDS in Society
- Listening to Music
- Affirmative Action and Civil Rights in the Labor Market
- Sexual Meanings
- Troubadours and Rock Stars—a Comparison

If you're a skeptic, so was the managing editor of a newspaper in Manchester, Connecticut. He asked the Yale administration: Could it be true, or was it just a silly sophomore parody?

Yale responded that while they didn't think it "likely," they acknowledged that the student curriculum was "technically correct." So much for Yale, circa 1997.

Harvard and Yale. The Bobbsey Twins of American higher education. Surely, the castle of learning on the Charles River must have a better educational system than Yale, a Johnny-come-lately some seventy years younger?

Hardly. Harvard *claims* to be more rigorous, insisting it has a true "core curriculum" that all students must take. But the reality is more semantics than factual. In foreign languages, for example, requirements are so minimal that two-thirds of the entering students meet them with their high school experience.

Instead of a true "core curriculum"—a specific list of foundation courses such as European History, Introduction to Chemistry, Philosophy 101, A Survey of American History, or Basic

Economics—the Harvard "core" is a flexible, sometimes thing. So flexible, in fact, that students have to take a total of only eight courses over four years, or *one* each semester. (As an aside, Harvard advertises among its graduate students for "teaching assistants," not mature professors, to handle these "core" courses.)

Most important, it's not a true "core" in the academic sense of the word. Instead, it's an often vacuous grab bag that can leave a Harvard graduate as uneducated as the product of a two-year community college. In the spirit of "student democracy" Harvardites can choose their "core" subject each semester from a list of forty-five, making the requirement as flexible as jelly, if not as thick.

It's really worse than it sounds. For example, from the Fall 1996-1997 and Spring 1997 lists (supplied to me by Harvard), students could take such solid courses as "Shakespeare, the Early Plays," "The French Revolution," or "World War and Society in the Twentieth Century."

Or they can brush away any such thought-provoking fare. Instead they can plead self-indulgence (a prime characteristic of the New Establishment student and faculty mind) and enroll in such superficial "core" fare as "Culture, Illness and Healing," or "Majesty and Mythology in African Art," or "Ethnicity, Modernity and Modernism."

That's hardly a core—or even a shell—of a good general education.

To fulfill their entire four-year-physical science requirement, for instance, Harvard "scholars" can take one fashionable course called "The Atmosphere." There is absolutely no requirement for basic courses in chemistry or physics or any follow-up. To meet their entire biological science requirement (the other half of the science core), they can take "The Biology of Trees and Plants." They'll then have completed their science work. Little wonder so many Ivy League graduates are notoriously ignorant of the sciences.

The same is true of history. Instead of survey courses in American and European history, Harvardites can satisfy their four-year history requirement with only two courses such as "Age of Sultan Suleyman The Magnificent" and "Modern Africa from 1850." (The question is: Can they satisfy their original desire to become educated people?)

Incredible. The history fare offered might be interesting, but whatever happened to Egypt, Athens, Alexander, Rome, the Medieval period, the American Colonial experience, the French Revolution, Napoleon, the American Civil War, the rise of the British Empire, World Wars I and II, and God knows what else?

Yet despite its watered-down required curriculum and almost absent academic discipline, the myth of Harvard as a great undergraduate educational institution carries on. Why? Because, like Yale, it rests on the native intelligence of its students and surely not on its vacuous "core" curriculum.

What about Princeton? Much the same. Princeton likes to sound impressive with such elaborate phrases as "Epistemology and Cognition." But it's also run by the same New Establishment theory of permissive, thin, uncoordinated education.

At Woodrow Wilson's old school, students are required to take eleven different courses in four major areas: Science; Social Science; Arts and Letters; and History, Philosophy, and Religion. Sounds great, but again there's a rub. They can choose whatever they want from a full catalogue of over *one thousand* courses.

What we're producing in college today are graduates with heads full of idiosyncratic, isolated bits of knowledge. There is no central organization of thought, no plan, no basics, no foundation. This gravely weakens their ability to think constructively and to distinguish truth from falsehood, a common failing of those influenced by the New Establishment.

Academics like to talk about "creative thinking," but that requires knowledge as a basis from which to create. The result is that the ignorance of our public elementary and secondary school system has invaded the realm of higher education, with catastrophic societal results for the future.

One of the gravest violations of college standards is the trend toward eliminating Shakespeare from the curriculum of *English majors,* a travesty that has already made Georgetown University infamous. Now we learn that this is part of a national movement in which the Bard is eliminated, then substituted for with trash literature. A recent study of sixty-seven leading universities showed that only twenty-three required English majors to take even a single course in Shakespeare.

"The survey confirmed our worst fears," states Jerry L. Martin, president of the National Alumni Forum, which conducted the study. "Dropping Shakespeare is not just a trend, it is the norm. Prestigious colleges and universities are contributing to the dumbing down of America."

The NAF looked at what Georgetown English students could take instead of Shakespeare. That includes such electives as "Film Noir/Hardboiled Detective Fiction" and "Prison Literature." At Duke, they make do with "Melodrama and Soap Opera."

"Shoddy propaganda is replacing the study of great literature," laments Professor Roger Shattuck at Boston University. "In fact, parents should sue for breach of contract."

This dumbing down of the American college serves the motives of the New Establishment, which now finds it easy to indoctrinate its undereducated students into its own biases and bigotries. Since college graduates, especially those from the Ivy League, inevitably end up as the nation's leaders, what does this say about the present and future of the American culture—its politics, literature, economics, journalism, films, and especially its philosophical direction?

Unless it can be turned around, it is a rather frightening prognosis.

Is there any Ivy League school left with a true core curriculum—one that even partly defines the "educated" man or woman?

Surprisingly, there is one. It is Columbia College, the three-century-old undergraduate school of Columbia University in New York City. Deans at other schools speak of Columbia as some sort of academic dinosaur because it has retained some of college's former rigor. But unlike the immature, permissive Ivy League schools, one can be sure that a Columbia grad at least knows *something,* if not all that an educated person needs to know. Their required courses for *all* Columbia students are the following:

- Literature Humanities (two terms)
- Contemporary Civilization (two terms)
- Art Humanities (one term)
- Music Humanities (one term)
- Logic and Rhetoric (one term)
- Science (three terms)
- Foreign Language (four terms)
- Major Cultures (two terms)

That basic curriculum ensures that all students take the first five specific survey courses, then fulfill the last three requirements. It's generally inescapable that Columbia grads know something about the ideas of Plato, Machiavelli, Locke, Adam Smith, even Marx. They are required to read such great books as *The Iliad,* Dante's *Inferno, Pride and Prejudice, War and Peace* and numerous others.

Not many would object to such a study of the works of Western Culture that have civilized us all. Would they?

Yes they have, and they do. At Columbia, minority students have organized a protest against the "Eurocentric" curriculum, which even educated minority members find a short-sighted view.

Jose A. Carbranes, a U.S. Circuit Judge born in Puerto Rico and a Columbia graduate, class of 1961, points out in a *Times* Op-Ed piece that *such a curriculum is invaluable for minority students.* He explains that it was designed in 1919 to teach immi-

117

grants and their children such as him the knowledge of Western civilization along with cues for assimilation they would never receive in their own lives or subculture.

"Those who yield to pressure to reject a Western civilization curriculum do minorities a singular disservice by depriving us of the great opening to the world . . . ," he writes. "We are demeaned by the assumption that our self-fulfillment and growth depend on a reinforcement of what we know, rather than a confrontation with the unknown. We are demeaned by the intimation that we are now and forever alien to the Western heritage."

Amen.

(One failing of the Columbia core curriculum is the absence of American History. A spokesman for the college said they assume the student has learned that in high school. However, as tests now show, that's no longer the case simply because the amorphous high school "social studies" courses shortchange hard history.)

Columbia is an exception in higher education. But since most American universities have diluted their education, how do they manage to persuade the gullible American public—who are paying small fortunes for their children's education—that they are doing a good job?

An easy way is to lie, and many colleges have taken just that route.

What is their answer to criticism? They merely pretend that they are turning out good students. How can they manage that? Simply by *inflating student grades*. If students are doing well, deans say, the college must be doing a good job.

Few parents are able to see through the scam or to truly gauge how much knowledge their children have absorbed. But they do know an *A* from a *C*.

The result is one of the great academic conspiracies of our time. Virtually every child in college today appears to emerge as "above-normal" among his college peers. Not only is that a bizarre statistical trick, but it's music to parental ears, the answer to a mother's dream that their children are at least "near geniuses."

Years ago, a *B* (3.0 Grade Point Average) generally won students cum laude honors. The typical student in the 1950s, for instance, was lucky to have a *C+* or *B–* average, the fashionable "Gentlemen's C."

And today? The *average* student receives a 3.15 GPA out of 4.0, a charitable B+ gift from the New Establishment. It is the perfect self-fulfilling prophecy. We must be doing a good job, college educators say, since our students get such high grades. Paying parents are, of course, pleased by the fraud.

At Cornell, the percentage of students receiving *A*s *doubled* from 1965 to 1993, up to a ridiculous 36 percent of all grades. Meanwhile the number of *C*s—a typical grade in 1965—dropped from 40 percent of students to only 12 percent today.

At Princeton, students and their parents are even more ecstatic about grade inflation, giving them bragging rights about their children and grandchildren. The number of *A*s granted by once-honorable Princeton now represents 41.2 percent of all grades, making permissive Cornell look academically Scroogelike in comparison. Harvard, the inner sanctum of the New Establishment, is the leader in false praise. There, the *average* grade is now an *A–* to *B+*.

So much for truth in college education.

(Stanford, which is also very generous with its grades, swears it intends to reform. It will even bring back the *F* grade, which had been abolished twenty-five years ago as unusually cruel academic punishment.)

In a panel discussion on inflated grades, a Harvard senior spilled the academic beans. "In some departments," she said, "*A* stands for 'average.' Since so many of us have *A* averages, our grades are meaningless."

An article in *Harvard Magazine* was quite confessional about the scam. It seems that law school admissions officers ignore magna cum laude and cum laude honors from Harvard as mean-ingless. Why? *Because Harvard generously handed out honors to an astonishing 84 percent of a recent graduating class!*

(To be armed as one goes out in the world as a Harvard honors student is misleading, since so few know that it is a grand anti-intellecutal scam.)

"*Relativism* is the key word today," Harvard instructor William Cole has stated. "There's a general conception in the literary-academic world that holding things to high standards—like logic, argument, having an interesting thesis—is patriarchal, Eurocen-tric, and conservative. If you say 'This paper is no good because you don't support your argument,' that's almost like being racist and sexist."

(All, of course, are fighting words in the university world of PC.)

Brown takes the prize in grade inflation by even continuing the charade *after* graduation. At that school, poor grades below *C* are not even entered on the student transcript!

"When you send in your résumé, do you put down all the jobs you applied for and didn't get?" asks Dean Sheila Blumstein in defending their policy. "A Brown transcript is a record of a student's academic accomplishments."

The ignorance of many college students has been verified by studies, including one of five hundred graduating seniors at the University of Florida and Florida State University. Only 22 per-cent knew that Alan Greenspan was head of the Federal Reserve system, and less—13 percent—knew that Lyndon Johnson origi-nated the Great Society.

Ivy Leaguers may sneer at the Florida brethren, but even though they did somewhat better in a *U.S. News & World Report* survey, there were enormous holes in their civic knowledge. Al-most one-fourth did not know the elemental fact that there are *nine* Justices on the Supreme Court. Three-fourths of the Ivy Leaguers did not know that it was Abraham Lincoln who said "a government of the people, by the people and for the people." Almost sixty percent of the Ivy Leaguers could not name even four Justices of the Supreme Court.

What are we to make of all this? Simply that the control of the university by the New Establishment is now near total. With its dominance has come the diminution of learning and the farce of pretended excellence. All supported by false grades.

The result? The contemporary American college most resembles the educational level of the high school of 1964, without reaching the level of such exceptional New York City public schools as Stuyvesant High or the Bronx High School of Science, where tuition is free and admission is solely by examination. Equally important, the new college is wedded to scholarly distortions that were not present in the secondary schools of a generation ago.

The New Establishment, which has encouraged academic permissiveness and grade inflation, is determined to alter reality by making almost everyone seem "smart." This is reflected in the new SAT scoring system, which has been "recentered." Before the change, the norm on the verbal test was 428 while the math was 479.

Since April 1995, everyone has been given a hefty lift in SAT scores, and by implication in intelligence, making them—at least to naïve observers—seem smarter than they are. Most important, it narrows the gaps among students, which is part of the fashionable ethos of false equality. That everyone is *almost* the same is the drumbeat of the American culture fostered by the New Establishment.

The new SAT scoring system moves the verbal scores up by over 70 points to 500, the new norm. It does much the same in math by advancing scores 25 points to 504. This affects the 1.8 million students who take the SATs every year, increasing their "self-esteem" if not their knowledge. No one will any longer have to sulk with a 428 verbal score, and most slow readers will be able to boast a respectable 500.

The smart will appear even smarter, even geniuslike, warming the hearts of mothers and grandparents. Before the change, only thirty-five students achieved the "perfect" SAT score of 800 on each of the math and verbal tests. Under the new system, you don't have to answer every question correctly to get a perfect score—which is a masterpiece of modern *relativism*. Thus, 550 seniors have been falsely elevated to "genius," the great magic of the New Establishment psychometrics.

Whatever their SAT scores, new college students face another dilemma when they enter college. They will undertake the study of a curriculum that changes rapidly to conform to the intellectually permissive society, one wedded more to fashionability than to knowledge.

The New York Times has published a piece on what college courses across the country can look like today. As hard subjects have declined, worthless elective courses have multiplied to fill the vacuum.

The following selection of electives is titillating, but it's also proof that much of higher education has become a shallow, often silly, activity.

At Bowdoin, one can study "The Souls of Animals." At Harvard Divinity, we have "Sports as a Metaphor for Life." At Sarah Lawrence, credit is given for "The Year My Voice Broke," while "Girl Talk" is considered academic at Wesleyan. Swarthmore offers "Renaissance Sexualities."

At New York University, an ad was placed in a professional journal seeking a faculty member for a performing arts course entitled "Gendered Performance." Encouraging applications from "women and members of minority groups," they described the duties as "drag, transvestite performance, queer theories."

With the denigration of academic standards has come another attack: the takeover of the college mentality by Political Correctness. At Stanford, once a leading academic center, PC leads the curriculum parade. In literature, Shakespeare's *The Tempest* is taught as *A Tempest*, a supposed moral study of the evils of "Western Imperialism."

Instead of concentrating on studies in Western Civilization— the force that created the modern university—Stanford excels in offering courses designed to raise student "self-esteem." That's easily accomplished through a narrow racial, sexual, and ethnic identity education.

David O. Sacks, a 1994 graduate of Stanford, and Peter Thiel, a 1992 Phi Beta Kappa graduate of Stanford, have delved into the new Stanford curriculum and found it not only wanting, but intellectually destructive.

The list of credit courses includes "Gender and National- ism," which preaches that nationalism is a male creation designed to oppress women; "Black Hair as Culture and History"; "Peace Studies"; "Feminist Studies 295," subtitled "How Tasty Were My French Sisters"; an English class entitled "Whitman to AIDS"; "African-American Vernacular English"; and "Religion in America," including a lecture on "Jesus Acted Up: A Gay and Lesbian Manifesto."

Many colleges follow Stanford's lead, offering a compendium of courses in Native American Studies, Black Studies, Women's Studies, Hispanic Studies, Jewish Studies, Chinese Studies, Filipino Studies, Hawaiian Studies, ad infinitum. These self-aggrandizing dis- ciplines, mainly filled with false and exaggerated "knowledge," are part of a college movement toward *segregation and isolation* rather than positive mixing.

Women's Studies is perhaps the fastest growing field. Ac- cording to the National Women's Studies Association there are 619 such programs nationwide. There is generally little academic content, but a great deal of "feeling" and theory about the sup- posed plight of women in America.

These narrow-focus programs are often the inspiration for

increased prejudice. At Queens College in New York, Professor Thomas E. Bird, the director of the school's Jewish Studies programs and an expert in Yiddish, was dismissed because he was not Jewish.

Bird argued that he was "the object of primitive religious bigotry at the hands of a few academic colleagues" who were Jewish. The editor of the *Forward,* a Jewish newspaper, expressed solidarity with Bird in a letter to the *Times,* pointing out that one need not be Greek to teach Ancient History.

Since ethnic studies seem *de rigeur* on campus, bias is obvious in the many ethnic groups ignored by deans and administrators. At Queens College, which is part of the City University, there is an Italian Studies program. Fair enough, but why not an Irish Studies program honoring another large immigrant group in Queens County, New York, the home of the school?

Or in addition to a Jewish Studies program, why not a Catholic Studies program, or a Presbyterian one? Or, in fact, why not a Muslim one as more Middle Easterners immigrate to America?

(A German Studies program would seem reasonable everywhere. That ethnic group has recently, and quietly, assumed the position of the largest "minority" in the nation.)

The idiocy of the whole idea of special studies for races, ethnicities, and genders should be obvious. (Where are the Male Studies programs?) Since America has over sixty minority groups, shouldn't we, in all fairness, accommodate each group's spectrum? Then why not eliminate all nonethnic or nonracial-based subjects and spend four years navel-examining each other's supposed differences?

At Stanford, perhaps the gravest damage to the college curriculum was the elimination of "Western Culture," once a required freshman orientation course in history and literature.

On that bucolic campus near one of the most affluent towns in America, 500 students and faculty listened to an address by a prominent African-American politician. Quickly, they broke out into a protest against the West, one totally inconsistent with the luxury of their school, primarily paid for by their parents, the government, and charities from the surpluses of Western Civilization.

"Hey, hey, ho ho, Western Culture's got to go," they chanted.

And guess what? The weak administration buckled under to their sophomoric demands. They eliminated the "Western Culture" survey course, replacing it with a pastiche called "Cultures, Ideas, and Values," quickly nicknamed "CIV." (One Comparative Lit professor quit in protest.)

To ensure that the emphasis on "Western Culture" was truly gone, the committee recruited minority teachers who could be trusted to attack Western values. In addition to small sops to Western thought, the CIV became a refuge for works by women, minorities, and persons of color.

A new academic thesis was put into place: that supposedly "oppressed" people, including those in the most primitive civilizations, ostensibly possess an inventory of truths that have bypassed the dominant Western culture.

Squeezed between Plato and Jefferson were new "insights" of individuals like Chief Seattle, a Native American, and "dreamtime" theories of Australian aborigines, including their belief that women become pregnant by crossing "spiritually enchanted" pieces of ground—a new geographic perspective on the problem of fertility and birth control.

Of course, CIV missed the whole point. The contemporary university is the creation of Western Civilization, which is the only culture now being imitated in every corner of the globe by non-Europeans, women, and people of color.

The anti-intellectual nature of "diversity" programs in colleges is obvious to scholarly observers, including Professor Rita J. Simon at the School of Public Affairs, American University in Washington, D.C.

"Diversity seems to go hand in hand with a conformity of thought that broaches few diversions from the correct political line," she points out in *Academic Questions,* adding that there is an overt university prejudice against Western culture.

"It is now de rigeur to regard non-Western societies as more worthy of study than Western civilizations, and the department that too enthusiastically promotes dead, white European males might risk its very existence," she adds. "Students are taught to adopt the perspectives of people who occupy the lowest social strata and then assess the culture, values, and morals of the society by their criteria."

Today's university environment bears an extraordinary resemblance to that of the Chinese Cultural Revolution of the 1960s, when traditional higher education, much of it Western in content, was attacked as counterrevolutionary. Professors were forced to wear dunce caps and were beaten by irate adolescent Red Guards mouthing the pronouncements of Mao Tse-tung.

As a result, the Chinese university system was destroyed and has never recovered. Instead, thousands of Chinese students have left the mainland to study in America and Europe, especially in specialized science schools, which despite attempts to weaken them by the New Establishment, are still functioning. (As a deserved backlash, many Chinese mainland students, including my former library researcher, never return home.)

The difference in the current American anti-intellectual revolution is that the professors and administrators are playing the role of the Red Guards. The students are not beaten, but they are introduced into the joys of the nonthinking, indolent mind and required to absorb and repeat back the banalities and dogmas of New Establishment professors and administrators.

One critic, who taught at both Brown and a state school, the University of South Florida, expresses his opinion that the prestige colleges are considerably less than they used to be.

Says an outspoken Jacob Neusner, a rabbi and a professor, in an article entitled "Cheers for No-Name U":

"A generation ago no one doubted the value of education among 'the best and the brightest.' The elite schools today lie in shambles and disgrace. Who wants to emulate them? Stanford has turned its curriculum into an engine of propaganda. Lacking requirements of weight, a Brown degree certifies nothing. The English department at Georgetown has repealed literature. Berkeley is a zoo, Harvard a jungle filled with prestige-hungry predators . . ."

Neusner believes students are better served at small, lesser known schools, and he may be right. But evidence exists that the New Establishment has taken control of many of them as well.

It is all part and parcel of the mass college hysteria of Political Correctness. The once-underestimated assault on free speech and free thought was initially greeted with laughter as a policy that would be dead on arrival.

Instead, it now dominates American campuses in a multitude of ways. PC, in fact, has created an environment of social and cultural madness that is doing grave damage to student minds. Its distortions have made contemporary college life a peculiar, insular, anti-intellectual experience with no real parallel in outside existence. The campus has become an incubator of adolescent rituals that are askew from the way normal, educated people usually think and behave.

One critic of PC campus life is a brilliant young woman, Wendy Shalit, who at the end of her sophomore year at Williams College in Massachusetts wrote an article on her experiences as a new student for *Commentary,* the publication of the American Jewish Committee.

The piece, entitled "A Ladies' Room of One's Own," is a satirical, but quite factual, introduction to the madness of college PC and how it has invaded one once-prestigious American campus. Giving us a private insight into the *required* freshmen rituals of Political Correctness, Ms. Shalit describes how the college began its orientation week with mandatory sessions on "Peoples and Cultures" and instruction in the "Harassment Codes."

"One must not be racist, sexist, or ethnocentric unless one happens to be a black or woman," she explained about the ethos of the Williams campus. "One must be positively sympathetic to diversity of gender, race, and sexual orientation but not to the diversity of ideas."

She describes how her freshman orientation included a "mandatory ritual" of "Feel-What-It-Is-Like-to-Be-Gay Meeting." All the students introduced themselves by declaring: "Hello, my name is . . . and I'm Gay!" Later that week, the students were herded into a darkened auditorium where, with eyes closed, racial, ethnic, and gender slurs were thrown at them from all directions as part of "Diversity Sensitivity."

The young woman also complained about campus dogma that left her without a ladies' room. She was forced to conform to the new PC use of a coed bathroom, with which—having had a traditional upbringing—she was uncomfortable.

A classmate told her she had once felt the same, but had gotten over it, becoming as she said, "comfortable with her body." Female students were told that if they had qualms about sharing a bathroom with men, there were any number of good campus counselors to talk to in "Psych Services."

It wasn't *her* body that she was uncomfortable with, Ms. Shalit points out. "It was the intracacies of the opposite sex's body which I wasn't necessarily so eager to study so early in the morning."

To avoid young hormonal men in her bathroom, she signed up for an all-women suite her second year at Williams. But alas, she again stepped out of the shower to find a man—"or rather the rear" of him. Finally, in desperation, she put up a sign: "This is NOT a coed bathroom—Ladies Only, Please."

The following day, her suitemate asked her to come into the

common room, where all four young women were sitting on the floor, wearing, as she says, "very grave expressions."

Ms. Shalit describes the scene:

"Andrea spoke first. 'Wendy, we've been talking and we were thinking, well . . . that sign of yours is really very exclusionary of one gender.'

" 'Exclusionary of one gender?' Was she serious? 'Well, yes, I admitted, but remember, that's kind of the point, isn't it?' "

(The point, of course, is that PC anti-thought is turning reality into a self-delusionary environment in which no other points are permitted except those of the New Establishment.)

"Sensitivity" seems to be a key concept on campus today. It is so blown out of proportion that whether it involves ethnicities, races, sexes, homosexuality, religion, or disability it often replaces education as the goal of the college. Every action and statement of students is painstakingly examined to see if it could somehow offend someone. Those who don't like that conformist practice risk being despised, even ostracized.

Again, it is much like the Chinese Cultural Revolution, about which Americans laughed long and loud, with its totalitarian techniques of brainwashing, self-confession, and "reeducation." Only now it has come back to haunt us as we expertly mimic those same practices on our campuses. PC is so oppressive that students who do not go along have even been labeled "fascist" or "Nazi," and attempts are made to "reeducate" them.

The list of PC edicts that students are supposed to adhere to, at the threat of serious punishment, is ever-growing.

Columnist John Leo of *U.S. News & World Report* has from time to time compiled a compendium of PC campus banalities, some of which perfectly reflect the social and cultural madness in our colleges.

• The assistant dean of the Harvard School of Public Health wrote a piece that the movie *Jurassic Park* was insulting to minorities because the dinosaurs killed mainly black characters and let the blond-haired ones escape.

• A student at Sarah Lawrence was punished for laughing during an argument when someone called someone else a "faggot." For that, he was charged with "Discriminatory Harassing" (new PC verbiage) and sentenced to ten hours painting campus benches and repairing flower beds. He was also forced to watch a video on homophobia and write an "academic" paper on it as part of his reeducation.

• At the university of California at Davis, the law review announced a new precedent. Henceforth it would use the female pronoun instead of the male pronoun as a matter of course. "Except," said the editors, "when referring to a criminal defendant, where male pronouns are used." They added that "Federal criminal defendants are overwhelmingly male."

• Phillips Exeter Academy (not a college but one of America's leading prep schools) gave its annual "Diversity and Cultural Awareness" award to a graduate who was killed while allegedly trying to mug a plainclothes cop.

• An introductory course in politics at Johns Hopkins University offered a reading list filled with books on American oppression, the evils of the CIA, the film *Berkeley in the Sixties,* and how AIDS was invented by straights to punish gays.

• Professors at Middle Tennessee State University were asked to count the number of times the pronouns "he" and "she" were used in their class readings, an attempt to equalize the impact of the sexes.

• At George Mason University, flinching when a homosexual touches your arm is a punishable harassment offense. Other such offenses include staring at homosexuals holding hands; keeping your distance from known gays or lesbians; *thinking* that a homosexual might come on to you.

• At the University of Massachusetts, the Minuteman mascot is under attack as "too macho, white, and violent. If you're a woman or a person of color, he really can't represent you." Indian mascot names are considered PC taboos and somehow offensive instead of flattering. The Marquette University "Warrior" nickname and logo are gone, the Saint John Redmen are now The Red Storm, and the University of Wisconsin has refused to play any team that uses Indian names.

There is a kind of desperation—even a pitiful desperation—in this crusade for supposed purity. This generation of new collegians is trying excessively hard to replicate the 1960s, when their parents were heavily involved in civil rights and political radicalism. Since there is no generation gap to speak of and real life is much the same as before, they feel driven to create an artificial gap, no matter how irrational, or superficial, the cause.

PC takes on many forms on the campus, including the housing arrangements for students at several American schools. In prior years, a brouhaha was created because of the segregation of men and women, Jews and Christians in fraternity houses, and blacks and whites at many levels. Much of this was eliminated by earlier campus movements that demanded the *mixing* of diverse Americans and their subcultures. And what better place to mix than at college?

Now, there has been an exact turnaround. Colleges are imbued with a new racist and bigoted attitude that doesn't seem to embarrass its proponents. Segregation, not integration or mixing, is now *official* policy for housing on several major campuses, a backward step put into operation by New Establishment administrators.

At Cornell, one of the nation's largest centers of the new segregation, Latino, African-American, and Native American students are encouraged to live, study, and eat separately in school-sponsored special dormitories or other living accommodations—reversing thirty years of work to integrate everyone into the American culture.

The Latinos mainly reside in the Latino Living Center, the African-Americans in a dorm labeled "Ujamaa," and the Native Americans in their own house, a separate building on campus.

The new President of Cornell, Hunter Rawlings, had second thoughts about the program put in by predecessors. He proposed delaying freshman from moving into one of the ten school-supported "Program Houses" until their second year. But he was met by a mass student protest, including a hunger strike by fifteen students. After that, he acted like most college administrators and relented.

Michael Meyers, an African-American who is the head of the New York Civil Rights Coalition, remembers his racial history. A former student at Antioch College, where he opposed the operation of a black dorm on campus, he has called for the abolition of all segregated campus residences as paternalistic and racist. Meyers has filed a complaint with the U.S. Department of Education's office on Civil Rights.

"Would they accept the demand for the white students who wanted a white dorm?" he asks, exposing the racist nature of Cornell.

Aside from its explicit damage, Meyers adds that there is also the loss of the chance to use college as perhaps "the first and only opportunity to get to know people without regard to their race."

Many colleges have set up this special housing, including the democratically infamous Stanford, where again there is an Ujamaa residence for African-Americans; Casa Zapata for Hispanics; Muhwekmataw-ruk for Native Americans.

At the once-prestigious University of Pennsylvania in Philadelphia, segregated housing masquerades under the euphemistically titled "Academic Programs in the Residences," giving a false rationale for the segregation. It features group housing for African-Americans (The W. E. B. Dubois College House). East Asians live together on certain floors of Harnell high-rise. There is a floor elsewhere for Latin-Americans, along with Casa Espanica, and the lower floors of High Rise North are reserved for Orthodox Jews.

Penn does not have special housing for Native Americans, because, according to the director of these programs, there aren't enough of them on campus. (Is this a case of racial discrimination in admissions?)

Under the guise of "diversity," American colleges have instituted a rigorous program of "anti-diversity."

All this activity violates the whole concept of the university, which stems from the Latin *universitas,* or loosely, "all together." By separating students into ethnicities, races, and even religions, the colleges are destroying the universal quality of higher education.

These residences become ingrown and are sometimes reinforced with special racial and ethnic academic programs to celebrate differences, rather than similarities, among students, which is the essence of a pluralistic university. Naturally, this type of fragmentation can also fire the flames of bigotry.

The implementation of self-segregation, with the financial and moral support of the university, was the beginning of a cultural war on campus. Today student and faculty bigotry makes continual demands on a weak administration, or on one dedicated to New Establishment principles.

At Stanford, a student head of M.E.Ch.A. the Latino-Chicano student group, has demanded a full-time dean for Hispanic Affairs instead of the part-time one now provided by the school. At Yale, the Dean of Chicano Affairs (a curious academic portfolio) was recently quoted as saying: "It is really important for students to have teachers and professors who look like them."

PC is pandemic. At the enormous State University of New York (SUNY), "multiculturalism" on campus is the rage. At all of its sixteen campuses, racial/ethnic subjects are not only offered to students, but are required. In fact, it is the *only* universal requirement on its campuses, from Buffalo to Stony Brook on Long Island.

PC, New York–style, has many forms. At the Albany campus, students must take three credits in a "Human Diversity" course, including such offerings as "Introduction to Lesbian and Gay Studies," and "Classism, Racism, and Sexism" in America. At Binghamton, their required PC course is simply called "Multiculturalism."

Old Westbury requires a course in "ideological institutions such as racism and sexism." At Stony Brook, the choice of required "Multicultural Perspectives" includes such courses as "The Modern Color Line." At the Cortland campus, students must take three semester credits in "Prejudice and Discrimination." At SUNY New Paltz, students are introduced to such "cultural diversity" material as "Women With Women."

The startling aspect of the PC curriculum is that it is more demanding of a student's time and energy than are the academic requirements. While multicultural courses are required on all sixteen SUNY campuses, math is required on only eleven; Western Civilization on only eight; literature on only four; and philosophy on only three. So while so-called "diversity" reigns, basic education declines.

As the Empire Foundation/National Association of Scholars report on the SUNY system concludes:

"It is one thing for a university or college to offer such courses as electives; it is quite a different matter when such courses are included as core requirements which must be fulfilled to graduate." The report adds that the courses are usually highly "politicized," and "focus on grievances of different groups, whether based on sex, race or class."

Historian Arthur Schlesinger sees these diversity studies as "degrading" to history. "Our schools and colleges have a responsibility to teach history for its own sake, and not to degrade history by allowing its contents to be dictated by pressure groups, whether political, economic, religious or ethnic," he writes.

These studies, of course, are not the province of a true university, where such phenomena can be examined but not advanced as sacrosanct truths.

Such a PC curriculum requirement is, of course, forced propaganda, which is increasingly creating a New McCarthyism on many campuses. Most students go along, either because they have been indoctrinated to conform to New Establishment principles, or because of peer and faculty pressure. There is also the fear that they are jeopardizing their social lives, even their academic grades, by not going along.

Several students interviewed by a writer confessed to fears of not conforming to strong campus pressure, especially of a political nature. At Yale, some anti-PC students say they are intimidated, much as gay students once felt they were. "He's in the closet (politically)," said one student about a classmate. "He won't be able to help you." Another student said: "So many could speak out but don't."

One history major spoke of the environment in the class as oppressive. "Every week it was a boxing match, except that it was fourteen against one." Another student feared that it was hurting his grades. "When everyone disagrees with you, including the TA (teaching assistant), you can't help but feel punished."

At Smith College, a student said she quickly discovered that the way to get an *A* in a feminist anthropology class "was to write papers full of guilt and angst about how I'd bought into society's definition of womanhood—and now I'm enlightened and free."

Michelle Easton, writing in the *Wall Street Journal*, elaborates on the fears of those who refuse to go along with PC academe. She quotes a mathematics professor at Oberlin, who says the goals of Women's Studies "sound more like a political party than an academic department. I have been supportive of women's studies in the past, but I am not willing to support a political party in disguise."

The atmosphere on many campuses is Orwellian, with administrations clamping down on the freedom of students and even those professors who refuse to play the conformist game.

When Timothy Maguire, a law student at Georgetown University in Washington, D.C., published an article in the school newspaper that claimed that there was a dual standard of admission—that some minority students were admitted with relatively low LSAT scores—he was disciplined by the administration and threatened with expulsion. But when he proved his charges and received legal help from the Center for Individual Rights, a nonprofit organization in Washington, he was reluctantly reinstated.

The New Establishment can be paranoic, seeing anti-PC thought everywhere, and clamping down before it can weaken its carefully constructed facade. At Hampshire College, a candidate for a post in Latin American literature was disqualified because his paper comparing Shakespeare and Mexican writers showed what they considered dangerous "Eurocentric" tendencies.

At MIT, Cynthia Wolff had to sue the administration for abridging her academic freedom. Despite the fact that she is an avowed feminist, she was excluded from teaching in the women's studies program ostensibly because she wasn't radical enough.

Even the federal government can be a partner in the stifling PC game, resulting in censorship of free speech and academic freedom. At the University of Alaska campus in Fairbanks, Judith Kleinfeld, a Harvard-trained psychologist, is a well-known advocate for better educational opportunity for Native Americans.

But at a meeting of the local Chamber of Commerce, she made a frank remark that sometimes professors in the teacher education program felt "equity pressures" to pass Native American students through the system. This not only created a furor at the school, but demonstrations were organized against her.

The ruckus soon came to the attention of Washington. Immediately an inspector was dispatched to Fairbanks from the Office of Civil Rights of the Department of Education, America's official

Thought Police. What was Ms. Kleinfeld's "crime"? The OCR came to find out if her remarks violated the law—specifically racial discrimination, which is outlawed by Title VI of the 1964 Civil Rights Act.

Title VI was written by Congress to stop segregated education in the South, but it has now been retrofitted by the Department of Education to police speech and behavior in schools, up through college. (As we shall see, Title IX of that same act is used to police "sexual harassment" in educational institutions.)

If a violation was proven, Washington could penalize the school by withholding its federal aid, a carrot—and stick—that gives them power over what is said and done on most American campuses.

The inspector was told to learn the following:

"What does (Kleinfeld) say was the basis for the comments? Fact or opinion? Supported by evidence? . . . Does she offer any witnesses? . . . What was her alleged intent or purpose behind making the remarks? . . . (Did) she properly qualify and limit her remarks to ensure they would be correctly understood?"

The federal attempt to "investigate" free speech was shocking to many. But the Department of Education regularly gets involved in such inquisitions. Kleinfeld protested that the investigation itself violated her rights under the First Amendment and the principle of academic freedom.

After weeks of snooping, the OCR finally sent a letter to the university that they did not believe her remarks violated Title VI. But the aftermath of this attempt at thought control is that Ms. Kleinfeld has been advised by the college not to get involved in research or teaching that involves questions of Native Americans, one of her academic specialties.

(Congress should take another look at Title VI to see if it is not, as it surely is, in violation of First Amendment rights of free speech.)

The specter of PC intimidation is recognized by independent

academics who speak out. Robert Cole, professor emeritus at the University of California Law School at Berkeley, best describes the method used on many campuses to achieve New Establishment goals. "The idea is, let's just shut these people up and we'll get equality," he says. "But you don't get equality that way."

The fight against campus PC is a difficult one. But sometimes student opposition to the conformity is underestimated, mainly because fear keeps many silent. According to a federally funded survey of Wellesley students, 30 percent of a women's study group were afraid to risk stating their true, unpopular, opinions in class.

Fighting PC is not easy since adolescent peer pressure is not something easily fought. But there are signs of revolt. A new journalistic industry has sprung up in which anti-PC students have put out unofficial newspapers in opposition to the official campus dogma. They are considered the province of angry white males, which is sometimes true, but several editors of alternate papers like the *Dartmouth Review* have been women or members of minorities.

They are labeled "conservative," which may or may not be an accurate description. "Anti-PC" might be a more appropriate label. But they exist only because the official, mainly PC, campus newspapers do not fight the New McCarthyism.

(I take pride in having openly opposed both Mccarthyisms in print, a generation or so apart.)

Naturally, these unofficial campus publications face an uphill battle. In addition to providing alternate news for students on campus, they try to get information about the schools out to mainstream media, who generally ignore anti-intellectualism on campuses. At Vassar, when a black student spoke out in an anti-Semitic manner, the administration tried to hush it up. But the *Vassar Spectator,* an unofficial paper, brought it to the public's attention.

In the spirit of little concern for First Amendment rights,

many college administrators have themselves tried to squelch the alternative papers. At the University of California at Davis, the unofficial paper could not be distributed in the same location as administration-approved student newspapers. Students had to go a distance to get it.

Anti-PC newspapers have been stolen or destroyed, as have official school newspapers when they print something that certain groups find offensive. *Editor and Publisher* reports that there were forty cases of stolen campus papers last year.

The catalyst was the theft of the entire press run—14,000 copies—of the University of Pennsylvania *official campus paper* in 1993. It was stolen by African-American students, who claimed the paper perpetuated "institutional racism." The Penn administration, in its usual PC mode, published a mild statement in support of press freedom, but did not punish the offending students, who claimed they were exercising their own right of "free speech."

In November, 1996, the entire print run of the *Daily Californian* at the University of California at Berkeley—33,000 copies— was stolen after it ran an editorial supporting the Regent's ban on affirmative action on campus. The thieves trailed the three delivery trucks, waited for the newspaper to be dropped off, then carted away all the copies.

Paper stealers claim that since the papers are free, there is no crime. (They obviously don't consider the costs to the newspaper or the groups funding them.) Maryland is the first state to pass a specific law making the theft of free newspapers a criminal act. That was prompted by the theft of bundles of a college paper found, and photographed, in the office of the Black Student Union at a Baltimore college. The police refused to make arrests and school officials ordered the editors of the campus paper not to print the picture.

Mark Goodman, president of the Student Press Law Center, speaking in Washington, D.C., at the Associated College Press convention, added his voice to those who fear that freedom of the press was being challenged on campuses.

"The increase of conservative columnists in the college press," he told his audience of two thousand editors and writers, "is matched only by the efforts of the protectors of political correctness to censor them, especially when their opinions range to race, sex, and affirmative action. No matter how offensive or unpopular their opinions, their right to write must be protected."

Of course, it should be pointed out that the fight is not one of "conservative" versus "liberal" students. Rather the struggle is for the right of all students—Socialist or Libertarian—to speak out, whatever their opinions, and for the administration to remain politically neutral, which too often is not the case.

Another group of eager censors are faculty members themselves. Professors have gone so far as to denounce anti-PC student editors in their classrooms for what they have written—surely no great stimulus to the freedom of expression universities are supposed to encourage.

Free speech is as much under attack on PC campuses as is freedom of the press. According to one survey, 383 colleges have some form of "speech codes," a totalitarian concept that controls what students can and cannot say. Supposedly designed to encourage civility between individuals and groups, it has instead become an offensive restriction on freedom.

A slip of the tongue, or a negative comment, could result in student expulsion. Or the statement might be a constructive piece of criticism, which in the oversensitive PC environment is often misinterpreted by students or faculty members falsely seeking "purity"—a common goal of totalitarian movements.

The censorship of student speech is often a broad based gag order, highly reminiscent of all fanatic attempts to control people's thoughts, including edicts against "biased ideas" and "offensive or outrageous viewpoints," "ill-timed laughter," and "intentional infliction of emotional distress." These dictatorial purveyors of New Establishment dogma forget that, in the final analysis, they are the truly offensive ones.

In an Op-Ed piece in *The New York Times,* columnist Anthony Lewis attacked the threatening wave of censorship on campus.

Speaking of a proposed curb on free speech at the University of Massachusetts at Amherst, Lewis pointed out that the proposed ban on speech that offends on the basis of "race, color, national or ethnic origin, gender, sexual orientation, age, religion, mental status, veteran status or disability" would be a step backward. He adds that the college's graduate student union had suggested still other curbs on speech, including those likely to offend on the basis of "citizenship, culture, HIV status, language, parental status, political affiliation or belief and pregnancy status"—a seeming compendium of all humankind.

"Orwell is the name that comes to mind as one reads this proposal," says Lewis. "It would create a totalitarian atmosphere in which everyone would have to guard his tongue all the time lest he say something that someone might find offensive. . . . Do the drafters have no knowledge of history? One wonders. No understanding that freedom requires as Justice Holmes said, 'freedom for the thought that we hate'? And if not, what are they doing at a university?"

Some students are starting to fight back against the New McCarthyism. At the University of California, Riverside, the Phi Kappa Sigma fraternity was officially kicked off campus when they printed up a politically incorrect T-shirt (designed by an Hispanic member) showing a sombrero-wearing man clutching a beer bottle. The fraternity sued the administration on First Amendment grounds and not only won reinstatement but forced two college administrators to go through "sensitivity training," the type of punishment usually meted out by speech cops.

Ira Glasser, the director of the American Civil Liberties Union (which surprisingly supports affirmative action even though it deprives certain Americans of their civil liberties) weighed in on the side of the fraternity, commenting that "when someone wears a T-shirt that others find offensive, too bad."

There have been other student revolts against undemocratic speech codes as well.

At Stanford University, anti-PC students objected to restraints on what the administration called "hate speech." Not that the students defended vulgarity, but they did want to defend the First Amendment, which they felt was more important than any individual's, or group's, sensitivity.

In a lawsuit, *Robert J. Corry v. The Leland Stanford Junior University*, Corry, a former law student, and eight other students, argued that Stanford's code of so-called Discriminatory Harassment was interfering with their right of free speech. In the case of Stanford, they pointed out that virtually any statement involving race, sex, religion, handicap, sexual orientation, or religion had been turned into illegal speech by the school. The code, as written, even proscribed "nonverbal symbols" that could be insulting, such as drawings, cartoons, or tee-shirts.

The judge of the Santa Clara County Superior Court agreed with the students, ruling that Stanford's "speech code" was unconstitutional. The code was crafted in 1990 after some students defaced a poster with racist caricatures. Corry pointed out that students themselves rejected the code in a nonbinding referendum and that it was "contrary to everything Stanford should stand for in free discourse." He added that it had a "chilling effect" on debate.

The school claimed that "hate speech" could stimulate anger and discord on campus. But the court referred to a prior case (*Terminiello v. Chicago*) in which the Supreme Court ruled that speech that "stirs the audience to anger" or "invites dispute" is protected under the First Amendment. The judge quoted former Supreme Court Justice William O. Douglas on the issue:

"(A) function of free speech under our system of government is to invite dispute. It may indeed best serve its high purpose when it induces a condition of unrest, creates dissatisfaction with conditions as they are, or even stirs people to anger."

Implicitly, the court was ruling that Stanford had falsely turned simple criticism of sexes, races, and ethnic groups into "hate speech." Not only was critical speech under the protection of the Constitution, but as Justice Douglas has pointed out, it might be highly constructive by stirring people to anger and change.

Like all previous attacks on the mind, from the Spanish Inquisition to McCarthyism, to facism and Stalinism, the New Establishment and its PC creation must be directly confronted lest its *abnormal* treatises begin to be viewed as *normal*.

At this juncture, we have some choices. Parents can send their children to a supposedly "better" American college, but understand that PC and a permissive curriculum can inflict injury on both their minds and their sense of morality. Or they can arm their children with that knowledge and prepare them for a confrontation.

Perhaps it is easier to avoid such colleges and search out those few remaining ones that maintain respect for individuals, knowledge, and above all, Western Culture.

For alumni, the challenge is to become active in the affairs of their alma mater and work to help restore the freer, more rigorous academic atmosphere of prior years. For the faculty, the challenge is to resist administration and student pressure to submit to New Establishment dogma in both curriculum and campus behavior. Students need to stop submitting to peer and group pressure, and instead openly battle the conspiracy of ignorance and conformity that has gripped America's campuses.

The challenge is also there for the average citizen. It is to fight, with words and actions, to protect our academic system, our youth, and our general culture from the ravages of the New Establishment and its Orwellian creation, political correctness.

CHAPTER FIVE

DIVERSITY, MULTICULTURALISM, BILINGUALISM, AND OTHER MYTHS

The Threat to American Culture

IN NEW ESTABLISHMENT LEXICON, TWO BUZZ-words stand out: *Multiculturalism* and *Diversity*.

Their meanings are as immutable or as nebulous as you want them to be, but their purpose is clear. They are used as weapons to counter the majority, or Eurocentric, American culture. According to the new dogma, that culture has supposedly been used for centuries to force various minorities into a rigid mold in which different languages, aspirations, and lifestyles were purposely minimized in favor of the majority.

The New Establishment seeks to break that mold by setting up alternate, separate cultures within America—stressing the importance of diversity.

What are the models for this effort?

The examples are seldom advanced by the New Establishment, but they exist worldwide. They include such multicultural nations as Russia, where dozens of languages flourish and feuding ethnics fight for independence; the Native Indian population in Mexico, which is rebelling against the central government; the

Hindi and Moslems in India, each with its own language and traditions, who are at each other's throats in that subcontinent of over one hundred dialects; the continuing war among three language/ethnic groups in Afghanistan; and in Africa, where the Tutsis and the Hutus, and scores of other tribes, have been killing each other mercilessly.

As a goal of the New Establishment, multiculturalism would encourage similar tribalism in America. It strives for a form of *separatism* in which each group's differences—foibles as well as assets—are not only tolerated and accepted, but celebrated.

Except, of course, for the Anglo-American Judeo-Christian identity that built America in the first place. But the New Establishment attempts to portray that vital culture as less important than those of minorities and their infinite sensibilities.

In fact, in the last thirty years the multicultural-diversity movement has evolved in America (and is similarly beginning to invade Britain, Germany, and France) as one favoring a program of anti-assimilation.

It is an obvious attempt to Balkanize America and undercut the unity that crafted a nation of once-diverse peoples into an effective whole through an extraordinarily successful *Uniculturalism.* By promoting Multiculturalism instead, the New Establishment is brazenly attempting to shatter that "oneness" and reward parochialism and sociological infantalism, the same tendencies that created the torn Bosnias of the world.

Before the advent of the New Establishment, immigrants had voluntarily downplayed their separate cultural identities and focused on what binds us as Americans.

What are the ties that hold us together? What is that "American" identity?

It is singularly Anglo-American. Not usually of blood anymore, but of culture. But what can such an identity mean to a Pole or a Jew or an Irishman or an African-American?

Everything. It is the identifying central core that gave us *all* freedom from political and religious dogmatism. It is the idea that makes America distinguishable and different from all other nations. The Anglo-American culture has specific guidelines and expectations, which after only a few years most newcomers begin to recognize and admire.

That culture has a defining ethos that describes and enables us. It has a central history going back to the 1600s (when almost none of our forebears were here), and a tradition of freedom, social mobility, youthful optimism, home ownership, a large active bourgeoisie, pluralism under a unifying ethos, the English language, and respect for Western culture, constitutional government, the rights of individuals, and fair play.

And despite the vainglorious boasting of the descendants of nineteenth- and twentieth-century immigrants from Europe (such as myself), it is almost entirely Anglo-American in its origins and content.

American culture has accepted numerous other identities into its sociological tent and has altered them, only slightly altering itself in the process. But overall it has produced a culture that is still basically one with its roots in Colonial America and England.

It is *not* a blending. Rather, immigrants from the 1840s onward—the Irish, German, Jewish, Italian, Greek, or whatever—whose descendants now make up a majority of Americans, assimilated their cultures into the Anglo mold, losing almost all of the their original identities over a period of three or four generations. Though America is now sometimes seen as a general "European" nation, it bears little relation to Continental Europe and is almost exclusively Anglo-American in content.

(One should not forget that America was forged in John Harvard's room at Cambridge University in East Anglia in 1628 when the Puritans signed the pact to come to these shores.)

This Anglo-American culture has many ramifications, subtleties, and subcultural offshoots. But in essence *we are all mainly Anglo*—whether white, black, Asian, female, male, Hispanic, Jew, gentile, or Mormon, straight or otherwise.

As our dollar bill proclaims: E PLURIBUS UNUM—From Many—One. Not as some falsely translate it—From One—Many. So thoroughly, and silently, has this Americanization taken place that a descendant of German immigrants, Dwight David Eisenhower, led the American victory over Germany in World War II.

Miulticulturalism and Diversity are, as we shall see, normal only among immigrants. It is an attribute necessary in the early stages of assimilation. But if maintained by false concepts of ethnic identity or sensitivity, it damages those who practice it and becomes the scourge of democracy, as it is today.

That is the threat: not just Western Civilization, but the unifying Anglo-American culture as well, is under attack by the New Establishment. Because of it, the cohesion of the nation and the future success of the still-not-fully-assimilated, whether Asians, Hispanics, African-Americans, or others, is jeopardized.

The white national population at the time of the American Revolution was well over 90 percent British colonials. This included the former inhabitants of England, Wales, Scotland, and the so-called Scots-Irish, who came to Northern Ireland beginning in the 1600s, then emigrated here, especially to the frontier.

There were a few other immigrant groups in the beginning: the Dutch, the Scandinavians, and some Germans. In fact, the first President under the Articles of Confederation was not George Washington, but John Hanson, a Swede from Maryland. But under the American social contract, which was already evolving, he was an Anglo in spirit. That culture was—and is—clear cut in its precepts and enhanced by the ideas of freedom espoused by the British-Americans, from Adams to Jefferson and Franklin.

That ethos still exists, but it is threatened by the New Establishment's misleading concepts of Multiculturalism and Diversity—two enemies which we thought we had already defeated through assimilation.

In the first half of the nineteenth century, there was a substantial emigration from Germany of tradesmen and small farmers who settled in Pennsylvania and further west, some of whom came here for religious freedom. President Dwight Eisenhower was the progeny of the German River Brethren group, which observed the Jewish Saturday sabbath.

In the 1840s and 1850s, a massive migration arrived in America from Ireland, where farmers fled as a result of the potato famine, coming to a nation that then had no immigration restrictions. It was a vast land mass in need of people to fill it.

The Irish provided the first large-scale incidence of Diversity and Multiculturalism in America. They were less well-educated than the Anglos. They were Catholic rather than Protestant, and involved, said their critics, in excessive drinking, bellicosity, crime, and the production of children. The Anglo majority accused them of being religious "Papists" and discrimination was rampant. IRISH NEED NOT APPLY signs were commonplace.

During the Civil War, $300 bought one an exemption from the draft. But being poor, many Irish provided cannon fodder for the North, prompting draft riots in New York.

The next wave of immigration, to provide workers for the Industrial Revolution, was even larger than the Irish migration. From the 1880s until Ellis Island—the entry point in New York— was closed in 1924, some 12 million new Americans arrived from Europe, the forebears of over 100 million current citizens. (My father's father arrived here from Budapest in 1893.) They were mainly Italians, Greeks, Austrians, Czechs, Hungarians, Germans, Jews, Slovaks, Poles, Russians, and any number of peoples, mostly Europeans.

If one wanted Diversity and Multiculturalism, the turn-of-the-century immigrants provided enough to fulfill a New Establishmentarian's dream. The American Anglo-Protestants were not so sure about the new arrivals. They needed the cheap labor, but common bias, including the opinion of some prominent academics, was that the new Southern and Eastern European immigrants were not equal to Anglo-Americans in native brain power and might be a serious drain on the well-established Anglo culture.

We tend to forget that at the time, before the great wave of European immigration peaked at the turn of the century during the presidency of Theodore Roosevelt, America was already the richest, most literate, and most productive country in the world.

Fortunately for the immigrants, they were treated with benign neglect, the proven milieu for survival and assimilation. They were given almost no help, except by a handful of private charities. They crowded into segregated ethnic areas in New York City, for example, where the smell and essence of the Old Country were often tangible. People spoke the tongues of Europe, published foreign language papers, opened restaurants to cater to their native palates.

In New York, the Jews were centered around Delancey Street, the Italians on Mulberry. The Irish, having arrived earlier in most cases, were further north and west in Manhattan, and had already spread to Brooklyn, Queens, and other parts of the city. (Together just these three immigrant groups now comprise some eighty million Americans.)

By World War I, the Irish had progressed well on the route to assimilation. The Catholic parochial schools, from first grade through college, were beginning to produce professionals. Politics and civil service jobs, especially in police and fire departments, were excellent stepping stones for Irish assimilation. By serendipity, the Irish similarity to Anglos, in both language and physical appearance, paid off as they lost their brogues and began to break out of blue collar into white collar, even onto the lower rungs of corporate management.

The Jewish immigrants found their way out of Multiculturalism through the routes of small business, especially retail stores, and rigorous education for the next generation. They capitalized on their passion for learning, developed in the old country in religious study, and were soon turning out professionals en masse. ("My son, the Doctor.")

Jews generally lived together, either out of desire or as a result of gentile discrimination. The West Side of Manhattan, with its elegant high-ceilinged apartments, was the home of successful New York Jewry, who were not allowed on the Anglo-Christian East Side, a barrier that did not break down until the 1950s, and later.

The Italians lagged somewhat at first, specializing in blue collar work and in certain small businesses including grocery stores, masonry, and other construction trades. Slower than the Jews in realizing the rewards of higher education, they too caught on, and made Anglo claims of their inferiority look ridiculous.

Through both the public and parochial schools, they rose in the professions and in politics, producing physicians, judges, lawyers, even several mayors of New York, including LaGuardia and Guiliani, Governor Mario Cuomo, and several national Senators, a Supreme Court Justice, and a President of Yale University.

The assimilation of the progeny of Ellis Island was taking place rapidly, creating new Americans.

The main method was *imitation* of the Anglo-Americans, the secret of assimilation. Each day, a piece of the Old World consciousness—thought processes, speech, dress, and habits—dropped away. Each day the children and grandchildren of the immigrants were becoming Americanized, which in essence meant *Anglicized*, more like the images they saw on the Hollywood screen and read about in their schoolbooks.

The schools played a vital part in that assimilation process, one that turned Multiculturalism into Uniculturalism, through the use of English and the hero worship of American icons, from Babe Ruth to George Washington. It was a victory without precedent in history. The children of all immigrants learning their reading and civics together were given no quarter by mainly Anglo (and some Irish) teachers, who insisted on English, spoken often and well, despite the immigrant languages used at home.

(I recall my civics teacher at JHS 52 on Kelly Street in the Bronx, the same school attended by General Colin Powell. Miss Moon, an Anglo spinster, spent much of the class time lecturing us on the superiority of English and the glories of America, and correcting both the grammar and accents of the youngsters.)

It was an atmosphere in which the Anglo-American culture, the world of Jefferson, Washington, Franklin, Jackson, Lincoln, Teddy Roosevelt, Hawthorne, Thomas Edison, Mark Twain and the Wright Brothers, was honored. We were all expected to learn it, absorb it, and become as much a part of it as any young Anglo graduate of Choate and Yale.

World War II was the final catalyst in integrating all Europeans into the Anglo-American bedrock. Fourteen million men, from the Bronx to Biloxi, were thrown together, advancing the meld. The postwar culture of suburbia completed that transition as Jews and Gentiles, Irish and Italians, Germans and Anglos lived side by side in the GI-guaranteed housing.

America, once only an Anglo nation, had become a full-fledged European one ethnically. But it was with the understanding that it was the historic Anglo culture, if not necessarily superior in all respects, that was still the dominant and unifying one. That was the social contract that other European-Americans agreed to, generally enthusiastically. The rewards of a single Anglo culture were there in the American Dream.

It has been estimated that of the Forbes 400 list of richest Americans, some one hundred are descendants of Irish immigrants. Further, the once heavily Jewish City College of New York has now passed Harvard and Yale in producing graduates who are CEOs of America's leading corporations. As Harry Golden was wont to say: "Only in America."

But one should not forget that the Italians, French, Irish, Jews, or Greeks could not do what the early Anglos accomplished. If any of those groups had founded America, it would have a different cast, physically, politically, and spiritually.

It would look and feel like the Old Country, with all its limitations, its rigid class and caste systems, its undemocratic outlook and established religions. But fortunately, America was founded by the Anglos, especially those seeking liberty from European oligarchy. It looks and feels that way—a nation in which the "Rights of Englishmen" have been greatly expanded and that had room to stretch across an entire continent.

Despite great individual contributions by immigrants over these two hundred years, they—often meaning "we"—have not been essential to the American experience.

By the 1830s, at the time of Andrew Jackson, when America was still heavily Anglo, the sense and physiognomy of the nation was formed. Since the turn of the twentieth century, immigrants from everywhere, including Europeans and Latinos, have gained enormously from the English-American forebears, considerably more than they have contributed, even when their contributions are individually superb.

It is the Anglo ethos that makes it all possible, a fact the New Establishment prefers to forget.

By the end of World War II, Diversity and Multiculturalism, which had been early impediments in the creation of a united America, had been conquered. (Only now to again raise their heads.) For the first time since the Civil War, we had finally created a giant nation of one people with a shared consciousness of its people, whether they came from the Polish Pale or the Italian boot. Each of us became Anglos in spirit, albeit with a private memory of the mores and myths of the Old Country.

Except. Except for American blacks.

While this assimilation of Europeans into the Anglo-American culture was going on, there were two separate black stories, one in the North, the other in the South, and only one a model of partial assimilation.

In the North, blacks lived somewhat like the European-Americans, but separated and generally on a lower economic scale. To blacks, their separatedness was a sign of white racism. For many whites, it was seen as the result of a long history of ad hoc, not legal, segregation and nonassimilation, with enough blame to go around for both races.

Much of the black population of New York City after World War I lived in Harlem, and in a few other places in Queens and the Bronx. It was not an enormous group, comprising less than one in ten New Yorkers by the 1940s. They spoke with less of a black patois than today, and even boasted a Black Renaissance of poetry, authorship, music, and art in the 1930s, 1940s, and into the 1950s.

Overall it was a quiet community, working like most others, if generally in lower-level jobs, but with good family bonds, church attendance, little or no welfare, and not much crime. They seemed to be making quiet, steady, if not extravagant, progress. It was this kind of a community that produced a Colin Powell.

Though one can hardly call African-Americans "immigrants," since many had come here beginning in the 1600s, they were still incompletely assimilated into the Anglo-American culture. In the 1950s, there was considerable hope that blacks would move forward rapidly since the economy was vibrant, work was plentiful. America had a solid manufacturing base in the cities (now virtually gone) and the blacks were beginning to participate in the general economy.

One would guess that, over time, the almost total separatedness of the two races—like the ethnics at the turn of the century—would eventually disappear.

But no longer. The New Establishment has moved in with a new, damaging *realpolitik,* and the black community has suffered in the process.

The contrast between those better days and today is illuminated by David Gergen of *U.S. News & World Report,* who explains that in 1950, two large factories employed people on the

153

West Side of Chicago: Western Electric had 43,000 workers and International Harvester, 14,000. "Both have since moved out," writes Gergen, "stranding thousands of black families who migrated to Chicago from the South for jobs."

The South, where segregation was enforced by law, is the second story of black existence in America. There, the blacks were not free. Unlike those in the North, they received truly inferior education, and also unlike those in the North, they usually could not vote.

The Civil Rights revolution of the 1960s changed all that. It also resulted in a massive migration of blacks to the North, drastically altering the demographics. While the original Northern blacks were urban people and somewhat educated, those who came from the south to New York, Philadelphia, Chicago, Detroit, etc., were rural and mainly poorly educated.

Unfortunately, as the migration moved northward, the Old Establishment, which had been the master of assimilation, was being replaced by the New Establishment, offering a pandering "Diversity" and "Multiculturalism" instead of "Assimilation" and "Success."

Through the schools, the media, and even the government, it stressed the differences with the white community and continually raised the specter of "racism" and "discrimination." Among the young, it harped on the slavery condition of some 130 years ago when most of our ancestors weren't here, fomenting anger and hatred.

In education, it stressed busing (and in many places, still does) as the panacea, while lowering the standards for the great tests of most young people's lives—eighth grade grammar and algebra.

Nothing illustrates this better than the situation in Yonkers, where there has been a ten-year fight to integrate the schools through busing.

In 1986, U.S. District Court Judge Leonard B. Sand ordered

Yonkers to end forty years of school segregation. The minority activists won their goal of racial balance, but it has been a Pyrrhic victory. Yonkers today has racial balance in all its schools for its 18,000 students but little else. Discipline suffered as teachers failed to criticize minority students for fear of being called "racist."

Students in Yonkers are schooled together geographically, but the honors classes are still comprised mainly of white and Asian students, while the minorities lag behind in achieving Regents diplomas and college admission, and are placed in lower-level classes.

The concept of helping minority students by promoting busing and creating physical proximity to whites is a spurious one. It has nothing to do with quality education. That requires the curriculum and discipline associated with the Old Establishment, not the New.

That New Establishment—in its white, black, and brown manifestations—is the villain of the piece. It has helped to delay and weaken assimilation into the mainstream with its constant advocacy of Multiculturalism and Diversity, especially in its false promises of an alternative civilization within the American experience. This is true not only in the African-American community but in other groups, including the rapidly growing Hispanic community, where the drive toward "separatedness" and maintenance of the Spanish culture is strong.

More than likely, the charges of "racism" and "sexism" are often just excuses for underperformance, whether low SAT scores or, as in the case of Connie Chung of CBS News, low television ratings. So common are such false charges that Americans are learning to listen to them less and less. (Observers find little "racism" toward such non-whites as Asian Ph.D.s from MIT.)

This is no small demographic matter. Just the African-American and Hispanic populations now number sixty million. Most important, the rewards of assimilation into the national ethos, which were granted to the European immigrants, are being denied to these other groups. The reality is that the more attention paid to so-called "blackness" and to "Hispanic" and other cultures, the less chance for economic and educational equality.

The academics, the media, and the government can shout and scream about Multiculturalism and Diversity, but no one changes the iron rule of sociology—that absorbing immigrants and minorities into the majority culture is the only route to success for the masses in any civilization.

The brightest and strongest among the minorities know this, and while mouthing the fashionable talk of "Diversity," they have seen through the blandishments of the New Establishment and preferred to rely on the old Anglo-Protestant ethic of work, study, and family. Understanding that assimilation requires imitation in education, speech, dress, and business and work attitudes, the black middle class is prospering. *So much so that the latest figures show that black women college graduates earn more money than their white counterparts.*

As African-Americans have moved forward and out of the ghetto, as is increasingly taking place, they have left the mass of others behind, mired down in anger and nonassimilation. They have left them subject to the half-baked "What ifs" of the New Establishment, and even with such racist attitudes that assimilation and success are somehow a "sell-out" and a sign of "Uncle Tom-ism."

Unfortunately, as the new black middle class has flourished, other African-Americans have languished. In no American subculture is there a greater gap between the assimilated and unassimilated than among African-Americans. And as the Hispanic community grows, the same is true: a disparagement of those who assimilate as being "fake Anglos." That, of course, is the self-defeating curse of minorities, one that is encouraged by the New Establishment's hollow pursuit of Multiculturalism.

To the extent that the New Establishment has accomplished

its eccentric un-American goal, it has left behind millions of victims, especially men.

Assimilation is a three-cornered stool, resting on marriage, education, and language. Unfortunately, minorities have looked to government to guide them in the pursuit of all three, falling into the best-advertised fallacy of modern society.

Welfare, for one, was supposed to raise millions out of poverty. Instead it has accomplished exactly the opposite after an expenditure of three trillion dollars. It has actually retarded marriage, forcing women to remain single and produce children out-of-wedlock in order to qualify for Washington's check. In retrospect, it has been one of the most debilitating programs in the history of Western society, an anti-charity move that masquerades as beneficence.

The result, as we have seen, is massive out-of-wedlock births among African-Americans and Hispanics as well. Among blacks, the rate was a manageable 19 percent in 1950, but it has risen to over 69 percent today. That assault on marriage has been very costly, socially and financially, for all statistics show that marriage definitely pays. As new figures indicate, married African-American families are rapidly approaching the affluence of whites. They now earn 87 percent of the income of white families, with the difference closing daily.

Education is the second leg of the assimilation progress, and once again, innocent blacks and Hispanics have futilely relied on the government. Most of the federal education money comes in the form of $12 billion a year spent on Chapter I and II—so-called aid to disadvantaged children. It *does not* come in a simple check from Washington, which local school districts can use as they please.

Instead, the money is mainly spent on "Chapter I" programs that provide federally paid teachers for a few hours of instruction a week. Too often it is in the form of "pull-out," in which the children are taken out of their regular (sometimes integrated) classes and placed in special, often segregated, classes for an hour at a time.

It is generally a waste, as even government evaluators confess. Professional evaluators at the Department of Education, which administers this program, have told me that they cannot claim any lasting value for the money spent. Their own studies show very minor gains in the early years, which disappear by the time youngsters reach the middle grades. A peer tutoring program by the brightest high schoolers, who would be paid to teach young children after school, would do more for less and would instill greater respect for scholarship in the schools.

More enterprising minority members eschew the false promises of government and enroll their children in parochial schools, where performance—without government aid—is much higher.

A report by economist Derek Neal of the University of Chicago shows the great advantage of a minority student attending a Catholic school rather than a public institution. Some 88 percent of black and Hispanic students in Catholic high schools graduate versus only 62 percent in public high schools.

Proof that this is meaningful is shown by the fact that minority Catholic school students who go on to college have more than twice the chance of graduating as do public school youngsters—27 percent versus only 11 percent. As Professor Neal indicates, this could be one vital answer to the problem of minority poverty in America.

The third leg of assimilation is language, as close to the King's English as possible. Studies all show that success is based less on a person's race or ethnicity than on his or her command of the majority language—English. The New Establishment performance here has been very injurious. In the case of African-Americans not only has it not promoted Standard English, but it has countenanced, even encouraged, the use of a patois called "Black English," with its failure of conjugation.

The same is true of the respect given to the daily use of a

foreign language—Spanish—among Hispanic-Americans. Notice, however, that prominent Hispanics like Federico Pena, the Secretary of Transportation under Clinton, speak perfect English, as do prominent blacks such as Vernon Jordan, a millionaire Washington attorney and close confidante of the President. Like most successful African-Americans, Jordan speaks the King's English, leaving the street patois to those left behind in the underclass, where they are imprisoned by poor speech.

Courtesy of the New Establishment, Black English has even been honored as a special language in some school systems. In 1982, black parents in Ann Arbor, Michigan, sued the city because their children who spoke Black English were supposedly being discriminated against in classes conducted in Standard English.

The court ruled in favor of the parents. It instructed the school system to treat the patois as a separate language. Teachers were to be educated in the structure of Black English. Why? So that they would no longer look upon the youngster's deviations from Standard English as a linguistic error.

In Oakland, California, where Black English has been labeled "Ebonics," school officials have applied for special bilingual funds from the Department of Education, initially claiming that it is a separate and distinct language deserving of study—and financial support.

The Ebonics furor captivated the country for a while, with strong defenses and attacks. But perhaps the sagest view of the problem was given in a short editorial in *The New York Times,* which exposed the anti-intellectual nature of the false "language" and demonstrated its harmful effect on the African-American inner-city population.

Pointing out that the claim that black street English is "structurally similar to West African tongues" is "absurd," the *Times* goes on to state that "defining broken English as black English is particularly galling, given that black poets, writers, and musicians have made eloquent contributions to the culture for at least 200 years."

(Nothing makes a better argument for one central culture and one language than the fiasco of Ebonics.)

All studies indicate that command of Standard English is the single most important factor in assimilation and economic success. But the message hasn't gotten through to the educational bureaucracy, which is an integral part of the New Establishment. Today, as part of their "sensitivity" to minorities, teachers throughout the nation fail to criticize the use of street language in their classrooms for fear of being labeled "racist."

Linguistic discipline in the classroom should be seen as constructive criticism. But in the skewed New Establishment environment, supposed "sensitivity" is more important than performance. Criticizing Black English is considered a put-down of African-American students, many of whom truly do not understand just how detrimental the patois is to their future. Among some, incorrect English is even a sign of racial pride. So much for New Establishment myopia.

This is all part of an anti-intellectual movement called "Bilingual Education," one of the most reactionary of contemporary New Establishment social movements. Mary Cuadrado, an Adjunct Assistant Professor of Sociology and a Ph.D. candidate at a New York college—and an Hispanic in whose home only Spanish was spoken—is relieved that she graduated before bilingual programs were made mandatory in the New York school system.

"Success here and in most quarters of this country," she wrote to *The New York Times*, "depends on one's ability to be fluent in English. Spanish is, and should be, an asset, not the liability I see it becoming for many thousands of New Yorkers."

She adds: "I find brilliant Hispanic college students who perform well below their potential because they cannot clearly express their thoughts in English or in the Spanglish they spoke in bilingual programs."

Much New Establishment nonsense stems from the failure of reason in leadership positions, whether in colleges, or in the boards of education of large cities. A professor of history at the City University in New York echoes these sentiments, stating, "The present policy guarantees failure for too many of the foreign-born students . . . expecting to earn a degree." He advocates total immersion classes in English.

Bilingual education is unnecessary and injurious to assimilation into the Anglo-American majority. We know that from our detailed experience with millions of immigrants at the turn of the century. Some fifty different primary tongues were then spoken at home, but almost no one failed to learn Standard English in school under the Old Establishment.

But today, harnessed to the ignorance of the New Establishment, millions of students throughout the nation are studying their three *R*s, including lessons in math, science, social studies, even art, *in the non-English languages spoken by their immigrant parents at home.*

In California, schools are now *mandated* to teach in forty-two different languages. Nationwide the number of tongues in bilingual education has passed sixty. The New Establishment is the villain, operating in such hydra-headed forms as the U.S. Department of Education (which doesn't educate a single child in the United States), various state education departments, and school boards, especially in large cities that attract immigrants.

Bilingual education has become an enormous program that now numbers 300,000 students just in Los Angeles and 147,000 in New York City. The number of children thrust into them rises each year. From the 1.6 million children nationally in 1986, the number of bilingual students has doubled in a decade to over 3 million, with a yearly increase of 10 percent. In California, over *20 percent* of all the students are enrolled in destructive programs in which foreign languages are the *primary* tongue for instruction.

It's also an expensive proposition. According to the National

Clearinghouse for Bilingual Education (operating on a federal contract), Washington now spends over $215 million a year on the program, just a small part of the over $2 billion involved nationally. New York City alone spends $305 million a year to teach children lessons in their parent's language rather than in English.

California, Texas, and New York are the main offenders, and Spanish the language most used instead of English. More than half of all bilingual students are enrolled in Spanish bilingual classes, while other languages with a sizable number of students include Vietnamese, Chinese, Korean, Tagalog (Philippine), Haitian Creole (popular in New York City), Russian, Hindi, and even Navaho Native American.

The theory is flawed. The idea is that by using the parents' language to teach children courses, they will learn more efficiently. Meanwhile English will be taught as a second language. This New Establishment theory flies in the face of all evidence that young children can learn any language effortlessly—but that the facility grows dimmer as the child gets older and may still be imprisoned in bilingual classes.

We have already had a spectacular success with English for immigrant children from the 1880s to the 1950s, with nary a failure. But evidence means little to educators who would rather rely on "experimental" ideas that are superficial or false but that *differentiate* them from the lay public, who, history indicates, generally know better when it comes to the education of their children.

Bilingual education has been studied by the New York City Board of Education, which has issued a report on its shortcomings. An investigative report by *The New York Times* also showed many flawed aspects of the program. One young girl who flunked the English proficiency test was placed in a class in which Spanish was the primary language. Why? Because of her Hispanic surname. The only problem was that she couldn't speak a word of Spanish!

When authorities protested that this was an "isolated case," a Spanish bilingual administrator confessed that there were at least twenty such cases of bureaucratic ignorance each year. This was the result of *testing every child with a Spanish surname*—a touch of racism.

Not until a new Chancellor of New York schools, Rudy Crew, came in was the ridiculous practice stopped in 1996. Even if a family had been here for ten generations and the father was a professor of English, and not a word of Spanish was spoken at home, children with Spanish surnames were subjected to testing, and many were placed in the bilingual program.

Other children are inappropriately put into bilingual education because they confess that a foreign language is spoken at home, even if by an eighty-year-old grandmother.

Perhaps more important, studies indicate that many children in bilingual classes do not move rapidly into regular English classes as planned. The New York law, for instance, states that students should attend a bilingual class for only three years. But many students get "locked in" and regress in English. In a recent year, 25,000 students in New York City alone were in the program for four or more years, and thousands more were floundering in place for six years or more.

"You can have kids who are completely dominant in English sitting in an English as Second Language program," says the assistant to a member of the New York Board of Education, "and that's where parents are upset that they haven't been able to get kids out of the program."

(When you put still another New Establishment theory into practice, you create "professionals" who profit from it and refuse to allow their clients to escape, just as has happened in the welfare industry. To their list of banalities and errors, we can now add a new phenomenon: *The Language Prison*.)

Are the children who are being pushed into bilingual classes by the reactionary profession all immigrants?

Hardly. Many are just youngsters who are penalized because their parents—unlike the older immigrants—are making little effort to have them learn the common language of English, or, exploited by the siren song of "multiculturalism," are even actively discouraging it. In just one school district in Queens County, New York, of 8,000 children in the bilingual program, over 3,600 were born in the United States.

But some immigrant groups who are astute enough to realize that the bilingual program is hurting their children, turn their back on bureaucratic New Establishment dogma. First among these protestors are the Russian Jews in New York, who want their children to soak up English like a sponge, as did Jewish immigrants a hundred years ago.

The city school system declared that 5,300 of the Russian children have "limited proficiency" in English and should therefore be placed in bilingual classes. But over 80 percent of the Russian Jewish parents refused to participate.

How did the bilingual system—which flies in the face of both reason and history—become a reality?

Actually it was the result of parents within certain ethnic groups, especially Hispanics and Chinese, who wanted to delay assimilation. They were intent on preserving their own heritage and language, all the while enjoying the fruits of American public education.

In New York City, the anti-assimilation idea moved into full gear when a group of Hispanics used the federal court system to stop English as the primary school language for their children. Aspira, a Latino youth group, sued the Board of Education, using the convoluted argument that unless they could learn their math and science and social studies in *Spanish,* not English, that they were being discriminated against! This was in 1974, just as the

New Establishment was beginning to make strong inroads everywhere.

The basis of the lawsuit was Section 601 of the Civil Rights Act of 1964. In a class action suit, Aspira claimed that Hispanic students had less "educational opportunity" because of their inability to speak English correctly. Because federal funds—even though a small percentage of school financing—were being funneled into the system, the federal district court had jurisdiction. They agreed with the convoluted Hispanic argument, which was an early anti-intellectual victory for the New Establishment.

"We had some bilingual programs, but as a result of the consent decree of the federal court, bilingual education was now *mandated* in the New York City public school system," says John Acompore, deputy director of the city's bilingual division. "We set up an entire curriculum in which the basic subjects were taught in Spanish. Hispanic students were directed in one of two routes. Those weakest in English would take their schooling mainly in Spanish, while those somewhat stronger in English would follow the ESL route—English as a Second Language course."

(One would think those weakest in English would get *more,* not less, English than the others students.)

In October 1996, the Census Bureau released its report that the poorest of all Americans were now Hispanics, having taken that dubious title away from African-Americans for the first time. In 1995, after six down years (and false claims about prosperity), the net household income of all Americans finally rose—2.7 percent. But among Hispanics it *dropped* 5.7 percent. Simultaneously, high school graduation among blacks rose closer to that of whites, but Hispanics lagged behind at 57 percent.

It was not a stretch to point out that Spanish bilingual classes, and the maintenance of Spanish as a primary language at home and in the class, are greatly to blame. They retard assimilation, the only known route for better education and general success.

Not only was the New York federal court swayed by specious

arguments, but the Supreme Court as well fell into the trap of separatism. As we shall see, cultural fashion—often cheap fashion—has been the criterion for many Court decisions in recent years.

The complainant this time, also in 1974, was the Chinese community of San Francisco. Many lived in Chinatown, in a separate enclave in which English was discouraged and the Chinese language heavily favored. Children born in Chinatown could spend their whole lives speaking only Chinese, barely bothering with English.

Many families purposely maintained the Old Country culture in the hope of someday returning there with their children, who were encouraged to stay "Chinese" and not be seduced by English or the American Dream.

Having turned their back on English, the Chinese community found that their children, including many born in America, were having a hard time in the public schools. The remedy? Learn English? No. Instead, they decided to sue the school system to demand that the *primary* instructional language be changed from English to Chinese.

The lawsuit, *Lau v. Nichols* (Lau was the name of the main plaintiff and Nichols was the Superintendent of Schools), was a class action that claimed that 1,800 Chinese children were not getting equal educational opportunity because they were deficient in English! That was obvious, since that was the intention of many parents in the insular, isolated Chinese community to begin with.

The plaintiffs stated that since the children did not know English, being taught in that language gave them unequal educational opportunity. They even claimed it violated the Fourteenth Amendment to the Constitution on the grounds that they were not receiving "equal protection of the law."

The federal district court in San Francisco denied the suit, holding that there was no violation of either the Fourteenth

Amendment or Title 601 of the Civil Rights Act since no discrimination was involved.

It was appealed, but again the Chinese community lost. The U.S. Court of Appeals pointed out that California state law required that "English shall be the basic language instruction in all schools," and denied the argument as specious.

"The plaintiffs were seeking *special* treatment and claiming that if they didn't receive it they were being discriminated against," says Burke Deventhal, a San Francisco city attorney who helped try the case. "Even Hubert Humphrey, the former Vice President, agreed that the state did not have the obligation to equalize accidental differences among citizens. He agreed with us that the courts should only uphold anything which violates the Fourteenth Amendment."

The case went to the Supreme Court, where the separatist Chinese community found a friend. In the high court's accelerating disregard for the Constitution, they reversed the Court of Appeals in favor of the Chinese plaintiffs. The majority decision did reject the argument of the Fourteenth Amendment, but held for Lau, et al., based on Section 601 of the Civil Rights Act which prohibited "discrimination."

There is no equality of learning if the children do not understand English, the Supreme Court ruled, failing to understand that the Chinese children had the same opportunity as anyone else, but their parents had turned their backs on it.

The Chief Justice concurred with the majority decision of Justice Stewart, but did—as if in a twitch of rational nostalgia—agree that "earlier generations of American ethnic groups have overcome the language barrier by earnest parental endeavor . . ." He added, almost sheepishly, that he was going along with his colleagues only because of the large number of Chinese children involved. "For me, numbers are at the heart of this case and my concurrence is to be understood accordingly."

Utterly and absolutely ridiculous. The decision was beneath

the legal sophistication of any court, let alone the High Court. The "numbers" are the main reason to reject, not support, the case. It was proof—to use the Chief Justice's own words—of the absence of "earnest parental endeavor" by the Chinese community to have the children learn English.

The Court edict was a masterpiece of judicial ignorance. It had ruled that the majority population had the *obligation* to provide all the funds and systems necessary to subsidize the will of certain minorities who wished to avoid assimilation and the English language, which had been the main avenue of success for prior immigrants. It had set in motion what are now called the "Lau Remedies," which were quickly issued by the Office of Civil Rights of the Department of Education.

That relatively new federal agency was a creation of the New Establishment and thus a fervent supporter of bilingual education over the traditional route, which was even stronger emphasis on English instruction in schools. But like all of the new dogma, it took the permissive, unreasonable, and anti-intellectual way out.

Today, these "Lau" edicts govern and legitimize the ever-growing bilingual programs throughout the nation, setting up language separation as the law of the land.

In San Francisco, the result, according to Raymond del Portillo, who was then an official of the San Francisco school system, was the establishment of a bilingual program not just for Chinese children, but for others whose parents spoke a foreign tongue and were having trouble with English. The San Francisco system now employs some 900 bilingual teachers, 150 of whom teach Chinese-American children their 3 Rs—in Chinese!

From the original Lau complaint involving 1,800 children, the number of all bilingual students in San Francisco has grown to 17,000—who take their lessons in Cantonese, Spanish, Tagalog, Vietnamese, Japanese, and Korean. So much for Diversity.

The "Lau Remedies" are now enforced nationally, and thousands of bilingual teachers are currently working assiduously to set back the American Dream.

The inanity of bilingual education reaches all the way up the ladder to college itself. In what could be the makings of a musical comedy, the trustees of the City University of New York (CUNY) decided that all holders of a degree from that institution should be literate enough to write basic English.

In a decree that shocked Hostos Community College, one of its institutions, trustees declared that graduating students of the June 1997 class should demonstrate that ability through an essay in English. The problem was that Hostos was a "bilingual" college mainly populated by Spanish-speaking students, a peculiar, if irrational, manifestation of the New Establishment. The school was up in arms. What? Write English? No one had demanded that before.

At the last minute, 104 students who had not demonstrated profiency in English were given the test. The result? All but 13 flunked.

It was not only the students who were at fault. The blame belongs equally with the administration that had—by its actions—falsely assured the college students that they didn't have to learn the language of America to succeed in America.

The injury to English as a national language has triggered a counterattack called "English Only." Years ago, such a movement was unnecessary because learning English was the main goal of immigrants. But today, especially with the enormous Spanish immigration—both legal and illegal—and the growing Latino birthrate, there are those who would establish Spanish as a second *primary* language in America, splitting the population, much as French does in Canada.

The idea that "any language" other than English is good enough is reaching epidemic proportions. In fact, the concept of separate public languages has even infected the workplace, where Spanish-speakers and others now claim they can exclusively use their native tongues on the job, whether or not anyone can understand them.

Several Hispanics who demanded to speak Spanish at work were fired because they were unintelligible to others. But in the last few years, twelve lawsuits by foreign-speaking workers have been filed in the courts against employers, claiming "discrimination" for being required to speak English on the job. Several courts have turned down their claims, but who has come to the rescue of no-English-on-the-job but the U.S. Government?

With taxpayer money, Washington is handling the cases of Spanish-only speakers in their lawsuits against American employers!

The growing threat of Spanish and non-English is evident as other languages adopt a semiofficial and even official status. Citibank begins its phone conversation with: "Would you like to continue in English?" ATM machines offer your money in a half dozen languages. Even voting ballots have fallen to the allure of the Tower of Babel.

In 375 voting districts nationwide, people can vote in languages other than English. Driver's licenses can be obtained in thirty states by taking your exam in languages other than English. In New York, the driving test is given in twenty-three different languages, despite the fact that all the road signs are in English.

The Los Angeles City Council prints all its public notices in six languages. The Texas Public Utility Commission requires telephone and utility companies to print Spanish translations of all their public information.

In one recent year, the IRS distributed 500,000 Form 1040s in Spanish and set up a hotline in that language, making English less essential for survival. And according to U.S. English, Inc., a nonprofit group seeking to make English the official language of the nation (which most people thought it already was!), the Immigration and Naturalization Service (INS) has already conducted a citizen swearing-in service almost entirely in Spanish and is testing a program to *conduct citizenship exams in foreign languages.*

The New Establishment is both winning and losing the non-English fight daily. Just as one school system after another and other institutions yield to Spanish or Chinese or Hindi or Haitian dialect, angered citizens are pushing politicians to sponsor "Official English" bills in the statehouses, localities, and Congress.

According to U.S. English, Inc., twenty-three states in the Union have already passed legislation making English the only permissible language in official actions. The movement—stimulated by a Tower of Babel in America—is growing rapidly. Just in the past three years, New Hampshire, Virginia, South Dakota, Montana, Georgia, and Wyoming have adopted English-only rules. The first state to adopt such a law was Louisiana in 1811, to fight the then prevalent French. The latest is Wyoming, in 1996. Locally, Suffolk County on Long Island, and other cities and towns are also passing "Official English" laws.

The fight has now moved to the federal level. In the summer of 1996, the House of Representatives, by a vote of 259 to 169, passed the "English Empowerment Act of 1996," which makes English the official language of the federal government. Similar legislation (S356) is pending in the Senate. However, if passed there, it must be signed by the President.

The bill, while making English official, does not make it illegal to use other languages such as Spanish in government notices when health or safety is involved. The U.S. English movement and its political allies are often seen as "anti-immigrant," but in reality it is designed not only as a safeguard for the majority language, but as a pro-immigrant initiative. By persuading immigrants to learn English when doing their civic and legal business, they are simultaneously hastening assimilation—the great secret of economic success.

This is not merely intuitive speculation. The U.S. Labor Department reports that English-speaking immigrants earn four times as much as those wedded to a foreign language. A study of Vietnamese and Laotian refugees conducted by the Texas Office of Immigration and Refugees found the following difference in hourly wages: No English: $4.35 an hour; basic words: $5.16; short conversation: $6.30; five- to ten-minute conversation: $8.45; fluent, $14.82 an hour.

Once again, a New Establishment concept—that any language will do—has been proven both false and detrimental to the progress of Americans at any socioeconomic level.

The movement to *many* languages in America is especially ironic considering that students throughout the world are struggling to learn English so they can communicate in what is becoming the universal language of world economics.

What is the solution to the damage being done by bilingual education and what it represents? The obvious goal is to increase the use of English and decrease the daily use of other languages, except as second languages of cultural or historic value. To accomplish that, several things must be done:

1. Pass federal legislation to make English the official language of the nation.
2. Encourage states to pass similar legislation. In the twenty-four states that have the Initiative—citizen rights to put laws on the ballot through petition—"Official English" propositions should be enacted.
3. Eliminate the $215 million a year federal subsidy for bilingual education courses, which will discourage school districts from continuing such programs.
4. Divert the billions now spent on bilingual education into stepped up programs to increase the teaching of English to children of immigrants.

The goal, of course, is to eliminate the use of foreign languages for the *primary* education of our children. This can probably be done state-by-state, or through federal legislation. Surely, such a move will be challenged up to the Supreme Court, but that body is infamous for changing its mind according to the public temper.

Multiculturalism, Diversity, and Bilingualism as words have infiltrated the American mind, the media, the government and the dominant culture so thoroughly that at first glance they seem almost like reasonable concepts. In reality, though, they are the antithesis of that which made this country great—Uniculturalism.

Over the past century, the entire globe has descended on America, much to our benefit. We have accomplished in modern times what no other nation has dared: turned millions from diverse cultures and varying races into one people, speaking one language.

E Pluribus Unum has been our secret. Yet we now face an onslaught from the New Establishment, which seeks to replace that magnificence with islands of selfish and self-defeating separatism.

Those who appreciate the American experience (and not to is to confess an absence of rational thought) must fight these alien concepts with the same energy we have used to create one nation out of many.

There is no alternative.

CHAPTER SIX

SEXUAL HARASSMENT

Assault, Vulgarity, or Romance?

IN A FIRE DISTRICT IN NEVADA, A WOMAN SOUGHT to become a firefighter, increasingly a female aspiration despite that gender's relatively weak upper body strength.

Long a male preserve, firefighting requires brute power to move ladders against buildings and to carry bodies, conscious or not, out of burning structures. Few women can meet these objective criteria, although an occasional female can compete with the men. Apparently this applicant wasn't one of them.

"She had worked for us in another capacity, but when an opening came for a firefighter, she applied," explains the local fire chief. "She passed the regular physicals, but when it came to what we call a multitask 'practical exam,' which puts all the work together, she failed. Then she sued us."

(This type of incident, the fire chief pointed out, is the result of political pressure placed on civil servants to hire female firefighters in order to avoid sex discrimination suits.)

The failed candidate didn't claim she had passed the test. Instead, she said she had failed because she was unnerved. By what? By sexual harassment in the firehouse. During her recruitment period, she lived in a common dormitory on a daily eight-hour shift with the men.

The cause of her anxiety? Pornography. She had been harassed by the *existence* of pornographic magazines and films in the firehouse.

A five-day trial in federal court was decided in favor of the plaintiff. Yes, the court said, her failure at firefighting was related to sexual harassment, which was related to the pornography. They awarded her $300,000, which was later reduced to $200,000—still not a bad reward for failing out of the firefighting business.

The woman was the beneficiary of the most extraordinary, vague, flexible, and often irrational legal charge in the history of Anglo-Saxon jurisprudence—sexual harassment.

As an offense, harassment is relatively new, less than twenty years on the books. It is still another manifestation of the New Establishment, which hangs this sword of Damocles over the heads of men (mainly) in order to extend its theocratic control of the American culture into the workplace.

In this aim, as we shall see, it is aided by the federal government, which has finally intruded into the one area of life that had been left to citizens—the normal, unpredictable, ungoverned relations between the sexes. In the New Establishment's zeal for a twisted "purity," another arena for mass hysteria has been created, one which rivals Salem's stalking of Hester Prynn.

Despite its short history, sexual harassment has expanded exponentially in recent years. From just a handful of cases in the 1970s it has risen to 15,000 claims each year, filed mainly with the EEOC, the Equal Employment Opportunity Commission, the Washington agency that now oversees the manners and mores of the sexes in the office environment, and increasingly elsewhere as well.

Sexual harassment is a much-used catch phrase, but few people understand it. What is it, and how does it affect the always sensitive relations between the sexes?

Originally, sexual harassment was defined as an attempt by a boss or supervisor to extort sex from a female by threat or intimidation: that is, to provide intercourse or other sexual favors or risk losing one's job or promotion. As actionable behavior, that makes perfect sense, morally and legally.

No one trying to earn a living should be placed in an intimidating position on the job, especially in relation to something as personal as sex.

There are always a few cases that involve such sexual pressure from the boss. But sexual harassment law and government edicts have now gone *far beyond that,* as its multiple definitions have expanded as rapidly as the number of cases. The result is that today virtually anything a woman finds offensive at work can bring a man to court, where he will be asked to pay for his alleged sins in cash, or to bill it to his corporation.

Since Americans have little idea of what sexual harassment really is, they read headlines and imagine the worst.

Contrary to heedless rumor, it is not rape or assault, or even usually a charge that involves any physical contact between the sexes. Neither is it typically harassment in the common meaning of the word, which conjures up the sense of "stalking," to hound someone moment to moment, as in a compulsive drive to achieve a goal—in this case, sex.

As used today, the phrase *sexual harassment* is a semantic distortion, one designed to bend the language to reach the level of melodrama that permits the New Establishment to market its dogma. The Random House College Dictionary defines harassment as: "(1) To be troubled by repeated attacks, incursions, etc., as in war or hostilities; harry, raid. (2) To disturb persistently; torment; pester, persecute."

This hardly jibes with the modern use of *sexual harassment,* which most often involves a case of modern metaphysics: what is in someone's head or on the tongue. Yet it is linked by the media, the courts, the attorneys, as being related to assault, even rape, presenting an absolutely false picture to the public.

In reality, the charge of sexual harassment, as we shall see, mainly involves curbing someone else's free speech, the right of anyone to say what they want—subject to such *real* laws as inciting to riot (falsely yelling "fire" in a theater) or slander and defamation. But in the new dogma, the speech itself, without proof of slander, suffices. And it generally has nothing to do with harassment.

In one case, at the University of New Hampshire, the definition of harassment was stretched so irrationally as to include "dirty talk" to no one in particular. A professor whose lectures were deemed a bit naughty was brought for discipline before the school's "Office of Sexual Harassment and Rape Prevention Program," a linguistic escalation worthy of any Star Chamber procedure or the New McCarthyism.

Let's look at some recent court decisions to see how the law views sexual harassment, and what men have to do to find themselves in legal jeopardy when dealing with supposedly sophisticated adult women at work.

Sometimes, a case does involve slight physicality, like touching or groping, as in the famous Tailhook Navy case in Las Vegas. In the landmark trial of Baker and McKenzie, a leading national law firm, the plaintiff, a new secretary, claimed that her boss had harassed her, including placing m&ms in her blouse pocket and touching her breast in the process. She was awarded $7.1 million for the violation, which a later court cut to $3.5 million.

But these cases are exceptions. Surely, there are villains in the office, but they are a small minority. Most of the contemporary sexual harassment claims would have been laughed off years ago—before the advent of what borders on mass hysteria.

Sexual harassment now ranks as one of the most aggressive of all social and cultural aberrations in a society increasingly bereft of sanity. The cases vary, but here's a fair sample of what workers and bosses are no longer supposed to do.

• At K-mart, a male supervisor was accused of touching a woman's shoulder and teasing her about carrying on with deliverymen. She received a $1.5 million award from the courts for his big mouth.

• In another case, a boss showed disrespect for his secretary, telling her she was "stupid," and often criticized how she dressed. She received $675,000 for her hurt feelings, interpreted by the court to be sexual harassment.

• At a mining company in Minnesota, forty-five women sued in a class action suit. For assault? Sexual intimidation? Hardly. Their claim was that the company had created "a hostile work environment" by allowing abusive graffiti and bad language to reach their innocent ears and eyes. (We must assume these women do not go to the movies or watch television.)

The federal court decided that since female sensibilities were offended, damages should be paid. Simultaneously, the state of Minnesota intends to collect for the same "offenses."

Language, once a protected activity under the First Amendment, is often behind the charges, as if ungentlemanly vulgarity is a crime or a cause for suit, an unprecedented concept in law promulgated by the New Establishment.

• At a Wal-Mart store in Missouri, a former employee filed a lawsuit in 1994, saying that her supervisor had harassed her with "abusive language," consisting mainly of crude comments about her body.

The court agreed with her. The award? $100,000? Try $50 million! It was so absurd that a federal judge later reduced it to $5 million, still a heavy punishment solely for bad-mouthings with no claim of sexual intimidation. An expensive mouthful.

• At Chevron Oil, four women received $2 million in damages for claimed sexual harassment. Had their bosses insisted on sex? Were they manhandled? Were their promotions held up because they were not free with their favors?

None of the above. What these women successfully claimed was that they were on the verbal and written receiving end of jokes, e-mail, and comments made by big boys with bad taste about their clothes and bodies.

Today, one of the most common sexual harassment charges is that men or their employers, are setting up a "hostile work environment," where female sensibilities are being violated, apparently in violation of the Civil Rights Act of 1964 as interpreted by the courts. At the Jacksonville Shipyards in Florida, a female complainant won a substantial sum of money because she was severely shaken up by pin-up pictures of pretty young women *en deshabille* pasted on a wall, creating what the court ruled was that "hostile" environment.

In other cases, men have been sued, and lost, not for criticizing a woman's appearance, but for *complimenting* it, as if that attention was proof of their true, more sinister, intentions.

Escaping punishment for what someone *says* to someone of the opposite sex is becoming increasingly difficult in any office in the land. Uncle Sam, in the form of the Equal Employment Opportunity Commission (EEOC) and its edicts, stands watch as the Big Brother of sexual morality—ready to apply enormous penalties for any male (or sometimes female) who steps out of churchly line.

The tension this situation creates has begun to stultify male-female relations at work, once fertile ground for wholesome flirtations. Many marriages blossomed around the water fountain. We have seen the magic of office romance portrayed in the Hollywood films of Katharine Hepburn and Spencer Tracy, sagas in which the wisecrack, sexual and otherwise, only added spice to office life.

And today? Perhaps no more. Surely, not even the EEOC can totally curb the hormonal instincts of young men and women.

But it is putting a nervous crimp into them. More than one executive has told of carefully guarding what he says in the presence of, and to, female co-workers—afraid (probably correctly) that someone, somehow, is listening, and preparing to sue.

There is also the grave danger that the First Amendment is being threatened, that in being forced to conform to government and court pressure, Americans will lose their freedom of speech in the workplace, a much worse forfeit than the newly prudish sensibilities of litigious women.

Given its way, sexual harassment law could turn male-female professional relations upside down as well, and make the office into a threatening atmosphere. How can a man freely interact with a woman on a business matter when he must fear that even the most innocuous comment of his could be misinterpreted and jeopardize his career?

Besides the EEOC, other watchdog groups have entered the fray in this latest variant of the battle of the sexes. Apparently, these bureaucratic agencies even entertain old complaints that may have become magnified with the passage of time.

A woman who worked at Tiffany's, the elegant jewelry operation on New York's Fifth Avenue, came forward ten years *after* an alleged "harassment" to complain to the New York State Division of Human Rights. On the recommendation of an Administrative Law judge, she was awarded $300,000 damages for "mental anguish" and "humiliation."

The charge? Was she grabbed, hustled, forced to submit, blackmailed for sex in exchange for promotion?

Nothing so melodramatic. There were no claims of sexual threat. She said only that she was the subject of sexually explicit remarks and comments disparaging to her religion. It was another case of oversensitive sensibilities, a kind of sophomoric pettiness that in Anglo-Saxon jurisprudence is normally nonactionable *except* in an era of social and cultural madness such as this. (Shades of old Massachusetts and modern Iran?)

The humorous, or tragic, aspect of the sexual harassment epidemic is that it is operating as a prim, pious neo-Victorian cause in the most sex-drenched, promiscuous, openly pornographic society in modern history. A $7 ticket to a movie house not only provides vulgar language by the minute, but female nudity, often accompanied by a vivid picturization of the sex act itself in all its orgasmic power.

Pornographic magazines are sold on virtually all newsstands and so-called "adult movies" are available for $3 or less in your corner video rental store. By opening virtually any newspaper, you can be regaled by images up to twenty-four inches high of young nubile adolescents with come-hither smiles dressed only in the scantiest of panties and push-up bras with little left to the sexual imagination.

We cannot escape sex in our advertising on television, or increasingly immodest dress and sex in our dramas and sitcoms. At the beach, immodesty is the rule as bikinis become smaller than intimate lingerie, all designed to attract and arouse the male sex to action, if not immediately.

Attracting the male is a $500 billion annual industry in fashion, cosmetics, jewelry, and hair stylists catering to women who seek family and security from men—as they should.

Yet in the office, all this sex-saturation must be forgotten as men, especially, are required to behave like fourteen-year-olds at their first prim, chaperoned dance. It is, to be generous, a ridiculous phenomenon, yet one taken seriously by the New Establishment, which then enforces its will on a frightened, conformist public that is afraid to speak out.

(Perhaps men should institute a class action sexual harassment lawsuit against women in offices who wear short skirts that ride up to their panties when they sit down?)

Rather than being a true threat to womanhood (that comes from insane rapists *outside* the office) so-called sexual harassment is mainly a cornucopia of social malapropisms, gestures, and comments: a dirty joke, a pin-up picture, a vulgarity, a body motion, a turned-down proposition, a comment that criticizes a woman's looks or clothes—or conversely, in the mad New Establishment world, compliments her.

For the female plaintiff, who insists on *not* being treated like an equal and an adult, it can provide an outlet and revenge for the frustrated, the denied, the excessively prudish. Or the motive can be a compulsive interest in large dollar court judgments, a new American payoff that rivals the lottery. And, we should not omit the thousands of willing trial lawyers salivating over the prospect of contingency fees in the millions.

For the defendant—and those fearful of becoming defendants (about 100 million men)—it can violate any rights contained within the First Amendment, which guarantees Americans free speech, on or off the job. But today, by some unseen, magical destruction of the Bill of Rights, it deprives Americans of those sacred privileges.

Or sexual harassment can be the distorted result of the age-old vexed relations between man and woman, from which almost anything can emerge. It can be the claim of a rejected suitor, a disappointed employee, or result from the pain of an angry quarrel.

The threat of sexual harassment is distorting the normal relations between the sexes. It might be triggered by a legitimate proposition, a saucy joke, or a sincere compliment from a man. Traditionally, in return, the male suitor could receive a polite refusal, a slap on the face—or even consensual sex, love, and marriage. But increasingly these days, the result is a lawsuit for harassment.

Since the payoffs for such suits have become so handsome, and the titillation so great, it is little wonder that cases make headlines in newspapers and tabloids, especially when they involve celebrities in our celebrity-mad culture. Most of the charges are dropped or settled but not before some unfavorable publicity appears in the media.

The New York Times has reported that the chief executive officer of W. R. Grace was ostensibly let go because of a secret sexual harassment situation. George C. Scott, the Oscar-winning film star, was sued for $3.1 million by his $1,500-a-week personal assistant for "groping" and making offensive remarks, a charge he denies but which still made headlines. Bill Clinton, the President of the United States, is of course being sued by a former Arkansas state worker for making a lewd sexual proposition in a hotel room.

The former head of the National Association of Colored People settled a sex harassment suit for $332,400. An official of the New York Racing Association was fired for ostensibly harassing female jockeys at Belmont Park, a first. The president of New York City's municipal hospital system, a thirty-four-year-old on his way up, was forced to quit because of charges that he used computer e-mail to make sexual suggestions.

Lisa Olson, a woman and a sports columnist for a Boston newspaper, sued three members of the New England Patriot football team for sexual harassment. After she walked into their locker room (a new privilege granted women reporters), several players who were stark naked allegedly made sexual suggestions with which she was not pleased. It was, said the outraged female football locker room fan, "nothing less than mind rape."

Even comedian Eddie Murphy received the harassment lawsuit treatment. When one of his female co-stars was fired on the set of a film they were making, she got her revenge by slapping Murphy with a $75 million sexual harassment lawsuit. She was fired, she said, only because she would not submit to him, a claim Murphy fervently denied. The woman stated that his "attempt to obtain a personal sexual relationship" led to her being fired, causing her "severe emotional and psychological damage." In fact, $75 million worth, though a verdict has yet to come down.

Celebrities make the headlines, but occasionally there is a corporate suit that has all the makings of sexual titillation and gets almost equal billing.

One such case involved IBM. A female former marketing representative of Big Blue sued in Santa Monica and was awarded $65,000. For what? She claimed she had been pressured into having a sexual affair. Not with IBM personnel, but with the director of the Pentagon's high-tech procurement arm. The reason? To help get enough military business to make up for IBM's $94 million shortfall in software revenue.

The court found against IBM, but not against her two supervisors, whom she claimed pressured her into her bedroom-business deal. The man involved in the affair denied that his *inamorata* was in any way coerced into having sex with him, but the jury apparently did not believe his story.

How does the government, the ultimate controller of libidinous sex (or more likely, impolite conversation about it) in the workplace, know what is and is not harassment? Its definition is loosening and expanding so rapidly that sexual harassment is becoming an amorphous, almost indefinable, if expensive, offense.

That definition is in the purview of the official Washington inquisitor, the EEOC. They spell it out in a piece of literature sent to me by that newly Puritanical federal agency, which employs 2,800 well-paid government workers and has a budget of some $223 million picked up by us all, sinners and innocents alike.

In 1996, the EEOC collected $27 million for plaintiffs, almost all women, in numerous sex cases. That sum does not include millions more collected by private law firms and state and local harassment overseers. Since 1990, the government has managed to collect $127 million from lecherous, crude, and often simply normal men trying to fend their way through the mating game while trying, unsuccessfully, to avoid the onerous pseudo-Puritanical political correctness in male-female relations that now permeates the

American workplace, and as we shall see, America's campuses as well.

On the federal level, the EEOC first hears and investigates the accusations. If it feels a case has merit, it tries to obtain a cash settlement, generally from the corporation for whom the "harasser" works. Failing that, it will supply an attorney and sue the alleged offender at no charge to the claimant, the bill being passed on to the taxpayer. If there is a settlement, the court will hand down a "consent decree," to enforce the award.

If not, the EEOC will go to trial, suing the defendant in the name of the United States of America, that glorious protector of American womanhood. (Except when it puts females in the same barracks and tents as hormonally-charged young male soldiers.)

The EEOC literature, which takes the tone of a Salem witch hunt, spells out what sexual harassment includes, which nowadays seems to be any action a prudish woman would object to, or at least has learned to object to because of the manna that can accompany her displeasure. Critics have characterized much of it as a "sexual shakedown," a charge that seems to have merit in certain cases.

Most of the EEOC harassment definitions were drawn up by bureaucrats, not by the Congress or the courts. Compiled by the staff of the EEOC, they were then approved by a five-person commission appointed by the President and confirmed by the Senate. Congress has not passed these EEOC rules, nor has the Supreme Court sanctioned them.

Yet they are enforced. What does that mean? Basically, that what is in force today in sexual harassment "law" is not true statutes set by Congress, but merely executive fiat. Still, that means little to losers in the sex war, who may lose their job and/or are required to pay up, willy-nilly.

Consider the federal enforcement agency guidelines: "Sexual harassment is a form of sexual discrimination that violates Title VII of the Civil Rights Act of 1964." They add that such violations need not be physical, but include anything "verbal" that "interferes with the individual's work performance or creates an intimidating, hostile or offensive work environment"—a highly subjective non-legal criterion if there ever was one.

One thinks back. Before the intervention of the New Establishment, was the workplace overrun by harassers, demanding sex for jobs or promotion? There may have been a lot of hanky-panky, as there still is. But intimidation? Surely not the epidemic one hears of in courts. Could the disease have been created by the medicine?

The EEOC guideline goes on to explain that *the offender need not be the victim's supervisor or boss or superior,* a turnaround of the original intent of the law. To be considered a harasser, the offender can be a supervisor in another area, or no supervisor at all! The law even applies to a co-worker, who would have no power over the "victim," or even to a nonemployee of the company, perhaps a guest or visitor.

The victim doesn't even have to be the person harassed. Anyone indirectly affected can make a harassment claim as well. And the conduct is punishable even if the victim is not discharged from the job or suffers no deleterious economic effect.

Then what the hell (excuse the expression) is sexual harassment?

It is whatever the EEOC, or any court, says it is. Sexual harassment is emerging as a kind of modern, subjective "junk justice," sustained by non-thinking bureaucrats and judges who have been indoctrinated by the New Establishment, and whose edicts are somewhat reminiscent of the former Soviet definitions of what constituted "an enemy of the people."

The definition of sexual harassment becomes more sweeping each day as firms—fearful of enormous punitive damages—write new guidelines, some of which resemble the behavior code of a Victorian girl's boarding school.

Gruntal & Company, a New York Stock Exchange Firm, has

codified its warning against sexual harassment in a newly classic semihysterical document worthy of an absurd age.

Says the Gruntal sex pony: Sexual harassment can be "jokes, pranks, or other forms of humor that are demeaning or hostile" in regard to gender or sexual orientation. Similarly, it can involve "written or graphic material (including graffiti) that denigrates or shows hostility or aversion" because of gender—whether those comments are placed on a wall, bulletin board, or personal computer.

Gruntal goes even further in warning employees that sexual harassment on its premises can also include "epithets, slurs, quips, or negative stereotyping."

Is that all?

No, the company also prohibits "staring." That of course is an easy charge to be raised and a difficult one to deny. Perhaps young brokers should avert their eyes as they walk the office corridors. That's especially true now that fashion in female skirts is short, and getting shorter. The code also outlaws comments about an "individual's body" as well as "sexual gossip."

The "staring" and the prohibition against comments on the "body" are tied to the newest EEOC fear—that men will excessively *compliment* women in the office, ostensibly making them uncomfortable. Comments like, "You look good today," or "I like your hair that way," used to be a polite sign of appreciation. Today, it is a red flag that, despite good intentions, someone might be falling over the edge of decency into the pit of sexual harassment, creating a "hostile" environment by trying to be nice.

"One compliment is not significant," says an EEOC spokesman, apparently with a straight face. "But if there is a pattern of such activity over a period of time, it could be classified as harassment."

In his solemn bureaucratic way, he had uttered one of the great inanities, and insanities, of our contemporary New Establishment culture.

187

When it comes to office romance, Gruntal is stingy.

Asking a fellow employee for a date is legal at Gruntal, but the man (we expect) has only *one* shot at it in the new nonromantic environment. Says the firm: "unwelcome flirtations," and "continuing to ask an employee for a date after the employee has indicated that he or she is not interested" is considered sexual harassment and punishable, first by dismissal, later by a possible lawsuit.

This might put a brake on suitors, except for the most persistent who are willing to brave the new pseudo-Puritanical sex laws. After the first denied request, the suitor can continue to seek the woman's hand, and more, but only if he operates on the sly.

(The case of such a persistent suitor comes to mind. That was Marty Ingles, former comedian and later Hollywood agent, who was smitten by actress Shirley Jones. He tells how when at first he failed to win her hand, he engaged in an almost around-the-clock courtship. Despite many refusals, he finally "harassed" her into becoming his loving, long-time wife. Today? That dedicated pursuit of romance could cost him his bonuses, his job, even his career.)

How did this madness all start? How did this latest flood of social insanity begin? What prompted a civilization to make a subtle touch on the arm, a flirtation, or even a good dirty joke, once the mainstay of cocktail parties and courtship, into a dangerous affair, a near-crime that can lead to bankruptcy? While we might add, turning a blind eye to truly hot sexual affairs known to the office gossip mill and implicitly sanctioned.

Sexual harassment as a basis for lawsuits has been around since the 1970s, when the lower courts ruled that even though it wasn't mentioned in the law, it was an implicit part of the "sexual discrimination" portion of Title VII of the Civil Rights Act of 1964, a broad leap into judicial speculation that started it all.

But not many cases were heard because "victims" had to prove too much—generally intimidation by a boss—and had little to gain. They could receive only "compensatory damages," mainly back pay if due, plus their legal fees if they won.

Then, in 1986, a case came before the Supreme Court that opened the litigation floodgates somewhat by widening the definition of sexual harassment.

The case was *Meritor Savings Bank v. Vinson,* in which the Court decided that the old criterion—dirty old bosses demanding sex—was limited and outmoded. Instead, it adopted the concept of "hostile working environment," which has since been defined as anything from leers to loose lips to insults to dirty jokes to physical compliments, to a display of *Playboy.*

Then in 1991, the big money breakthrough took place. The Civil Rights Act of 1991, passed by a Democratic Congress and signed by a Republican president, George Bush, made sexual harassment a trial lawyer's dream. After that, a decision of sexual harassment meant that the person could also receive "punitive damages," awards that have since reached the $50 million mark from overstimulated juries.

The next step forward (or more likely backward) came in 1993, when the Supreme Court heard its second sexual harassment case, *Harris v. Forklift.*

Before that, the U.S. Court of Appeals for the Sixth Circuit, out of Cincinnati, had ruled that in sexual harassment cases, the plaintiff had to prove that she had suffered "severe psychological damage." This followed common law precedent that no one should receive financial damages unless the person actually suffered damage, not mere annoyance.

Using that standard, a lower court dismissed the case of Theresa Harris, who worked as a manager of a truck-leasing company in Nashville. She claimed that her boss, the owner, had insulted her, saying: "You're a woman, what do you know?" and "Let's go to the Holiday Inn to negotiate your raise."

The court ruled that although her boss was crude, even "vulgar," that on a commonsense basis, the incident wasn't serious enough for a lawsuit. Besides, there was the issue of free speech.

But when the often-fashionable Supreme Court heard the case, it set a new precedent that was to invite thousands of sexual harassment complaints. In the original hearing before the High Court, Judge Ruth Bader Ginsburg, who became the leader of the debate in favor of the plaintiff, tried to show how the boss's comment was sexual harassment. At the original hearing, she insisted:

" 'You're a woman and what do you know?' means something different from 'you're a man, what do you know?' " she insisted.

However, Justice Scalia didn't buy that argument and commented: "You've never had anyone say that 'you're a man, so what do you know?' You must live in a different family environment than I do."

The shocking part of the dialogue between the two justices is that they were arguing about what someone said to someone else without ever interjecting the question of free speech guaranteed by the First Amendment to the Constitution, a document the Justices are not only sworn to uphold, but who are its main guardians.

At any rate, Justice Ginsburg won the argument overwhelmingly. Not only did the Court overturn the lower court ruling and hold for Ms. Harris, but it also overturned the Appeals Court ruling that "severe psychological damage" would have to be shown for a victim of sexual harassment to win damages.

What the Court did was to rule that the plaintiff did not have to show any psychological damage at all, violating all precedents in Anglo-American common law.

It also upheld the earlier 1986 decision on so-called "hostile" environment, adding to the legal swamp of harassment, which to mix two common metaphors, has become an albatross around the male neck.

Obviously, the Court, as it often does, had taken the fashionable, cowardly, unconstitutional, way out.

Several decisions regarding the conflict between so-called sexual harassment edicts and the First Amendment are wending their way through the lower courts and will eventually reach the Supreme Court, which has now heard two cases of harassment. When the subject finally arrives at its bench, its decision, like its forward and reverse decisions on affirmative action, will depend heavily on politics, public opinion, and fashionable ideas, rather than on the law.

The true question of free speech versus excessive sensitivity of adults is squarely faced by a former government official.

"Concerns have been expressed that the EEOC's definition of workplace harassment in its proposed guidelines forces employers to do what the government should not and legally cannot do: punish offensive speech," says Ms. R. Gaull Silberman, former Vice Chairman of the EEOC, and apparently a skeptic, who adds: "Is the commission unwittingly importing into the workplace notions of political correctness that are tearing our universities asunder?"

Sexual harassment law is still in the making. Today, it is coming to grips with a new challenge—same-sex cases. Can one homosexual or one lesbian be harassed by another? The potential here for titillating hearings and super-sexism is enormous.

According to the EEOC, 90 percent of the 15,342 sexual complaints in fiscal 1996 were made by women, and 10 percent by men. Of that small minority, some were made by men against women in the workplace, but others were *same-sex* complaints made by homosexual men against homosexual men, and similarly, lesbians against lesbians, as well as "straight" complaints against homosexuals, and any gender combination thereof.

The EEOC has no exact figures on each of these categories, but they say that the number of such complaints is growing.

Same-sex cases are now the bane of the courts because there

is indecision, from judge to judge and court to court, about whether they are covered by federal Civil Rights sexual harassment codes at all.

In Baltimore, Judge Alexander Harvey II of the Federal District Court heard the case of a man who was an employee of a public utility. He claimed that his male supervisor has made unwelcome sexual advances, including pointing a magnifying glass at his groin. In the men's room, he had allegedly pretended to lock the door, saying, "Ah, alone at last."

The defendant denied making the comments, but the judge dismissed the case anyway. In his opinion, same-sex cases were not covered by the law. The Maryland Human Relations Commission, which enforces harassment cases, disagreed with the judge, stating: "This agency will continue to investigate and prosecute cases of same-sex harassment so long as it is harassment based on a person's sex, whether it is a male harassing a female or a male harassing a male."

Another turndown took place in Oklahoma, where a three-man panel of the Fifth Circuit Court of Appeals ruled that same-sex cases were not valid. They threw out of court a claim by an oil rig worker who said that his supervisors held him down in a shower and sexually harassed him.

But almost simultaneously, two other federal appeals courts have backed same-sex harassment claims as legal, and have upheld claims. A lower court in Montgomery, Alabama, for example, heard the case of a man who said his male boss grabbed his crotch and kissed him on the neck. In the summer of 1995, the federal district court jury held in favor of the complainant.

"This is one of the first, if not the first, that has gone to trial with a plaintiff verdict involving male-on-male sexual harassment in the workplace," said the plaintiff's attorney.

Despite the indecision from court to court, same-sex complaints are becoming more common. An openly gay worker in a restaurant in Philadelphia complained to the Pennsylvania

Human Relations Commission, that his boss fondled him, rubbed his body against him, and asked for sex. The plaintiff has since filed in federal court and is awaiting trial.

What about the federal government? Once again it tries to carve out still more control over social mores. "The courts have not yet decided on the legality of same-sex complaints," says an EEOC spokesman in Washington, "but we still treat them like any other harassment case."

Among the 10 percent of male complainants before the EEOC, men versus women are the more common, a situation which gave birth to the movie *Disclosure,* from a novel by Michael Crichton and starring Michael Douglas and Demi Moore.

The first such case brought to trial took place in November 1995 before a federal district judge in Florida. The plaintiff, the manager of a Domino's Pizza store, claimed that his female supervisor harassed him by squeezing his buttocks and making sexual comments about his body.

When he heard that she had told his store workers that she loved him and wanted to live with him, the plaintiff said he blew up. "Get out of my office," he shouted. Six days later he was discharged. The judge, Henry Lee Adams Jr., awarded the man $237,257.

"As more women get power," says attorney Stephen Cooper in Minnesota, "they are just as likely to be the perpetrators as the victims." Cooper, who has represented hundreds of women and several men, handled the case of a male aide who successfully sued a female city official for sexual harassment. His client received an award of $105,000.

"Her behavior ran the gamut," Cooper explained, "from verbal comments such as 'I'd like you in my harem,' to running her hands along his thighs."

Perhaps the most famous "turnabout" case—men versus women—in which males claimed sex harassment and discrimination—involved eight men from the Boston area who worked as counselors at the local office of Jenny Craig International, the weight-loss operation run by and for women. Of its 4,300 employees, 90 percent are women, as is the chief executive.

In what has been called the "female chauvinist" case, the men charged that they were subject to speech and behavior they found demeaning and intimidating. The eight men, who say they either quit, were fired, or weren't promoted because of their sex, filed complaints with the Massachusetts Commission Against Discrimination, which agreed that there was probable cause of gender bias.

One of the plaintiffs complained that the girl talk of "who to marry, who is pregnant, how to get pregnant" was offensive and made working there difficult. Some men claimed that they were given "sexist" tasks like shoveling snow, emptying the trash, or fixing the boss's car.

They say they were insulted by comments about their bodies—their "tight buns"—and forced to wear the company uniform, a smock and neck scarves. One male "victim" claimed he was told he would never get ahead in that company unless he wore a push-up bra and got a sex-change operation.

The men have also filed complaints with the EEOC and are waiting for their cases to come up in federal district court in Boston.

Another man-bites-dog story, that of males being harassed by females, came up in the federal government when male employees of the Federal Aviation Administration accused the government of naughty behavior. The FAA paid for "diversity training" in which men had to walk past women co-workers who were told to fondle their private parts and make disparaging remarks about the men's sexual attributes.

"This thing went way off course," says an air traffic controller who didn't appreciate the fondling and is suing the government for $300,000 for toying with him.

All combinations of cases are evolving as claims of sexual harassment become common in the workplace. One woman has sued the Metropolitan Opera Company for discrimination, claiming she was discharged from her job as an assistant stage director because she was a *heterosexual woman,* which is usually considered "normal," if the word has meaning anymore. Her superior was prejudiced against heterosexuals and people over forty, she claimed, and favored younger homosexual men and women.

She claimed that her dismissal was prompted by her objection to lewd pictures of half-dressed men put up near the stage, creating a "sexist" environment. Her New York attorney, David Scott, explains that the Opera has not settled and that the case will go into federal court.

There are even women-to-women complaints, some of an eccentric nature. This has created a new type of "hostile" environment, which is *not* considered sexual harassment by the courts, which seems a blatant case of legal bias.

Such a situation took place in California, where women employees filed a sexual harassment claim against their women bosses at a mortgage company. According to the employees, their supervisors started a conversation about the relative size of their bosoms. One women said her boss had her lift her blouse in front of a mirror to see how large her bust was.

The case was heard in federal district court, where the judge ruled that the plaintiffs did not have a viable complaint. He held for the female bosses, saying the sexually suggestive activity did not have the same impact as if men were involved. But he did admit that the workplace sounded a lot like a "bawdy sorority."

Whatever the outcome of particular cases, the sexual harassment epidemic is alive and spreading, from the workplace to the campus to the schoolyard to the armed forces.

Claims of sexual harassment have grown everywhere, but in a recent four-year period, according to EEOC, they almost doubled in colleges and universities.

On campus, it has become a vital part of political correctness, creating enormous nervousness on the part of professors, who see it destroying their valued independence of thought and threatening their careers. The concept that "speech" can be harassment is outside the tradition of Anglo-Saxon law—unless it is slanderous, which has strict legal guidelines. It becomes most dangerous when applied to the college classroom, where open discourse is the purpose of the endeavor.

Journalist Nat Hentoff made a strong contribution to the argument for free academic speech versus exaggerated modern sensibilities. In Hentoff's piece, published in *The Progressive,* he tells how Professor Graydon Snyder, a biblical scholar at the Chicago Theological Seminary, almost lost his academic career because of a female student who took exception to the teachings of the Talmud.

Though a Christian member of the Church of the Brethren, Snyder's lesson involved that medieval Jewish book of ethics, and contained a piece of philosophy based on sex, an allegory meant to illustrate the question of intent or accident in moral issues.

It seems that a rabbi tells of a roofer who took off his clothes because it was hot, while in the courtyard below, a woman did the same. The man lost his footing and accidentally fell on top of the woman, penetrating her vagina with his penis.

Ethically, the roofer must pay the woman for physical damage and any pain inflicted. *But,* says the Jewish good book, he is not liable for rape or adultery for the indignity involved. Why? Because the act was not purposeful, and it did not emanate from desire or lust.

A few days later, a young female student tape-recorded the lecture on the Talmud. She then filed a complaint with the seminary's Sexual Harassment Task Force, one of many academic equivalents of Robespierre, the French Revolution's dispenser of terror.

A report in the *Washington Post* quoted the female student:

196

"She said she was offended because men in her life and men generally say that they don't intend to do anything, and they do it anyway."

It was quite a leap from the Talmud. In normal times, the woman would have been laughed off. Instead, Snyder was placed on probation and an official memorandum detailing his supposed sin was placed in the mailboxes of all 250 faculty members, staff, and students. Snyder is suing the school to regain his position.

Michael McDonald of the Center for Individual Rights, in the *Chronicle of Higher Education,* writes of his fears of such censorship under the umbrella of political correctness. "The mission of a university, where the ideal is Socrates . . . . ," he writes, "has been replaced with an amalgam of Alan Alda and Phil Donahue. . . ."

A similar case in New Hampshire twisted a professor's meaning to accommodate the exaggerated Puritanism of offended women students. It seems that Professor J. Donald Silva, at the University of New Hampshire, was delivering a lecture on technical writing, his specialty. He compared the focus in writing to the focus in sex. In another case, he used a description of belly dancing as one example of a "simile," saying it was "like Jello-O on a plate with a vibrator underneath."

Some women in the class filed a complaint with the college. The school suspended Professor Silva for a year without pay and directed him to undergo professional counseling (Chinese Cultural "reeducation") at his own expense, as if free speech was a mental illness.

The penalty was a symptom of the misplaced purity and piety of America's campuses, perhaps the most active centers of sexual promiscuity in the world. We should be reminded of another case of exaggerated Puritanism, that of Antioch College—which has its own strict petting and fornication code that requires student agreement at each stage, with verbal assent to such romantic queries as "May I touch your breast?" and "May I unzip your fly?"

It is laughed at by an Antioch student who explained that the coeds "are still doing it like rabbits," a charge echoed by other Antioch students who speak of nude bathroom orgies.

Professor Silva refused to yield. He did not take counseling and he sued the university in federal district court. The judge found that the school's sexual harassment code, which is much like those on campuses everywhere, had violated his First Amendment right to free speech. Silva was granted $60,000 in back pay and damages and $170,000 in legal fees as compensation for the college's attempt at thought control.

The lower court's opinion applies to Silva, and perhaps to the university. But unfortunately it has had little effect on the upsurge of controlled speech elsewhere in academe.

Discussing the case in the *New York Review of Books,* Richard Bernstein cast a skeptical eye at the charges. "It is important to note that throughout all of this, there was not a single charge against Silva of physical contact with students, no invitation to meet women after class, no fixed staring, nobody alleges that there was ever a single private encounter," he wrote.

In the vernacular, Silva had been accused of talking a little "dirty" in class for a few minutes, a laughable indictment that has been magnified out of proportion by falsely pious New Establishment fundamentalists.

In another case, this one at the Virginia Polytechnic Institute (VPI), a charismatic teacher of economics, Allan Mandelstamm, was one of the most popular professors on campus. Using humor as part of his dramatic pedagogic presentation, he had invented a fictional character, Handsome Al, who had a patter laced with innocent sexual innuendos—like a tie printed with a woman who undressed as he manipulated it.

The school, like many today, had a female executive who headed Women's Affairs in the Equal Opportunity/Affirmative Action (EO/AA) office. She received a few complaints about

Mandelstamm from female students and visited him, claiming his jokes had inhibited women from asking questions.

In rebuttal, Mandelstamm put out a questionnaire to the students stating: "I am afraid to ask questions . . . because he makes sexist comments in reply." The women answered as follows: 279 "No," and only 3 "Yes."

But the EO/AA officer pressed on, using the local press and pressure from women's groups, finally achieving her goal of getting Mandelstamm to leave the school.

Henry H. Bauer, professor of chemistry at VPI, who wrote an article on Mandelstamm for *Academic Questions,* an intellectual journal, explains that the EO/AA is like a separate empire with social change, not education or intellect, as its goal.

"The EO/AA bureaucracy operates independently of the rest of the administration," Bauer writes. "It ignores academic traditions of due process, cares little for learning, teaching, and scholarship. At VPI, all charges against faculty are handled by faculty committees—*except* charges of racial or sexual harassment."

He concludes: "Immediate causes of the Mandelstamm debacle lie in the university's politicized atmosphere, in the expansive definition of sexual harassment, and in the existence of an independent EO/AA bureaucracy."

That bureaucracy exists in some form in most colleges and has taken on the job of thought control. Political correctness officers with extra-organizational power have enormous control over the faculty.

So convoluted are the rules governing sexual harassment on campus, and so arcane their interpretation, that the Harvard Law School has issued a nineteen-page single-spaced document, "Sexual Harassment Guidelines," in three parts. Designed to help faculty and students divine the orthodox view on how to talk to and treat females on campus, the document reads like a court brief and is just an unintelligible to laymen. Its closest relatives are the guides given to tourists when visiting an exotic Oriental nation with customs deemed eccentric to Westerners, who must be careful not to offend the indigenous people.

Usually, claims made by aggrieved women, at Harvard or elsewhere, are against one male who deviated from the proscribed manner. But at the University of Minnesota, an entire department was accused of sexual harassment, *en bloc*. How could that be? The complainants were four female graduate students in the Scandinavian Studies Department, which existed because of the large number of Scandinavian-Americans in Minnesota.

The case began when the Dean called in the entire faculty of the department and gave each of them a letter from the Office of Equal Opportunity and Affirmative Action (EO/AA), which is charged, as in most schools, with policing sexual harassment and/or inappropriate language. In addition to the individual complaints, there was one against the department itself, a unique philosophical and biological leap considering it involved sex.

The four graduate students signed each complaint, even though not all had done course work with some of the named faculty. The prevailing atmosphere on campus—one of intimidation of the faculty—helped to stimulate the accusations. Large posters showing young women with professors leering over their shoulders had been placed around the school grounds, inviting students to make complaints. YOU DON'T HAVE TO SUFFER ALONE—COME SEE THE EO/AA OFFICER.

The official college booklet, entitled "Sexual Harassment," acknowledges that the school definition of sexual harassment need not necessarily involve either sex or sexuality. Sexual harassment at the University of Minnesota, the school says, "is broadly defined to include behavior that may not be considered overtly sexual." The definition goes on to say: "Sexual harassment can be as blatant as rape or as subtle as a look. Harassment . . . often consists of callous insensitivity to the experience of women."

Startling. The edict requires that all males on campus, both students and professors, can only escape the charge of harassment if they learn the "experience of women." Otherwise, there is little chance for free speech or a decent discourse.

The University of Minnesota was apparently serious about its non-sex disclaimer on sexual harassment. Several of the harassment complaints in the Scandinavian Studies department had nothing to do with sex. In one case, a student complained that she had been unfairly denied a teaching assistantship. In another, a professor was accused of being cool and unsupportive by not giving sufficient attention to a paper she was writing.

In still another case, one of the four female graduate students complained that her professor had compared "love and rape" in class. Actually, he had discussed a story by Isak Dinesen in which the protagonist falls in love with a woman he has raped, which is not quite the same thing.

In several cases, the complaints marked a desire to reduce professorial power and increase power among students under the guise of "sexual harassment." After a seven month investigation by the EO/AA, all the charges were dropped, apparently having been without merit. But the head of the department says that two of his colleagues are "psychologically devastated" (should they get compensation, then, from their accusers?), and that faculty from other departments who know little of the facts still assume that "where there's smoke there's fire."

The grave danger here is twofold: that *real* sexual harassment, which does occasionally happen, will become an academic joke, and that professors will be held hostage to semihysterical students egged on by New Establishment dogmatists. Many faculty around the nation have decided—like gynecologists—not to hold conferences with female students in their offices unless a third party is present.

As for free speech in the classroom, there is a considerable damper on frankness, a reflection of the fear of the sex police. One professor says that since some women students regard Freud as "sexist," he avoids discussing Freud. There is always the fear that someone will "snitch" to the EO/AA bureaucracy, and that thought control and political correctness, rather than intellect, will prevail.

The epidemic of sexual harassment has no bounds, infecting even grade school, as in the case of the six-year-old boy from North Carolina who was chastised and barred from an ice-cream party for complying with his female classmate's request for a peck on the cheek.

The case aroused the ire of *Newsweek* columnist Meg Greenfield, who quickly gets to the root of the matter, which she terms as "preposterous."

Says Greenfield: "The case against young Jonathan Prevette for kissing a little girl on the cheek told you where we have come to in the culture of counterintuitive and bloodless, not to say pointless, rulemaking in our civic life today." Lamenting the situation, she adds, correctly, that life once wasn't always like this.

Today, the situation in the local schoolroom has become more tense as officialdom, in the form of the U.S. Department of Education—a New Establishment stronghold—has put in its bureaucratic two cents.

The Big Brother villain here is Washington and the federal courts in the form of Title IX of the 1972 amendments to the Education Act, which prohibits discrimination and is enforced by the Civil Rights division of the Department of Education. We once assumed that harassment had nothing to do with Little Brother and Little Sister. The innocent byplay of boys and girls— a form of precourtship that has its own natural rules, long worked out by children of both sexes as they grew up—was once considered off limits to government.

If it came into conflict, parents, teachers or the school system intervened to work it out. So far that system has resulted in children successfully growing up into adults and producing millions of families and children of their own.

But no. The New Establishment considers nature a vacuum

that has to be filled with regulation, constraint, laws, and punishment. Au naturel, as in Penrod and Sam and Tom Swift, busybodies of Washington and the New Establishment are sure, was the breeding ground of evil between boys and girls, particularly to the detriment of girls. Whatever children had been doing all these centuries had to be stopped.

(This from an Establishment that makes it convenient for hormonally active young people to cohabit and fornicate, whether in college or in the armed forces, and that pays teenagers handsomely to have premature sex and produce children out of wedlock, then go on the federal dole.)

The social control of schoolchildren by the federal government is quite recent, but it is burgeoning. In 1992, the U.S. Supreme Court ruled in *Franklin v. Gwinnett County (Ga.) Public Schools,* that under Title IX, students could collect monetary damages from the school system if they were "discriminated" against.

In that case, it was a charge of alleged sexual harassment by a male teacher of a high school girl. Other court cases involved lawsuits by girls who claimed they were discriminated against in school sports. But when it came to sexual harassment cases involving students versus students—usually girls complaining about boys' behavior—the area was still legally gray.

By 1994, school officials became frightened as cases started to reach the courts, especially those involving students at the fringes of puberty. One twelve-year-old girl sued the school board in Delaware County, New York, saying the school did not stop boys from snapping her bra and grabbing her breasts. But in other cases, the courts were not sure if they had jurisdiction, especially among younger children.

Then a fifth grader in Macon, Georgia, complained to her teacher that the boy sitting next to her was using vulgar language, rubbing up against her, and trying to touch her breasts. The teacher changed the girl's seat, but when the harassment continued, the mother went to the principal, who said he would threaten the boy. Finally, the mother sued the school district. The federal district court dismissed the case, saying that Title IX was not written to cover student-to-student complaints.

The case was appealed and was heard by Judge Rosemary Barkett of the 11th Circuit Court in 1995. She ruled that Title IX did indeed cover sexual harassment of one child by another, and that since the government had jurisdiction—because of federal aid to education—the girl could sue the school district, which was ultimately responsible for the actions of all its students, including those of nasty little boys.

In a modern society, Judge Barkett was in effect saying, *nothing can be left to traditional social negotiating, even among children.* Everything must be legally decided, and the national government, not schools or parents, had the ultimate power to regulate children's behavior. Only the federal courts, lawyers, and damage decrees, the more sizable the better, were ostensibly the answer to societal conflicts, even those afflicting tykes as young as five or six years of age.

(Perhaps if Washington were to regulate sexual behavior down to the infantile stage, it could revive the reputation of Sigmund Freud.)

This has moved the New Establishment into control of children versus children, some fifty million strong, almost as large a market for their power as the workplace. Once Judge Barkett had ruled, the trial lawyers quickly entered the picture.

Some of the new cases have been settled out of court for as much as $800,000. "School boards are becoming more and more worried about the potential liability," says an attorney for the National School Boards Association. "What scares them is that they know they can do everything they're supposed to, but that's not necessarily going to stop the boy who's bothering the girl next to him."

The dilemma was commented on in a *New York Times* editorial about harassment as it involves young children. In Queens, New York, a bright seven-year-old boy who finishes his work before the other children was suspended from school for five days after pestering at least two young girls. (At ages five to seven, boys seem to find girls attractive, an urge that disappears soon after, turning to indifference, even disgust, only to be reawakened at puberty.)

In the boy's latest incident, he kissed a girl and tore a button off her skirt. Says *The New York Times:* "Both cases [including the North Carolina one] are examples of how even enlightened rules can become harmful when they are blindly followed. Small children are naturally subject to impulsive and disruptive behavior. The art of education involves teaching acceptable behavior without criminalizing the child."

There seems to be an historic, biological pattern of boys flirting with and pestering girls, which is part of an early courtship ritual that we can assume will outlive us all. But is the court system, especially the federal court system, the answer, as it increasingly seems to be in this litigious, New Establishment society?

Hardly.

If school behavior of boys and girls is a problem, one can imagine how it escalates upward when we get into a newer phenomenon, the mixing of the sexes at the young adult stage in the armed forces of the United States.

The problem began with the initial mistake of bringing the sexes into close proximity in a profession designed to win wars by killing as many of the enemy as possible.

As we read the headlines about sexual harassment in the Army and other services, we are somewhat shocked, as we should be.

The dismay is on two accounts. The first is that there should be so much sexual harassment of female soldiers by males, especially by drill sergeants. But the second is that the Army has set up life on base so foolishly that it encourages sexual activity, including petting, kissing, and even intercourse between soldiers. At the same time, the permissive mixing of the two sexes increases the possibility that the other side of the sexual coin—harassment—will take place.

The headlines tell one sordid story, *but what is generally unknown is that never before in history has there been so much opportunity for amorous activity between the sexes than in the armed forces, once the setting for celibacy and self-control.*

As paradoxical as it sounds, the military has become a vital mating and dating center for the new experimental society.

In theory, the service is supposed to be "sex neutral" so that young men and women, many as young as eighteen, can easily work together. "Side by side," as Togo West, Secretary of the Army likes to say, without having sex on their minds. But that is a New Establishment myth. Hormonally charged young men are hardwired to seek out sex. In fact, their psyches are often dominated by that one driving thought—as nature intended.

Rather than discourage the sex instinct, the modern U.S. Army says "Be All You Can Be" and arranges life in the barracks and in the field so as to encourage it.

To go behind the headlines of hundreds of cases of harassment, we have only to look at how the sexes mix in the Army, which to my old Army eyes is still shocking. In former days, soldiers, isolated in their barracks or in war, could only gaze at a pin-up of Betty Grable or Marilyn Monroe and *dream.*

But today, all they need do is virtually stretch out their arms. And there she is.

"I have had a number of commands," says a Major who is now acting as an Army Pentagon spokesman, "and we treat the woman like any other soldier. In terms of living conditions, if it is a two-story barracks, a typical arrangement—because there are more men than women—is to have the men on one floor, and split the second floor between men and women. In the field, if we're dealing with a twenty-four-foot tent, then the men and women will also live together—sometimes for a week or more. We'll put a kind of curtain up to separate them. But they mix freely together if they're in smaller tents."

However, the Major explained, the new barracks being built have no open bays. Instead, they are broken up into rooms, two to four soldiers to each. Men and women have separate rooms, but they are often side by side. That is, a young man can walk just fifteen feet down a common hall and enter a female soldier's room, a proximity that defies reason, tradition, and human nature.

"Does sexual intercourse go on right in the barracks between male and female soldiers?" I asked.

"Well, we assume that soldiers will be responsible professionals. But they are still human beings. Sexual intercourse is prohibited in the barracks, but yes it does go on. When I would make a morning inspection with my sergeant, we would sometimes find men and women soldiers in bed together."

"What was the punishment?" I asked, incredulous.

"According to the Uniform Code of Military Justice it is not a judicial matter, so I would mete out the punishment."

"And what would that be?"

"Perhaps a letter of reprimand in their record and confinement to base for seven days."

But wouldn't that just increase the chances of still more sex between the "perpetrators?" I wondered.

Still startled by what I heard, I asked the obvious: "But what about sex during the night in the barracks after lights out and before the morning inspection?"

The Major hesitated. "There's nothing we can do about that—if we don't know about it."

"Do some of the unmarried female soldiers get pregnant? Are they discharged as a result?" I asked, still trying to relate what he was saying to the Army that I had served in.

"No, pregnancy is not grounds for discharge or reprimand, even if the woman is unmarried. We just arrange for prenatal care at the base hospital. The female soldier continues her duties as usual. She even goes to field exercises until the fifth or sixth month of pregnancy."

"What happens when the baby is born? Does she have to leave the service then?"

"No," he responded quickly. "We arrange for the baby to be taken care of by couples on base who have set up child-care businesses in their homes. She continues as a regular soldier. It makes no difference to us if the mother is married or single."

The conversation was most revealing, especially as the Major continued to defend the mixing of the sexes in the service, which is now 14 percent female. But since females are barred from regular duty in infantry, artillery, and armor, the percentage jumps to 30 percent in other units such as signal corps, or air defense, or engineers, where men and women serve together in the same squads and platoons—marching, running, training, including coed hand-to-hand combat, together, and living as one.

The situation is, to be generous, ridiculous. The attention has been focused on drill sergeants, who are not supposed to fraternize with their young female charges, not even to smile at them. As the headlines have told us, a number of these drill sergeants have been charged with sexual harassment, even rape. But one aftermath of the cases has been the revelation that much of the sex was actually consensual and not rape. Five women soldiers announced that army investigators had pressured them into making the felony claims.

But the real attention should be focused on the permitted, even encouraged, relations between male and female privates, corporals, and sergeants. The only verboten activity is that enlisted personnel and officers are not supposed to mix and those in a supervisory position are not supposed to fraternize with anyone under them. But otherwise—it's Hellzapoppin.

Being naïve, I asked the Major why they did not have sexually segregated barracks to cut down on the amorous activity between soldiers. With less opportunity and less proximity, perhaps not only sexual intercourse, but harassment, might be lessened.

He pondered that question, as if it were coming from an alien world.

"I suppose that's possible, but it might be inconvenient. We need the barracks close to the orderly room so that when the soldiers fall out into formation, the men and women are there together at the same time."

The outrage against sexual harassment, particularly assault, is justified—*except* that the Army (and the Navy by having women aboard combat ships) has arranged it so that perhaps it is surprising that there isn't much more of it.

The solution? Very simple. The concept of a sex-neutral service is ludicrous. Young men and women eye each other continually, and when they are compatible, sex results. When they are not, sexual harassment is often the end product.

To avoid the plague of harassment *there should be no females in the regular Army or Navy or Air Force.* We should return to the sex-starved arrangement of old. And as I have already suggested, if women are to participate in the armed forces, it should be as auxiliaries, as were the segregated WACs and WAVES in World War II.

Despite the New Establishment equation of "What if women can be real soldiers or sailors?", men and women cannot mix side-by-side in the service, either in combat, or in the barracks, or in platoons, or in the field. There is too much sexual tension, sexual competition, sexual interest, and sexual activity to make such an experimental arrangement work.

There is too much human nature involved, in love affairs consummated, and those rejected, one major cause of sexual harassment. The entire situation destroys concentration on the task at hand—to prepare and fight wars, which unfortunately, is the *only* job of the armed forces. Gender equity should be no part of that deadly equation.

The philosophy of the new feminized military was inadvertently summed up by a woman consultant hired by the Pentagon to evaluate problems that have evolved from the mixing of sexes. The trouble with the armed forces—that well-honed killing machine—she concluded, was that it was just "too masculine."

The question of regulating sexual harassment must be more thoroughly examined. The increasingly vague definition of harassment has taken much of it out of common jurisprudence and placed it in the realm of subjectivity. Taste, rather than the law, has become involved. In such a situation, the odds are stacked against men, whose word is taken less often than that of accusing women.

But some men are fighting back, starting a counterrevolution needed to restore sanity to the current hysteria. Robert C. Clowers, a law enforcement officer in Houston, was accused of running his hands up and down the leg of a female subordinate. He said the charges were false and sued for defamation in federal court. This time they believed the man and awarded him $3 million.

In another countersuit, a former general counsel at Morgan, Stanley, the securities firm, was the subject of a complaint to the EEOC. Three secretaries charged him with sexual harassment, one of whom claimed that he scandalously commented on a woman's "nice legs."

The counsel said that secretary was seeking revenge after she received a poor performance review, the same reason the two other women were allegedly fired. The EEOC found the charges against the counsel to be baseless and he has filed a $1 million defamation suit.

These cases offer hope that some sanity will return to the sexual relations environment. But thus far the hysteria has not abated and frivolous charges are becoming more puerile and more frequent.

Where rape and assault are involved, it is an easy situation.

They are covered by *real* laws. The thorny question is how do you mediate the relations between the sexes where the law has not been traditionally involved, and where the New Establishment is intent on setting up control in the office, the colleges and even in the grade schools?

In the case of children, those disputes should be resolved by parents and schools and not by the government. In the case of adults, charges that involve vulgarity and insult should not be the province of the law, for two reasons.

First, there is the small matter of the First Amendment. Working in an office doesn't deprive one of the right of free speech. If the speech is reprehensible, then the firm—not the law—should take action if it wishes to do so.

Second, if women want to be treated as equal adults, they should act like equals. *There should be no recourse to lawsuits for any behavior that is not physical or is not outright intimidation.*

In sex discrimination suits in business, women claim equality. Therefore, they must act the part of mature adults. If a man insults a woman, she should—if she wants—insult him back. The *only* actionable behavior should be the original context of sexual harassment: demanding sexual favors in return for business rewards, or vice versa, threatening employment or promotion if refused.

Acting like an equal adult to men means that females must be responsible for their lives, just as they always expect men to be. Whining to the law because someone fails to treat a woman as a lady is oxymoronic since she wants the law to recognize her as an equal, not as the squeamish victim of boorish men.

Propaganda and falsely pious morality have made clear thinking on this issue difficult. But it is about time for us all, men and women, to break through the miasma set up by an aggressive New Establishment, and tangle with the sometimes harsh truth.

CHAPTER SEVEN

AFFIRMATIVE ACTION: THE NEW RACISM AND SEXISM

Are You One of the Preferred?

NOT LONG AGO, VIACOM, A GIANT MEDIA CON-
glomerate, wanted to sell most of its cable television operation in
what turned out to be a $2.3 billion deal. To whom? AT&T? Or
Ted Turner? Or MCI?

No. They chose a relatively unknown black entrepreneur who,
not surprisingly, turned out to be a partner of another media
giant, Tele-Communications, Inc., which was decidedly *not* a minority firm.

So why didn't Viacom sell directly to the large corporation?

The answer was obvious to anyone familiar with the manners
and mores of the New Establishment. Through the FCC, the
United States Government was granting an enormous break in
the form of an IRS "Tax Certificate" to anyone selling to a minority owner. By dealing with the African-American businessman
instead of directly with Tele-Communications, Viacom would
have saved some $400 million, a boon for it and an enormous
loss to taxpayers.

Once the press broke the story of this unique (and expensive) affirmative action, only the intervention of the 104th U.S. Congress in 1995 halted what looked like an original twist to racial charity. But Viacom was not taking special advantage; it was abiding by the law. In fact, there had already been 300 cases of special affirmative action at the FCC.

In July 1994, the FCC showed how generous it could be with the people's money. It auctioned off 600 interactive video licenses, many to another class of "preferred" bidders—women.

One female licensee received a 25 percent discount, which saved her company $7 million, with a similar loss to taxpayers for their gentlemanly attitude. Conveniently, she turned out to be the fiancée, then wife, of an entrepreneur.

(How many "female-owned" businesses are fronts for husband-and-wife teams where the woman is handed "majority control," making the firm eligible for preferential treatment from a naïve government?)

The long arm of affirmative action, choosing who shall and who shall not succeed by fiat, has indirectly, and directly, intruded into virtually everyone's life and business as a contemporary form of social madness. It includes not only preferences for capitalists, but advantages for women and *supposed* minorities in colleges, government employ and in entering most professions, from medicine to law. What started out as an experiment to help "victims," has burgeoned into a sociological scourge that is changing the face of America, generally for the worse.

In little Piscataway, New Jersey, the school district was in an affirmative action program dictated by the New Jersey Department of Education. It clicked in when, for budgetary reasons, the district had to lay off one of its two business administration teachers.

Sharon Taxman, a white teacher, and Debra Williams, a black teacher, were considered equally talented, and both had begun work the same day. What did the school board decide? They laid off the white woman.

Why?

"I believe that by retaining Mrs. Williams it was sending a very clear signal that our staff should be culturally diverse," said the head of the school board, apparently a loyal member of the New Establishment.

(Culturally diverse? Was he implying that black teachers have different cultural values than white teachers?)

Mrs. Taxman was one of thousands of victims of "reverse discrimination," the penalizing of people because they are white, or because they are male, or both. She sued the school board and won $140,000 in back pay, a rare victory in the fashionable world of American jurisprudence.

Affirmative action was ostensibly begun to dampen the raw practices of racism and sexism, a noteworthy goal supported by most Americans. But instead, that modern destabilizing program has taken those ills to an all-time high by sponsoring preferences for one American over another based on skin color and gender, the exact *opposite* of the original intent. In fact, in no other area of American life, has racism and sexism raised a more ugly face than in the attempt to secure preferences for a whole range of "victims."

Affirmative action is the creation of the New Establishment, which sees it as still another chance to increase its control over society. By providing special privileges to certain groups, it increases public instability and encourages separatism and racial and gender conflict.

It is a cleverly designed plan that fits neatly into the New Establishment dogma: It triggers the sense of "compassion"; it satisfies the need to expiate Freudian guilt, earned or otherwise; it sets up a hierarchy of victims and oppressors. But simultaneously it convinces millions of its good intentions while doing grievous harm to fairness and democracy.

Affirmative action is an unusual charity. It is not food, clothing, shelter, medical care. In fact, contrary to myth, it is not generally for the poor or the downtrodden. It has been designed for those who can take advantage of it, in business or college—the socially mobile, already up-and-coming women, blacks, and ethnics.

They receive it in an unprecedented form: a gift of power and achievement—rewards Americans once believed were the result of work and merit. Instead, the nation has entered a period of advancing anti-merit, a debilitating policy it must contend with or abolish.

In Jackson, Michigan, white teachers with seniority were laid off while relatively junior black teachers kept their jobs under a pact between the teachers union and the school board. In Milwaukee, the city government ruled that 51 percent of all hires had to be women. The chief building inspector had no philosophical objection, except that he couldn't find any licensed female plumbers.

In effect, affirmative action has evolved as a method of rewarding failure and punishing merit.

Affirmative action has spread beyond reasonable borders. Washington has even developed a new class—DBEs or Disadvantaged Business Enterprises. In one recent year, these minority- and female-owned companies received $6.4 billion of preferential federal contracts, one of which went to that needy bond dealer, Alice Walton, an heir to the Wal-Mart fortune.

The DBE racket is widespread, especially in work set-asides from such agencies as the Pentagon. At some military bases, the *majority* of construction contracts were given to minorities and women. At the Anniston Army Depot in Alabama, the figure was 52 percent; at Andrews Air Force base outside Washington, 75 percent; and an extraordinary 100 percent at Barksdale AFB in Louisiana.

"We were being discriminated against as a white, Anglo-Saxon business," complains Edward Agee, president of a construction firm in Shreveport.

When all set-asides, including those for supposed "socially and economically disadvantaged people" under the Small Business Administration program are tallied, the bill to taxpayers comes to $14.4 billion. And for each such beneficiary, many of whom are quite well-heeled, there is a white male (excuse the expression) who was discriminated against.

GEOD Corp, a "majority" company in New Jersey, says it lost $500,000 a year in surveying work because of affirmative action given to someone else. "Time after time, I'm told: 'Sorry, John, but we're giving the survey effort to a DBE.' I sometimes wonder what kind of country we're living in."

Meanwhile, a construction firm called Promotech admits that it received 70 percent of its business from the government because it was owned by a woman.

Besides favoring one person or firm over another, modern affirmative action deals in group quotas, the newest form of discrimination. The "Q" word is not usually used because several courts have held it unconstitutional and the New Establishment is nothing, if not deceptive. Instead, quotas are disguised as "proportionalism," "diversity goals" and "underrepresentation" or helping "victims of past discrimination," even when no such specific discrimination ever existed.

Santos Garza, a female entrepreneur who has cashed in on the modern sexist formula, did so because she was doubly blessed as a woman and someone of Mexican ancestry. Using both credentials, Ms. Garza expanded her security business into a 375-employee operation that grossed $10 million a year. Her secret: *three-fourths of her business came from a Small Business Administration program that steers government contracts to ostensibly "disadvantaged" persons.*

Disadvantaged? That's often the comic punchline of affirmative action. Ms. Garza had a reported salary of $100,000, plus any profits from her operation.

One of her competitors, a white male in Falls Church, Virginia, says it's "disgraceful," that skin color can determine who gets federal work. Ms. Garza is not dark—just savvy enough to take advantage of a bizarre, rather idiotic, government operation.

The SBA program is one of the most corrupt of all affirmative action programs. It actually gives a *cash* bonus to prime contractors who subcontract to minority- or female-owned firms, a form of bribery that uses taxpayer money for the pay-off. The ludicrous nature of the SBA program (they of Susan McDougal fame), was highlighted when a court in Washington, D.C., declared a white contractor eligible for preference because he was working in a predominantly black community.

Arnold O'Donnell, a partner in a small Washington, D.C., contracting company, fought the SBA set-aside program for years, even testifying against it before Congress. His argument: the program was unfair and un-American. In Washington, a white man such as himself was an oppressed minority. Why wasn't he in the SBA preference program?

The SBA laughed at him for years, but he persisted until finally an agency administrative judge agreed with O'Donnell. He ruled that in the heavily African-American city of Washington, O'Donnell was in fact "socially and economically disadvantaged."

O'Donnell chuckled with glee. "It's bizarre. I've been a vocal critic of their programs and now I'm in one. Hey, if this gets me business, I'll do it."

The black construction community was less than entertained. "It's outrageous," said one African-American builder about O'Donnell sharing the largesse.

Not only is the SBA set-aside program skewed against white men, but it appears that the government minority gravy train is not spread around evenly. Instead, it seems concentrated in a few favored hands. The General Accounting Office discovered that only *1 percent* of the 5,155 companies in the SBA's women and minority programs were receiving *25 percent* of the contracts. The majority of the firms received none of the gravy.

Much of affirmative action is based on quotas, and a major

user of the illegal quota system is the federal government itself. Though Washington swears it never indulges in quotas, an IRS lawyer in Atlanta shows the opposite. Lynn Abernathy calls the system "Ethnic Cleansing in the IRS." At the Atlanta IRS office, she says, managers are required to hire the same number of women and minorities as their proportion in the population.

This involves every government grade (GS-1 to GS-15), including attorneys, accountants, managers—often without regard to merit or competence. *Race and sex* is the name of the game. Abernathy says that white men are purged at the IRS or must work in an antagonistic environment.

An employee in the U.S. Forest Service reveals the existence of the same quota system, a form of poorly disguised *sexism*. To boost the number of female firefighters in California from 28 to 43 percent, quotas were installed that ended up in one of the great fiascoes of the affirmative action program.

Fire Captain Bob Grate of the Northern California Lasen National Forest explained the improbable, but true, tale when interviewed.

"A women's group in San Francisco sued the Forest Service because they said there weren't enough women working in the California area, including in our firefighting service. They sued in court and the Forest Service agreed to accept a consent agreement which forced us to hire many more women. The trouble was that although we had a pool of qualified men, there weren't enough qualified women to satisfy the 43 percent quota. That was strange in itself. That percentage was equal to the women in the general labor pool, but had nothing to do with working in forests."

When the Forest Service realized that the couldn't fill the orders of the court with qualified women, they placed one of the strangest ads in the history of affirmative action, or any other employment situation.

"So help me," says Chief Grate, "the notice read: 'Only *unqualified* personnel may apply.' The reason was simple: they couldn't mention gender and they didn't want more qualified men to apply."

The fiasco brought in all the *unqualified* women they wanted and several hundred were hired, and are still working for the Forest Service in California.

"On behalf of the qualified men, we first put in a complaint with the EEOC, but they turned us down," adds Grate. 'Then we filed our own lawsuit, *Levitoff v. Secretary of Agriculture,* which was a male class action claiming discrimination. The federal district court ruled against us, saying that because of the 1991 Civil Rights Act, an outside party could not question a consent decree. In 1994, we were heard on appeal by the Ninth Circuit Court and lost 2–1. Then we appealed to the Supreme Court, but late in 1996 they refused to hear our case. Meanwhile the work force is demoralized because it knows the courts are more interested in false gender equality and *unqualified* people than in good forestry personnel."

As a result of this case, Congressman Wally Herger of California has put in HR 61, the "Forest Service Equal Opportunity Act of 1997," which states that employment and promotion shall be solely on the basis of "merit."

The case is historic. The "unqualified" ad is the masterful end product of the affirmative action program, surely the most biased and distorted one in the history of the American government.

The government likes to say it is unbiased, which is an outright fabrication. A U.S. deputy labor secretary had admitted the department gives high priority to women and minorities. When white males won only eleven of the fifty-eight attorney jobs, a career Labor lawyer called it a "racial spoils system."

The government quota system rides roughshod over merit to achieve so-called "diversity," which is surely one reason why the federal government is the worst-managed large business in America.

In 1970, women and minorities made up 48 percent of all civil service grade (GS) jobs and 23 percent of the middle management (GS 9–12) positions. After a push was made to increase females, blacks, and Hispanics, by 1990 "minorities" held 77 percent of all government graded civil service jobs, and 60 percent of lower and middle management positions. Even top-ranked jobs jumped from 8 to 30 percent, and the percentage is growing.

How come? The 1978 Civil Service Reform Act endorsed the idea of a "representative bureaucracy," a new, undemocratic concept in government that calls for "a work force reflective of the Nation's diversity," the antithesis of a merit system. We seem to be returning to the days of Andrew Jackson, when the victor took the "spoils." Today, the spoils are divided by race and sex. And the victor is the New Establishment.

The government has issued detailed instructions to "correct" female and minority "underrepresentation" (read "quotas") in high-level positions and within a timetable. President Reagan relaxed those goals in 1987, "permitting" but not "requiring" affirmative action numbers. But the policy continued unabated.

How did this un-American racial and sexist concept become legitimate to begin with?

It started with noble goals, to help those who had truly been discriminated against in the past. Not women or Hispanics, but black Americans who had been segregated in the South by law. They were poorer than whites, more apt to be involved in welfare and crime, had lower academic achievement, lower SAT scores, and less representation in college and the professions.

That troubled many Americans, who wanted to help *qualified* blacks enter the inner sanctum of business and higher education. One result was the Civil Rights Act of 1964, especially Title VII, which made discrimination in employment against any person because of race, color, religion, sex, or national origin illegal. At first it was limited to companies of more than 50 employees, but that was changed in 1972 to fifteen, and courts keep lowering that threshold as well.

Early on, the law was enlarged to protect women, then in 1967, the Age Discrimination in Employment Act gave safeguards to those over forty. In 1990, the disabled were added to the potential "victims" list, and in 1991, President Bush signed a new Civil Rights Act that broadened all protection.

But all this was allegedly done to prevent discrimination, not to provide affirmation action to anyone.

In fact, Title VII—the granddaddy of the movement—specifically states that nothing in the act should require any employer "to grant preferential treatment" to any individual or any group. Affirmative action was declared illegal from the outset, which is one of the great legislative jokes of our era.

In 1965, Lyndon Johnson, in Executive Order 11246 set up the EEOC, the Equal Employment Opportunity Commission. That was followed by Labor Department regulations that gave the EEOC the right to investigate and negotiate claims of discrimination. If discrimination was proven, the plaintiff could receive back pay and reinstatement or promotion. (The 1991 Civil Rights Act signed by President Bush also enabled people to receive *punitive* damages.)

Despite the fact that affirmative action *had not been authorized* by law, the EEOC was set up as a vehicle to enforce it. The first direct affirmative action was launched by President Richard Nixon in 1969. His "Philadelphia Plan" used the Office of Federal Contract Compliance to achieve "minority group representation in all trades," the beginning of preferences.

The plan demanded jobs for blacks in Philadelphia construction firms working for the government. The contractors sued, but in 1971, the Third Circuit Court of Appeals upheld Nixon.

It was a dramatic shift in emphasis—from stopping discrimination to demanding affirmative action for minorities. But no one really noticed, and many even approved. The numbers of people given preference were small. The white male working population was only barely affected, and the public believed that trade unions were discriminatory anyway, which was quite true.

From there, the EEOC started branching out into private industry. It sued AT&T and won $38 million in compensatory damages. The movement soon gained approval—more or less—from the Supreme Court, if on shaky legal grounds. In 1971, in *Griggs v. Duke Power Company,* the plaintiff claimed that the company's demand for a high school diploma and an intelligence test to screen applicants was unconstitutional.

The Court agreed, saying the use of tests was unlawful discrimination, even though they were routinely used by corporations and colleges. The argument was now joined, and Congress jumped in. In 1972, in the Equal Employment Opportunity Act, it gave the EEOC more power, and extended Title VII to schools, states, and local governments. Several attempts were made in Congress to rule out quota hiring, but they all failed. That alone seemed to give respectability to group-think, quota affirmative action.

Title VII's prohibition against *any preferential treatment* still stood, although it was increasingly ignored, particularly by the government that wrote it.

Affirmative action soon blossomed into a major industry. Pushing its claim of "good intentions," it has mushroomed into a racket that substitutes preferences for the original intent of fighting discrimination. The result is a series of programs that massively distort racial, ethnic, and sexual equality in favor of racism and sexism.

This un-American concept rivals the old European system of merit by birth. Considering the damage to our institutions, it would be cheaper in the long run to give checks to these supposed "victims," providing welfare for the upwardly mobile as well as for the poor.

Although the courts are only now beginning to face the issue (they haven't really done it yet), the problem is that "preferences" in public-supported activities is not only a violation of Title VII, but is totally unconstitutional.

Where does it say that? In the "due process" language of the Fifth Amendment, part of the Bill of Rights adopted in 1790, and more specifically in the Fourteenth Amendment to the Constitution passed in 1868 to give legal rights to freed slaves.

The courts may be confused, but the Constitution is so simply written that it can be understood by a sixth-grade child. The Fourteenth Amendment clearly states that neither the federal government nor the states "shall deny to any person within its jurisdiction the equal protection of the laws." That, of course, applies to white males just as much as it does to blacks, Asians, Hispanics, or women.

Despite the Fourteenth Amendment, the New Establishment continues its crusade against white males, the historic backbone of the nation. As Harriett Sussman, president of a Massachusetts employment consulting firm has said, "White male is the newest swear phrase in America."

Though Title VII was written to stop discrimination, some observers at the time feared it would turn out as it has—as a weapon for discrimination against others. Senator Hubert Humphrey, one of its proponents, promised that if it was ever used to discriminate against anyone because of race or sex, he would *eat* the bill.

Unfortunately, Humphrey cannot make good on his gastronomical promise, but that's exactly what Title VII has countenanced, even encouraged. Through arm-twisting and "consent decrees" the EEOC has regularly forced companies to hire people according to racial, ethnic, and gender guidelines—or in plain language, it has put in quotas.

This was a new form of social action, what might be called "statistical justice." Every group has to measure up to white male employment or it was considered proof of an "unbalanced" and discriminatory society. Naturally, this is blatant nonsense.

Such affirmative action quotas have become commonplace even if illegal. Edward Lynch, a congressional aide whose civil service committee was investigating quotas in government hiring, singled out the Departments of Energy and Agriculture. "Most citizens would be aghast at the amount of hiring by the numbers," he said.

So ludicrous has this concept of "proportionalism" and quotas become (remember the analogy of the short, white basketball players?) that it has even been enforced in the opposite direction.

Discipline in schools, a court ruled, had to follow that same proportional formula. In 1980, a federal judge declared that the Kingston, New York public schools were discriminatory against one group of students—black youths. Because these monitory students were more often on the receiving end of discipline, the school system had to make *sure* that in the future black and white students were disciplined in exactly the same proportion.

The ultimate villain in the school environment is the federal government, specifically the Office of Civil Rights of the Department of Education. That bureaucracy has even ruled that the common "tracking" system, which separates students by ability in order to facilitate learning, can be a vehicle for "discrimination." Why? Because usually there are more whites and Asians than minorities in the faster tracks.

(Federal government intrusion into local school affairs, which constitutionally belongs to the states and communities, is mainly made possible because of the pittance of federal aid to schools. It represents only six-percent of school budgets, but it allows Washington and federal courts to intervene in the local schools. By refusing that aid, school systems could be freed from much of the escalating intrusion by the federal government.)

Affirmative action law is a swamp of "reverse discrimination," which former Supreme Court Justice Lewis Powell made clear was illegal. Said the Justice: "Preferring members of any one group for no other reason than race or ethnic origin is discrimination for its own sake. This the Constitution forbids."

But the federal government *apparatchiks* thumb their noses at the Constitution. In a classic case of quotas, the Equal Employment Opportunity Commission (EEOC) enforced an edict in North Carolina based solely on gender statistics.

It involved the penal department of North Carolina, which the federal government claimed did not have *enough* women as corrections officers. The federal agency stated that there was a "statistical shortfall" of 618 female hires over a ten-year period—just as if this was a number ordained by God. It was, of course, another case of government sexism, with a strong totalitarian twist.

Deval Patrick, an African-American and then head of civil rights at the Department of Justice, sued the North Carolina Corrections Department, demanding that they hire women in "numbers that reflect their availability" in the local labor market, an obviously illegal quota scheme.

The EEOC then inflated its demands. It insisted that the state corrections department set aside $5.5 million in back pay for women. Which women? Not only those who had applied and were not hired, but for women "who would have applied" but didn't. Why? Because they feared they wouldn't be hired! (What better confirmation of the New Establishment theory of "What if?")

The EEOC even advertised for "victims," then sent them road maps so they could apply for the money in person. It also insisted that the state set up a twelve-person organization to monitor the corrections people, at a yearly cost of $1.3 million.

North Carolina could have fought, but faced with the cost, it capitulated and signed the "Consent Decree." The EEOC faced one more obstacle. It needed a federal judge to sign on. By chance, the decree was given to Judge Terrence W. Boyle, who in February 1996, delivered a written tongue lashing to the EEOC.

"Not only does the agreement appear to be unlawful and unreasonable," he wrote, "it is also doubtful that the agreement comports with the Constitutional requirement that male employees and prospective applicants be afforded the equal protection of the law."

What happened to the EEOC as result?

Nothing. *When it comes to quotas, lawlessness has become the modus operandi of the federal government,* still another example of American social and cultural madness.

Deval Patrick, who left the EEOC in late 1996, claimed that quotas did not exist and that there was only one "set-aside" program that favors people by race. Sounds reasonable. But a more reliable agency, the bipartisan Congressional Research Service, says that it has found 160 such racially based federal operations.

Not only is the EEOC unlawfully promoting racism and sexism, but so potent are its threats that frightened employers indiscriminately hire women and minorities just to get the government off their backs. Some companies even risk breaking the law by telling employment agencies they want *only women* for management job openings in order to keep themselves on the right side of the quota frenzy.

Corporate Directions, a California search firm, says that several companies have asked it to recommend only women for top jobs. "We will interview men," they say firms instruct them, "but we are only going to hire women." (What goes around apparently comes around.)

The quota theory, or "balancing" or correcting "underrepresentation," is now rampant. Even the FBI has yielded to the concept that "G-Men" should be chosen by race and gender. As a result of a class action suit by Hispanic FBI agents, a quota of 30 percent women and minorities has reportedly been established by the agency, although it denies it.

Sounds fair and equitable. No?

No. If the mind-set that divides Americans into segments is enlightened, then this same treatment should be equitably extended to all groups. How many Seventh Day Adventists should receive preferential treatment? How many Greek-Americans? How many short people? (Notice all those *tall* presidents?)

At first glance, "proportionalism" seems attractive, even fair, but it is a trap of mindless bias. Former President John F. Kennedy warned against preference quotas, saying: "I do not think we ought to begin the quota system. We are too mixed, this society of ours, to begin to divide ourselves on the basis of race."

JFK was correct. The "slice-of-pie" theory may apply to pizzas but not to an open democratic society. There can be no "shortfall" or under- or overrepresentation of any race, gender or ethnic group in achievement. It makes absolutely no difference if there are none or one hundred African-Americans in Congress, as long as they are all fairly elected. The same is true of Jews and gentiles, Mormons, Hispanics, Asians, men, or women.

African-Americans make up over one-third of the Army, some three times more than their "representation" in the population. Should divisions be dissolved and the black soldiers discharged to equalize the portion of races? Or perhaps only white young men (and women?) should be drafted to achieve racial balance. Such simple analogies expose the madness of "proportionalism," the current affirmative action rage.

A long-time watcher of absurd "proportionalism" and other cultural nonsense is Daniel Seligman, who pens his "Keeping Up" column for *Fortune* magazine. By the end of the century, Seligman points out, the minority population of America will be thirty-percent. That fact, he explains, has set up anxiety in the ranks of The American Society of Newspaper Editors, which is determined to reach that same proportion in their newsrooms. But why? asks Seligman, giving his always frank, if unpleasant, answer.

"Newsroom jobs require college graduates with above average verbal skills," he writes, "and ethnic minorities have fewer of them than do whites."

He delivers a similar attack on the U.S. Navy, where 11 percent of the officers are minority members, but where the goal is 29 percent by the year 2000. That irrational proportional argument, he explains, has even spread to the national convention of the Democratic party, where the 1996 delegates were chosen by race, ethnicity and gender. Not only that, but party delegate slots were supposedly open, by proportion, to folks regardless of their "philosophical persuasion."

"Clearly," needles Seligman, "this means that Nazis, having an identifiable persuasion, are now eligible to participate" in future Democratic conventions that choose one of our presidential candidates.

Perhaps the whole quota concept will become clearer if and when it is turned against its beneficiaries. Statistics show that women, for example, receive three times as many graduate degrees in education as men. Should we limit their numbers and push men into their slots? Conversely, men receive four times as many graduate degrees in engineering. Should we hold back the men and draft women into greater use of the slide rule?

Had affirmative action been restricted to black Americans, the movement, as undemocratic as it is, might have retained public support. But as more groups were added to the "protected" categories until they became a super-majority of the population, the public began to lose interest, even became angered. According to a poll by the National Opinion Research Center, only sixteen percent of white Americans favor preferences for African-Americans.

The California law on who was eligible for preferences (before passage of Proposition 209, which ostensibly made it illegal in that state) shows the ridiculous reach of affirmative action.

The law declared a minority to be "An ethnic person of color and who is: black (a person having origins in any of the black racial groups of Africa); Hispanic (a person of Mexican, Puerto Rican, Cuban, Central or South American, or other Spanish or Portuguese culture or origin regardless of race); Native American (an American Indian, Eskimo, Aleut, or Native Hawaiian); Pacific-Asian (a person whose origins are from Japan, China, Taiwan, Korea, Vietnam, Laos, Cambodia, the Philippines, Samoa, or the United States Trust Territories of the Pacific including the Northern Marianas); Asian-Indian (a person whose origins are from India, Pakistan, or Bangladesh.)"

Such a broad racial and ethnic listing—which, with women, paradoxically covered 73 percent of the state's population—raises embarrassing questions for the New Establishment:

1. Why Japanese, whose "home" country is among the richest in the world? If Pakistan, why not Afghanistan or Turkistan or other non-Pacific Asians? And since members of the "Portuguese culture" are also "protected," should a Brazilian millionaire from São Paulo receive a "leg up" over an American businessman? And why Cambodia and not Malaysia or Singapore?

2. In California, where 25 percent of all residents are foreign-born, who decided to give immigrants preferential affirmative action over unprotected American-born citizens?

Not only have these programs increased tension between blacks and whites, Hispanics, and Anglos, and men and women, they have even split the minority population, pitting one group against another. Once you put in quotas, as President Kennedy warned, where does it end?

One female professor applying for a position at a Midwest university had the advantage of being black, the new tradition in much of academe. The child of a black Cuban mother and a white father, she was attacked in a three-page memo by another professor for not being black enough! The complainant was also black, but being a descendant of American slaves, she claimed she was purer since the other professor was not really an African-American!

In Los Angeles, organized Hispanics want a larger share of county civil service jobs, arguing that black employees are "over-represented." In Ohio, the tussle has gone to the courts, where blacks are fighting Asian-Indians for greater preference in public contracts.

Torso Del Junco, an Hispanic and Vice Chairman of the Postal Board of Governors, was angered because "too many" African-Americans are working for the Post Office, at the expense, he said, of Hispanics. While blacks represent only about 10 percent of the labor force, he pointed out that they make up 63 percent of all postal workers.

The "overrepresentation," Del Junco claimed, was created by a racial network operating in violation of the Civil Rights Act of 1991, which states that if race and ethnicity do not match the available labor pool, it is grounds for a discrimination lawsuit.

So grotesque have some types of affirmative action become that a Pentagon hiring directive actually read: *"Special permission will be required for promotion of all white males without disability."*

That same Pentagon has gone overboard in setting up contracting preferences for minorities and women. In one instance, it granted 57 percent of all its long-distance telephone services to minorities!

Unlike the SBA, which had set aside a portion of its business for supposedly "disadvantaged" women and minorities, the Pentagon gave minority contractors a ten point pricing advantage on their bids. (This of course made such contracts more expensive for the taxpayers.) The result? In the tight profit margin long distance telephone business, the *majority* of the work went to affirmative action companies to the detriment of other firms.

"We're losing business left and right," said Craig Roberts,

president of Electra, a small white-owned company. "What about us? We're a small business too."

The General Accounting Office has examined the sweetheart minority and women deals and concluded that they should be closed down. But the director of Pentagon procurement says it must stay. Otherwise the Defense Department could not meet its overall 5 percent quota of contracts for "disadvantaged" minority business.

(No one has yet explained how any operating business is "disadvantaged." Previously that term was applied to the poor, who had more important things—likely eating—on their minds.)

Often, firms receiving preferences are too small to actually handle the business. In several SBA and FCC cases, for example, they operate as "fronts" for so-called "majority," or white-owned, companies. This is often the case in municipal bonds issues (remember Alice Walton?), where minority companies front for larger firms who compensate them for bringing in the affirmative action business.

Says a *Business Week* editorial on the subject: "Fronting has been a problem in government set-aside programs in construction and cable TV for years. Now it is becoming a similar issue in municipal finance. . . . It may be legal, but it isn't right."

When the list of "victims" defined by various civil rights acts was completed in 1991, some 80 percent of all Americans (everyone but white males under forty, not disabled and not on welfare or SSI disability) were classified as "minorities." It has become such a statistical joke that most citizens, including many of the "victims," have finally become angered.

Initially, affirmative action had been sold to charitable Americans as "common decency," the New Establishment's favorite platitude. By instilling the public with false guilt, the New Establishment was implying that anyone who didn't support the program was badly intentioned. And many Americans agreed. But the public has now become resentful, seeing the unreasonable way in which the program is administered by the government, and the favoritism given to people who don't need it.

What had been sold as "common decency," soon seemed to border on the immoral—especially in its punishment of the white male, the "minority" incorrectly labeled as a "majority."

The passage of Prop 209 in California was one indication of public opinion. A *Washington Post*/ABC poll of 1,524 adults nationwide found that three-fourths opposed preferences for women and racial and ethnic groups. Two-thirds of the women even opposed it for women. Almost a majority of blacks (46 percent) opposed it for themselves.

Consider the following futuristic scenario if affirmative action continues. Why stop at a 30 percent quota, as in the FBI? Why not a 70 percent proportion for "minorities" in all walks of life, as is already happening in government employment? The danger is first in accepting such irrationality as reasonable, then institutionalizing it into law.

Under the quota system, the men who now head 498 of the Fortune 500 Corporations, for instance, would be brushed aside for others with the politically correct skin color or gender. This despite the fact that the boards of directors and stockholders (including millions of women) of these mainly public corporations prefer these men—such as the brilliant Louis V. Gerstner, Jr., who heads IBM—to run their firms.

The same would be true of generals, professors of science, members of Congress, even as we have already seen, heart surgeons. The New Establishment theory—"What if power is divided along gender and racial lines"—fails because it seriously penalizes the most talented of Americans, and thus society itself.

In a free society, leadership must flow from individuals, not genders or races or ethnic groups.

In a quota system, such as the one we are developing, consider the future of Jewish-Americans, one group that would be heavily penalized, as they once were. They make up only 2 percent of the population, yet are heavily "overrepresented" virtually everywhere, from medicine, law, business, and the arts even to some 30 percent of the President's 1996 Cabinet.

Would they, under the new concept of quotas, be legally replaced by others, much as happened in Hitler's Europa? The same is true of Asian-Americans who are taking the lead in schools of science, a fact that will soon become highly evident in society.

The same, of course, is true of white males in general, those who shaped our democracy, our science, and our industry for two hundred years. The danger of relegating them to a secondary position is an irrevocable threat to our civilization.

One hole in the affirmative action theory is that many "protected" groups are not, as claimed, victims of past discrimination. That is a commonly held, oft-repeated, myth, especially when it comes to women, as we have seen in medical school admissions.

Instead of past discrimination against women now being alleviated, there has been a distinct change in sexual sociology. In the 1940s and 1950s, the overwhelming majority of women worked only until their first child was born. Many actually quit college the day they were married, preferring a "Mrs." to a B.A.

Most became "homemakers," some returning to the working world only after their children had finished school. The situation remained reasonably constant into the 1960s until the advent of *The Feminine Mystique* by Betty Friedan, which followed Simone de Beauvoir's *Second Sex*. The change that was to follow was the advent of working women, feeling their way, seeking to persuade employers, themselves, and the nation that they could handle families and work simultaneously.

In the 1940s and 1950s, few women aspired to be doctors or professors or lawyers or soldiers. Today, many do, and claiming "past discrimination" receive affirmative action to help them. But past discrimination is often a false claim. The true lever is the enormous female political power, which they take advantage of.

Plain and simple, a "majority" has classified itself as a "minority" and is making good use of the label.

In fact, brighter, wealthy women have been the major beneficiaries of affirmative action, not women en masse or their sisters in the underclass, especially African-Americans and Hispanics, who are still stuck in the sociological mud.

Women have had the luxury of choice, something denied to men. Men know they must work, from late adolescence until retirement. Women can choose either to work with full commitment as men do, to work only part-time, or not to work at all. Surprisingly, a study shows that almost half of women (48 percent) do not work for self-fulfillment, but for money to support their families. If not for that need, they would prefer to stay at home and raise their children.

That dovetails with the theory that much of the women's revolution was created by the need for two paychecks where one once sufficed. Sociological fashion then followed the pocketbook. Perhaps the IRS, not female thinkers, should be given credit (or blame) for the enormous number of working women.

Proof of the theory that money counts in this revolution comes from a decided new trend among the affluent. *Increasingly, women whose husbands earn enough to support the family are staying home once they have children—just as they did in the 1950s.* In fact, it is becoming a new status symbol, a sign of affluence that rivals the honor given to such "comfortable" women in Thorstein Veblen's "Theory of the Leisure Class."

The myth that past discrimination usually justifies affirmative action is also seen in the case of the foreign-born, many of whom receive affirmative action. In California, some 25 percent of the population is foreign-born and could hardly be victims of past discrimination—unless it happened in their countries of origin. Yet many are eligible for preferences over native-born Americans, a distortion that alienates most citizens.

Mortimer B. Zuckerman, editor-in-chief of *US News & World*

Report, made that point in an editorial showing that blacks who have come here from the Caribbean, for instance, never experienced the historic rejection of American blacks, yet are equally eligible for preferential treatment.

The number of those who can receive affirmative action, he explains, is rising exponentially because of immigration. The American-Asian population, which was only 1 million in the 1960s, is now 8.5 million. Latinos have increased from 3.5 million to 23 million. Without immigration, the self-defined Native American population has zoomed from 500,000 in the 1960s to 2.2 million today.

"What began as a measure of justice and grace," Zuckerman concludes, "has become itself a source of injustice and envy."

Several observers point out that true civil rights protect everyone and favor no special groups. "I was clerking for Justice Byron White in the year the Supreme Court heard the Bakke case," recalls California State Senator Tom Campbell. "My job was to read the entire history of the Civil Rights laws. And it was clear to me that the conclusion that should be drawn from it is that the intent of the law was to be colorblind."

But what of American blacks, who truly were victims of legal discrimination in the South? Should they alone receive affirmative action, or is that just another false palliative?

To answer that we should understand that most African-Americans *do not* receive affirmative action, unless one considers welfare and fatherless homes to be a "leg up." Glenn Loury, an African-American professor of economics at Boston University, points out that the bottom one-fifth of the black community, the underclass in the inner cities, hasn't been helped at all by the program. "It is now beyond dispute," Professor Loury says, "that the principal beneficiaries of affirmative action are relatively well-off African-Americans."

Is the racial and sexual preference machine slowing down?

Absolutely not. The EEOC has become a rogue agency, continuously expanding its purview and creating its own rules without the permission of Congress. It operates by the simple vehicle of issuing its own edicts to millions of Americans in virtually every area of life, with little or no basis in law or the Constitution.

Recently, it issued an edict—that if actually enforced—will make the American workplace not only ineffective but totally confused.

The new order, issued in April, 1977, would force employers to "accommodate" the mentally ill when they act out their hostilities and irrationality on the job.

Most Americans are sensitive to the problems of the mentally ill, especially their inability to perform well in the work environment, with all its tensions and competitive requirements. For that reason, most of the mentally ill do not hold formal jobs and instead receive income from the government under various programs including SSI.

But claiming that it is merely carrying out the Americans With Disabilities Act of 1990, the EEOC, according to *The New York Times*, has issued guidelines to employers that they "may have to allow extra time off from work, alter work schedules or assignments, and make physical changes in the workplace as a 'reasonable accommodation' for employees with mental disabilities . . ."

Most importantly, the EEOC's new rules say that employers "should be alert to the possibility that traits regarded as undesirable—chronic lateness, poor judgment, hostility to co-workers or supervisors—'may be linked to mental impairments.' "

For the first time, poor behavior on the job has taken on the cover of the insanity defense, with no end of illogic in sight. The remedy? The ultimate cure is to eliminate the EEOC, or failing that, for Congress to create truly strict oversight of the renegade agency so that the EEOC's own "mental impairment" is strictly contained.

The EEOC has a backlog of 80,000 cases, and the pressure

to settle suits in favor of claimants is becoming intense. The problem rests in the courts, where confusion reigns. In the lower federal court system, there are decisions on both sides of the fence: that preference is the law of the land, and conversely, that reverse discrimination is illegal. The courts go back and forth on this question, as does the Supreme Court itself.

One reason the courts cannot seem to make up their minds—even though the legal concepts are crystal clear—is their adherence to political fashion, which heavily influences judges, who after all, are usually chosen by the political parties.

The case of *Firefighters Local Union No. 1784 v. Carl W. Stotts* shows the confused state of mind of the courts. It involved the Memphis Fire Department, which after a "consent decree" from the EEOC, was forced to hire more African-Americans to eliminate what the government charged was discrimination.

That charge is often false. Discrimination means rejecting a qualified candidate because of his race, gender, or ethnic background, a law (Title VII), which the courts should strictly enforce. What the government is talking about is quotas, that there aren't "enough" women or blacks in the fire department, or elsewhere.

The city of Memphis became embroiled in the quota dispute when budget cuts forced it to rely on seniority in laying off firefighters. Since most of the African-American firefighters had been hired under court order and generally lacked seniority, they took the brunt of the cutbacks.

The African-American firefighters sued. The federal district court judge, Robert McRae, Jr., agreed that the layoffs were discriminatory and ruled that the firefighters be reinstated. But the case went to the Supreme Court, which, by a 6-3 vote, surprisingly reversed the decision. They found in favor of the fire department—that seniority counts.

"It is inappropriate," stated Justice Byron R. White, a Kennedy appointee, "to deny an innocent employee the benefits of his seniority in order to provide a remedy . . ."

Was this a clue that the Supreme Court was against affirmative action? Not really. It was more a sign of its indecision, which has been going on for thirty years, one that seems to mirror what is "in" or "out" on affirmative action at any particular point on the sociopolitical landscape.

The most celebrated Supreme Court case came in 1978, when the Justices made such a confused ruling on affirmative action that legal scholars and the public are still dumbfounded. A white student named Allan Bakke, who applied to medical school, sued the University of California at Davis. Despite the fact that his grades and standardized test scores were higher than those of several black and Hispanic students who were admitted, he was rejected.

It appears that Davis had formally set aside sixteen places for minorities out of one hundred in the entering medical school class. The court ruled for Bakke and he was admitted, which seemed like a clear-cut vote against affirmative action. But paradoxically, it was not. In fact, it even advanced the preference racket.

How was that possible?

The Supreme Court Justices, *while holding for Bakke, also ruled that race could be taken into account in making decisions for admission to schools*—as long as the cases were decided on an individual, not group, basis. Basically, it was legal as long as it was not a "quota." The high court stated that the lower courts could "use race as a criterion and could order such affirmative action as may be appropriate."

What seemed like the death knell for affirmative action turned out to be quite the opposite. That double-faced ruling reinforced the schools that wanted affirmative action, only cautioning them not to be as blatant as the University of California at Davis.

So in trying to straddle, or appease, both sides in the argument (instead of relying on the word of the Constitution) the Court had, in effect, given its blessing to affirmative action.

When I inquired of a dean of the Harvard Medical School how long it had used affirmative action in admissions, he frankly answered—"Ever since the Bakke case."

This type of lawlessness has flourished for almost twenty years. In the 1980s, the court reaffirmed affirmative action for minorities and women on at least two occasions, which gave encouragement to Presidents and the EEOC to continue.

At the same time, some lower courts put a temporary finger in the affirmative action dike. In Atlanta, a white man won a lawsuit against the city because he was rejected as director of a Civil War display in favor of first a black man and then a white woman. It was a symbolic victory against "reverse discrimination" but it had absolutely no national significance.

Nor has it slowed arrogant New Establishment activists. Former Congressional Black Caucus chairman Kweise Mfume of Maryland went so far as to demand the resignation of the Capitol Architect. Why? Because women and minorities were "underrepresented" (that word again) among the higher-paying jobs in his staff.

This Achievement-on-Demand has become a form of social blackmail. In prior times it would have been laughed at as an absurd concept, one that violated every precept of the merit culture that built Western society. But today, with New Establishment potency in academe, government, and the courts, "groupthink" has achieved a dangerous form of respectability.

Supreme Court Justice Sandra Day O'Connor has issued a warning against official quotas, but it has been ignored. She has pointed out that the Fifth and Fourteenth Amendments do not protect groups, only individuals. Programs based on race, she said, "should be subjected to detailed judicial inquiry to ensure that the personal right to equal protection of the laws has not been infringed."

Justice O'Connor can be assured of two things: (1) They do

infringe on Constitutional rights; (2) they have *not* been subject to detailed inquiry.

But underneath the surface, the American public—though still frustrated by lack of success of many blacks and Hispanics—has become increasingly annoyed at favoritism. A citizen revolt finally showed itself in the passage of Prop 209 in California, and the beginnings of similar initiatives in twenty other states to cut out affirmative action.

Proposition 209, which would have eliminated preferences in public jobs, contracts, and institutions in California, was heavily opposed by such groups as the major foundations. The Ford, Rockefeller, and Carnegie foundations put up $1.5 million to fight it. It passed nonetheless, but was initially blocked by a federal court. (See Chapter Nine.)

Ever-aware of growing public opinion against preferences, the Supreme Court finally agreed to hear a case involving affirmative action for minority contractors, few of whom are poor. The decision came down in June 1995, and with it, some of the legal ardor for affirmative action was diminished.

The case was pressed by a white contractor named Randy Pech, the head of Adarand Constructors, who sued Secretary of Transportation Federico Pena (518 U.S.—1995). Adarand had put in a subcontractor bid on highway guard rails with that department. Even though it was the lowest bid and he had a good reputation as a contractor, it was turned down in favor of the Gonzalez Construction Company, which had officially been declared a minority Hispanic firm.

"It was very discouraging to . . . go to a lot of trouble of bidding on a project," said Pech, "and come in with the low bid and then find they can't use you because of their (minority) goals."

This type of complaint was common among contractors. Thomas Stewart of Spokane, Washington, who like Adarand installed guardrails, said he was sick and tired of "Sorry Tom" phone calls explaining that the business had gone to a DBE female or minority firm even though his bid was the lowest.

The main contractor on the Adarand case, the Mountain Gravel and Construction Co., was given a cash motive to choose Gonzalez. For subcontracting 10 percent of its work to a "socially and economically disadvantaged" individual—actually a minority business firm, no matter how wealthy—the federal government promised Mountain a 1.5 percent bonus. That comes to a handsome cash gift of $150,000 on each $10 million in contracting, an enormous waste of taxpayer money.

This type of freebie preference was upheld as "constitutional" by the federal district court in Denver, then by the august Court of Appeals for the 10th Circuit.

But Adarand decided to petition the Supreme Court, which agreed to hear the case.

In a historic decision that was thirty years in coming, the Court ruled in favor of Adarand. Affirmative action, they stated in a 5–4 decision, was only Constitutional if it was "narrowly tailored" to "redress discrimination against persons, not groups," and was "of compelling interest to the government."

Delivering the majority (5–4) decision, Justice Sandra Day O'Connor said the government must keep "racial politics" out of the picture when dealing with discrimination. "We have long felt that equal protection of the law is a personal right, not a group right," she ruled. "Laws classifying citizens by race pose a great threat to that right."

She added that the racial classifications the Court had previously upheld "can only exacerbate rather than reduce racial prejudice," and "will delay the time when race will become a truly irrelevant, or at least insignificant, factor."

Justice Scalia added that under the Constitution, the government can never have a "compelling interest" in penalizing one race to help another. "In the eyes of the government," he said, "we are just one race. It is American."

The Adarand decision also rebuked the Supreme Court's own ruling of 1990 (*Metro Broadcasts v. FCC*) which upheld the agency's affirmative action in awarding broadcasting licenses for female and minority-owned firms. It also cast doubt on the decision in *Fullilove v. Klutznik*, which upheld a federal program that set aside 10 percent of the value of government contracts for minority firms.

Some lower courts quickly picked up on the Adarand decision. In Los Angeles, just two months later, Superior Court Judge Dzintra Janavs declared unconstitutional the Metropolitan Transportation Authority's preference policy in getting contracts.

A white male San Diego engineer-contractor was denied a piece of the $5.8 billion subway project because the MTA was reserving 29 percent of the business for minorities and women.

It seems the MTA was not just handing out social charity, but wasting the public's money. The judge found there was no reason to allow preferred groups to bid up to 10 percent higher than others and still win the contract. "MTA's policy was discriminatory and a waste of taxpayer's money," the plaintiff's attorney said.

Much of this preference not only robs the taxpayers but supports companies that would otherwise go out of business. Without favoritism, they are not efficient enough to make it on their own.

Just before the Adarand decision, Governor Pete Wilson of California issued an Executive Order closing down all affirmative action in state contracting. Soon after, minority and women-owned firms felt the pinch of true competition, the natural law of commerce.

A woman-owned asbestos removal company suddenly came to a near halt. It had been getting thirty faxes a week from large contractors hoping to use the company in state-funded projects just to fulfill affirmative action "goals." Now, says the owner, her fax machine is no longer busy.

A woman general contractor in Wrightwood, California, says

that estimators for large companies used to eagerly solicit her, but now don't even answer her phone calls. The president of a trade organization of minority owners says that business is poor and "there is no way to count how many have gone out of business."

Is that bad? Of course not. Apparently the "leg up" is no preparation for the *realities* of the commercial world. It is reminiscent of firms in the former Soviet Union that stay in business only with subsidies from Moscow.

Washington has been in turmoil ever since the Adarand decision, hoping to salvage as much of the affirmative action–diversity program as it can. Assistant Attorney General Walter Dellinger has issued a thirty-seven-page memo to government general counsels, confessing that "many existing federal affirmative action programs are not specifically mandated by Congress."

But he makes it clear that affirmative action is far from dead, just that those programs should undergo "strict scrutiny" and there must be a "compelling government interest" in supporting them. (This is entertaining. The High Court, in effect, ruled that the Constitution is paramount, *unless* the government has a "compelling interest" in waiving it.)

Most important, Dellinger did explain that Congress, like state and local governments, *"may not predicate race-based remedial measures on generalized, historic societal discrimination."* Thus, supposedly no quotas.

But despite Adarand, the Court has still not fully conformed to the Constitution. It has left the door ajar for "narrow tailoring" affirmative action, an opening bureaucrats and admissions officers will use to keep afloat programs that should be closed.

There have been a few positive steps since Adarand. The FCC declared that they would no longer give "discounts" to women and minorities on wireless auction bids. Instead they will grant those preferences to small businesses, which one spokesman pointed out, might work out much the same way.

Many bad habits still linger in the federal government. Despite Adarand, the Transportation Department, which was the agency sued, gave Oregon officials the green light to continue a program in which all states are *encouraged* to set aside highway construction work for women and minority owners. As usual, lawlessness reigns in Washington.

What is needed is a simple definitive statement by the Supreme Court upholding the Fourteenth Amendment and declaring all affirmative action unconstitutional.

Only that will force governments, business, and schools to find ways other than race, ethnicity, and gender to help those individuals (not groups) who find it difficult to achieve in our complex society.

Not only the workplace, but our colleges as well, have been heavily involved in preferences in choosing one student over another for admission. As the Harvard dean pointed out, this has been going on apace ever since the Bakke decision of 1978.

Prior to that, there was another type of "affirmative action," the preferences given to the rich, the alumni children, and the graduates of such prestigious prep schools as Andover, Exeter, and Choate. With the new strength of academic achievement, including SAT scores and financial aid, college admission has become more democratic.

But "minority" preferences are just as skewed as the old patrician ones, and much more widespread. The first beneficiaries (and still the largest group) of affirmative action were women. Even though women score some 40 points lower than men in the SATs, they now occupy a *majority* of the places in our colleges.

The next step in affirmative action was affording preferences to students because of race or ethnic background—mainly blacks, Hispanics, and Native Americans. Despite their lower SATs, which fall behind white males by 100 in the case of African-Americans and 70 in the case of Hispanics, these groups have a higher rate of acceptance than any. Simultaneously (and perhaps there is a connection), the academic standards and curricula of our institutions of higher education have been substantially lowered.

The closing of "Western Civilization" courses, the implementation of such paper-thin subjects as African-American and Hispanic and Women's Studies, along with the elimination of such required subjects as literature and science are all hallmarks of the new ignorance that has come to campus. Is it related to affirmative action policy? In many ways it is, especially as preferences also increase ethnic and racial study programs and inject the divisive theories of multiculturalism and diversity into campus life, as we have seen.

Beginning on May 20, 1988, the Regents of the University of California codified its affirmative action program, stating that it "seeks to enroll on each of its campuses, a student body that . . . demonstrates high academic achievements . . . and encompasses broad diversity of cultural, racial, geographic and socio-economic backgrounds characteristic of California."

Fine sentiment. But a member of the Board of Regents of the University of California system (the largest in America with nine campuses and 162,000 students) explained how blatantly that affirmative action system was actually carried out. At the Irvine and Davis campuses, all "underrepresented [that word again] minorities" were automatically admitted. If you were white or Asian and had a perfect 4.0 grade average you could be turned away in favor of a black applicant with only a 2.8 high school average.

The affirmative minority admissions were often carried out with a secret point system, he explained. At UC San Diego, blacks, Hispanics, and Native Americans received an automatic 300-point bonus.

Point distinctions even put one minority ahead of another, placing racism on a statistical basis. At UCLA and Berkeley, the academic stars of the system, "Chicanos"—those of Mexican heritage—were favored, receiving 250 more points toward admission than a "Latino," a student from South or Central America.

Supposedly, California has since eliminated affirmative action in its top nine campuses by order of the Board of Regents. Henceforth, from 50 to 75 percent of the students will be chosen "solely" on the basis of academic achievements. That is still much less than the original aim of the University of California, which was to be the mecca for the best brains in the state. In addition to the up-to-50 percent of students being chosen for other criteria, six percent can be admitted without even meeting the original cut-off, to be in the top 12.5 percent of high school graduates.

I say that affirmative action will "supposedly" be eliminated because many officials at the University fear the change, which is scheduled for 1998, and will seek ways around it. They have developed a projection, at which they tremble, which shows that if *academics* are fully taken into account, that Asians, who now make up 43 percent of the student body, would jump to well over 50 percent, while whites, who now make up 30 percent, will rise to 35 percent. Meanwhile, Hispanics would be cut down from 15 to 6 percent, and African-Americans from 6.5 to 2 percent. If they institute "socio-economic" preferences instead of race and ethnicity, it would be somewhat better for the minorities, if not as "affirmative" as at present.

The most important aspect of the whole incident is that the university officials should not shudder at the new prospect. Perhaps they shouldn't be counting at all, but concentrating instead on colorblind, gender blind and ethnic blind higher education, the true goal of academe.

Professional schools are prime participants in affirmative action as well. Not only on behalf of women, as we have seen in medical schools, but also for minorities. A spokesman for the Association of American Medical Colleges (AAMC) frankly admitted its bias for affirmative action, apparently even if these would-be doctors are less qualified than others for that life-and-death job.

The AAMC view is backed up by its report, *Minority Students in Medical Education,* which opens by defining a new category of future doctors as "URM," or "Under-Represented Minority" students. The implication is that the medical profession should have the same proportion of racial, gender, and ethnic groups as Americans in general, regardless of their qualifications. Hardly a rational view of medical practice.

Leapfrogging from that dangerous assumption, the report profiles the URM students: lower grades in college and lower scores on the MCAT (Medical College Admission Test) by a factor of 30 percent—too low to guarantee that they can properly practice medicine. Yet minority students have a greater rate of admission than higher-scoring applicants.

From 1990 to 1995, mainly because of affirmative action, the ranks of female medical students have grown annually until they now make up 43 percent of the student body. The number of blacks grew by 26 percent, Native American medical students by 81 percent, and Mexican-Americans by 60 percent.

And white male students? Their drop has been precipitous, and continues in a downward spiral.

Did these minority doctors-to-be come from poor families who take the brunt of lowered opportunity? Hardly. AAMC figures show that the *average* annual income of "URM" minority families was $61,952. Surely not the downtrodden of the inner city.

But if minorities come into medicine with lower credentials, won't they flunk out? No. As we have seen, entrance into medical school virtually assures an M.D. degree and a license to practice.

The charity is evident, but the concept of "underrepresented minorities" smacks of racism.

Something of the same order also takes place at law schools. At the University of Texas Law School, four white students who were rejected sued the school, claiming their places had been taken by less qualified minority students.

The conflict began in 1992, when fifty-five Mexican-Americans and forty-one African-Americans were admitted into the first-year law class at Texas. An internal school memo showed that they had lower college GPAs (Grade Point Average) and lower LSAT (Law School Admissions Test) scores than other students. Without affirmative action only a third of those students would have been admitted.

The "Hopwood Case," named after Cheryl Hopwood, one of the plaintiffs, was heard in federal district court in an eight-day trial. The University of Texas rallied its allies—the deans of several law schools including Michigan and Stanford—who testified in favor of affirmative action.

The federal government pitched in as well in the presence of Kenneth Ashworth, the Commissioner of Higher Education of the Department of Education. He advised the court that the school *had* to admit those students under a discrimination "consent decree" with Washington signed in 1983.

In August 1994, the judge, Sam Sparks, hedged his philosophical bets and seemed to come out for both sides, simultaneously. Yes, he admitted, the University of Texas program did discriminate against the white students in violation of the Fourteenth Amendment.

Did that end it? No. New Establishment ideas had infiltrated his mind, and thus the court. While ruling that affirmative action was probably unconstitutional, he declared that the law school could continue its policy.

Said the flexible judge: "Until society sufficiently overcomes the effects of its lengthy history of pervasive racism, affirmative action is necessary."

(An interesting sociological comment, but hardly the opinion of a jurist. Was there a history of turning away *high-scoring* blacks and Hispanics from law school admission? Apparently not.)

The disappointed white students appealed to the Fifth U.S. Circuit Court of Appeals, the body just below the Supreme Court in Texas, Louisiana, and Oklahoma. In March 1996, the three-judge panel issued its decision. Dramatically, the judges reversed the Sparks' ruling. Affirmative action in law school admission was declared a violation of legal rights under the Constitution.

"I was really quite surprised," said Robert Berdahl, president of the University of Texas. "I think everybody was."

The first clear-cut decision for the Fourteenth Amendment sent the academic community into shock. But since the U.S. Circuit Court only covered those three states, it was the "law of the land" only there.

The Attorney General of Georgia, for one, issued a "recommendation" that considering the Adarand case and the Texas law school decision, race should not be a crucial factor in admitting students to the state's 206,000-student public college system. He was quickly rebuked by the black chairwoman of the state's Board of Regents. "The ruling that he refers to in the Fifth Circuit," she reminded him, "applies only to Texas, Louisiana and Mississippi, not to us."

The next step was up to the Supreme Court, to whom the University appealed for relief. Meanwhile, Drew S. Days, Solicitor General of the United States, filed a brief asking the Court to hear the case.

Admissions offices, government agencies, and businesses everywhere waited for its decision with bated breath. *But, once again, the Court system failed.* If they were to follow the Constitution, the Nine August Ones knew they would have to support the Appeals Court judges in Texas and declare all affirmative action based on race, ethnicity, and sex as being unconstitutional.

What did they do? On July 1, 1996, they announced that they would "pass"—they would not hear the case at all.

What does that signify about the High Court? Surely its confusion, even cowardice. It means that affirmative action is illegal in three states by order of the court, and in California by order of Proposition 209—if that is ever enforced. But it also means that it will probably be ignored in forty-six states. Only in America.

Most courts are obedient to New Establishment dogma, but when they act otherwise, as in the Hopwood case, they tend to be brushed aside. Byron A. Wiley, who runs "social equity" for the state schools in Pennsylvania, believes the Appeals Court decision, if liberally interpreted, still "makes it possible to proceed (with affirmative action) absolutely as we have before."

The federal government, which disapproves of the Hopwood decision, has decided to ignore the ruling of its own court, a brazenness unprecedented in pre-New Establishment days. In March, 1997, the Department of Education issued a warning to Texas, that they must ignore the order of the federal court, or else. *If the state of Texas were to obey the decision of the federal Court of Appeals in favor of the white students in the Hopwood case, they said it would lose all its federal higher education money!*

Intimidation, even if it violates law, is a favorite New Establishment tool. Despite the court order, the Department of Education in Washington insists that Texas *must continue affirmative action as before* or lose the $500 million in federal grants in federal student scholarships, work study programs, and research grants.

Is affirmative action worth it? Should the proponents continue to press their argument that social charity is more important than the Constitution? Is it necessary to flout the real law to help those who are not competing effectively, for whatever reason?

That's a philosophical, not a legal, question. The program has been a great success for women, giving them an unequal advantage over men in virtually every area of life. It has placed many women in colleges and medical, legal, engineering, and other professional academies, where they would never otherwise have been admitted.

Affirmative action has been less of a success for African-American and Hispanic students. But it has helped a *few*, generally the more affluent, who would never have entered our better colleges—from Harvard to Stanford—without it.

In response to the two arguments for affirmative action, there are at least nine arguments against it:

1. Affirmative action for women and minorities has turned federal judges into arbiters of philosophy and dispensers of personal bias rather than interpreters of the written law, their true role. This is dangerous and gravely injures the whole judicial system.

2. Most of the achievement charity goes to the middle and upper middle class, even to the rich, not to those who truly need a "leg up."

3. It gives minority students a false impression of life—that preferences can replace study and dedication. The few places in prestige schools granted minorities are less important than the situation that most never attend any college. According to the Department of Education, only 3 percent of bachelor's degrees go to African-American men, half the number in proportion to their population.

4. Affirmative action is unfair. Places denied to ambitious young white males, as in the Bakke case, invite a sense of inequality that is disturbing to the national ethos, setting up rivalry and conflict between races, ethnic groups and genders.

5. Schools alter and reduce their curricula and lower their grading standards to accommodate affirmative action students. A college degree means less and less each day.

6. Affirmative action helps create a harsh campus atmosphere in which racial, ethnic, and sexual identities are exaggerated, making assimilation into the majority culture that much more difficult.

7. It breeds disrespect for the law and weakens the competitive merit system on which this nation operates—or used to operate.

8. It gives women an unfair advantage over men in school placement and subsequent success in life.

9. It is blatantly unconstitutional.

What then should we do?

The first step would be to amend all the Civil Rights Acts and Executive Orders from 1964 onward to make it clear that one form of discrimination cannot substitute for another.

The next step is for the Supreme Court Justices to hear *Hopwood v. Texas* and rule on the Appeals Court decision that affirmative action in public colleges is unconstitutional. Once they do, they have no choice but to rule that the Fourteenth Amendment protects *everyone,* closing all preferences in public institutions and in many private ones as well.

(Harvard, Yale, and Princeton, all believers in affirmative action, might claim they are not *public* institutions, which, of course, is nonsense. They receive huge sums of federal money for research grants, overhead, and aid to medical education, for starters, plus a fortune in government-guaranteed loans for their students.)

Another route for reform is being offered by Congressman Charles Canady of Florida, who is proposing a bill he calls the "Equal Opportunity Act of 1997." It seeks to enact "a prohibition against discrimination and preferential treatment in federal contracts or subcontracts, federal employment, or any other federally conducted program or activity."

Affirmative action must be ended if America is to move ahead with greater opportunity, initiative, education, and assimilation for all. Representation by groups, no matter how attractive it may sound, is a noxious racist and sexist concept that violates everything American.

Representation in any field must be determined by individual skill and its acceptance in the marketplace of commerce and ideas, and cannot be either fixed or counted by race or gender. If by using good nondiscriminatory standards *every* physician turns out to be an Asian or Jewish man, that is not just acceptable, but ideal. The same is true of female elementary school teachers in lower grades, or Korean vegetable dealers.

Nor is affirmative action simply a case of "common decency," as New Establishment propagandists would have us believe. That is a misreading of the Judeo-Christian ethic on which we stand, which demands fairness for *all*.

If affirmative action is ended, what would replace it?

For women, their natural abilities and determination will suffice, though they will have to face increased male competition for places in college, medical school, law school, government contracting work, and business, instead of enjoying their present favored position.

As Laura A. Ingraham, a lawyer and board member of the Independent Women's Forum says, enough is enough. Pointing out that over 40 percent of all middle management positions are now held by women, she believes that continued affirmative action would be "patronizing." By demanding real, not rigged, competition in every profession, she says, "women would fulfill the real goal of feminism."

Whatever one's race or sex, individuals should have the right to achieve to the highest level of their ability. But group statistics and underrepresentation, which demean the efforts of the individual, carry us just one more step down the primrose path of cultural stupidity and eventual destruction.

But what about African-Americans and Hispanics, who lag behind the rest of the nation? How can they achieve the American dream without affirmative action?

The way the European immigrants did—by *Education*. Despite such New Establishment campus nonsense as ethnic and women's studies, coed bathrooms and segregated dorms, and PC in general, higher education is still the best route for assimilation into the majority Anglo-American culture. Educated people, whatever their race or gender, have more in common with each other than they do with the uneducated of their own group.

There are some positive signs in that direction, though affirmative action is not one of them. African-Americans are approaching whites in the percentage graduating from high school, and those African-Americans in Catholic parochial schools (a holdout from New Establishment orthodoxy) are surpassing the graduation rate of whites in public high schools.

The problem is that black males, particularly, lag far behind whites in college attendance and graduation. Affirmative action has helped some middle- and upper-income African-Americans, but as Professor Loury of Boston has pointed out, it has not reached the mass of minorities in the inner cities where assimilation into the Anglo-American ethic is weakest, unemployment and negative social factors strongest.

How can that be changed without affirmative action?

The African-American community itself must make a decision for education, much as an evangelist might make for religion. The youth need to become *compulsively* involved in schooling, eschewing sports figures as role models. Instead, these students must concentrate on such individuals as Colin Powell, who graduated CCNY without affirmative action. Hispanic youth need to do the same, seeking out similar models who have successfully emerged from the barrio and assimilated into the majority American culture.

But there's a grave problem that must be faced. Too many young African-Americans view full assimilation as a "sell-out," as a yielding to "Uncle Tom–ism," and therefore a defeat. In the Hispanic community, where things un-Spanish are not fashionable, there is a similar self-destructive impulse. In the final analysis there is only one successful culture, and that is the Anglo-American Judeo-Christian model that founded the nation.

One can *pretend* that there are alternative lifestyles, as does the New Establishment, but that's a sociological fantasy, especially in a high-tech era. Even when minority spokesmen condemn the Eurocentric experience, they usually do it in the best of English and with historic references to Western ideals.

To open the route to full assimilation and success, the path to college must be widened. Not through affirmative action, but through access.

The good public high school of old, in which standards were high, is a thing of the past. The present secondary school is not academic enough, not disciplined enough, and too involved in New Establishment nonsense.

To reproduce the high school experience of old (which was once the passport to Americanization and work) now requires at least a two-year community college. We should view that as the natural, automatic extension of high school, and the future basic education for all youngsters.

This suggestion does not require affirmative action. Most community colleges are *required* to accept all high school graduates. The problem is twofold: money and motivation, which go hand-in-hand. High school is free, but the tuition at community colleges is rising, not dropping. The Manhattan Community College in New York costs $2,500 a year, plus books, travel, etc. For a poor eighteen-year-old, often without a father at home, the tuition is not only too expensive, the cost destroys the motivation to even make the decision to proceed with higher education.

The success of a free institution of higher learning is clear. That is shown by the story of the City College of New York, whose graduates now rank first in the number of corporate chief executive officers. For over a century, it was open to the brightest of the poor, with no means test, at absolutely no cost, except for $2 for the General Organization pass. (Had it been $10 at the height of the Depression, some families might have been deterred.)

That same model could be adopted for all community colleges, a system that would funnel minority youngsters automatically from high school into a *free* two-year higher education experience, which they can either accept or reject.

At first glance, the idea seems unfair. Why should one group of people receive special attention such as *free* community college while other families must pay, and other students often work, to gain the same advantage?

The answer is simple. Today's public high schools are so abysmal and so mired in psychobabble and educational bureaucratic stupidity that they mainly de-educate black and Hispanic youngsters, especially in not providing a learning base for proper English usage and diction. The schools excessively honor the subculture and its liabilities. Instead they should rigorously try to replace them with stronger mainstream academic and cultural values, much as the schools did in assimilating the enormous immigration beginning in the 1890s.

How bad is the present education? Judge for yourself by looking at John F. Kennedy High School in the Bronx, the largest secondary school in the New York City system, with 5,000 students, most of whom are black or Hispanics. While 500 is the national norm on the SATs in verbal, the Kennedy average is 335 on the verbal. That low score defies analysis since the student receives 200 points just for signing his or her name. Such a performance is almost a sure passport to later failure.

That situation—unless the educational establishment is replaced, which is politically unlikely—is not rectifiable. The minority student population has to find another route to education. Where is that possible? In the local two-year community college, where the instructors are academics and not graduates of the infantile "education" establishment.

New Establishment or not, college faculty do not look at students the way "educators" do. They are seen as youngsters to be taught, without excuses or condescension, rather than "victims" to be saved.

But should everyone receive this free two year college instruction, as some have suggested? Obviously not. Two criteria should be set up: (1) Screening exam, or good high school grades, which would indicate that they can benefit from college work (2) Inability of the family to pay the tuition.

Surely it is not a cure-all (that must come from a cultural change in inner-city attitudes), but it can become a ladder out of ghetto failure.

The cost to society? Substantial, but cheap in comparison to that of crime and social welfare. The burden should be borne by a consortium of the federal government, the states, the cities, and private philanthropy. In fact, the $12 billion a year federal subsidy to schools for the present ineffective Chapter I and II programs for disadvantaged children could easily be shuffled to the support of community college education for the same youngsters with far greater returns.

Education and assimilation, not achievement charity for the few, is the key to enrolling *everyone* into the American experience.

The present system of affirmative action, which is exploited by the New Establishment (no true friend of minorities), is not only a failure, but a deception that promises much but keeps most of the underclass in its current unsatisfactory condition.

In this era, we face an extraordinary choice: either to advance people mainly because of race or sex or ethnicity, which will eventually debilitate the entire system, or to raise millions to new heights of *earned* achievement.

In the short run, charity is always the easier choice. But there are no shortcuts, as we have seen with the infamous debacle of government welfare. In the long run, only gains through study, merit and greater opportunity can create, and maintain, a superior society for all.

CHAPTER EIGHT

THE NEW IMMIGRATION

The Plot Against the Europeans

RECENTLY, ON A CRUISE ON WHICH I WAS LEC-turing, a young Frenchwoman was telling me about her enormous desire to immigrate to America and become a citizen. Young, attractive, and a college graduate, she seemed like a perfect immigrant. But she was frustrated, having waited three years without success. She had applied at the American Embassy at Paris, but was not encouraged.

It seemed she lacked the right credentials for entry into America. She had no family here with whom she could be reunited, and she had no crucial skill like engineering. She was working in the ship's store, which was as close as she could get to America.

"But isn't there a quota for French citizens?" I asked, reminded how many of the French, from the Huguenots who founded New Rochelle to the settlers of New Orleans, Detroit, and Saint Louis, had enriched America.

She laughed at the question. "No, there is no French quota anymore. It's almost impossible for a French person to become an immigrant to America," she said. "I have just about given up."

"Then why not just get off the boat when it reaches Fort Lauderdale and disappear in the crowd?" I asked, playing the devil's advocate and knowing that some 200,000 illegals did that each year at America's airports. "Illegals just come here as tourists—and stay, and stay."

This time her demeanor became more serious. "No, I wouldn't do that. It's immoral, and I wouldn't want to begin life in your country as a criminal. I suppose I'll never get to live in America unless I win the immigration lottery."

So a moral, intelligent, educated Frenchwoman could not become an American, I mused.

Meanwhile, it is obvious that the nation's cities are flooded with new immigrants, legal and illegal, from the Third World—Mexico, the Caribbean, Central America, China, India, Pakistan, Korea, the Philippines, and elsewhere. So why not France?

I mentioned that to an official of the Immigration and Naturalization Service who responded: "I don't know, but I suppose now that Europe is doing well, they don't want to come to America anymore."

That sounded reasonable and in fact, that is the current consensus in the media, at fashionable cocktail parties, and even in barbershops where people shake their heads about the changing demographics of America.

They watch the march of non-European immigrants into America and assume it's true. America had just better get used to the idea that the European base will soon be overwhelmed by immigrants from Asia and Latin America—what some call "The Third Worldism of America."

As demographers tell us, the European base that founded America and established its mores is changing so rapidly that by the year 2040, European-Americans—from the Anglos to the Irish to Germans to the Poles to the Jews—will become a minority if major changes are not made quickly.

However, as I learned, the lack of Europeans wanting to come here is a total myth. The reality is that millions of Europeans want very much to come to America, but they have been locked out by our convoluted, nonsensical, biased immigration laws.

Over the last thirty years, through a series of little-noticed "reforms," the federal government has made the Third World poor the primary market for immigration. Courtesy of our politicians and bureaucrats, they have frozen out the educated middle class and workers of Europe. If one wants to give way to just the slightest touch of paranoia, it's possible to see the fine Machiavellian, multicultural hand of the New Establishment at work.

How do we know that Europeans are being discriminated against? Isn't that just another case of misplaced, perhaps wish-fulfilling Eurocentrism?

First, let's look at the present immigration numbers to see the enormous disparity in favor of Third World immigrants. In the last fiscal year available, the totals are as follows:

Of 804,000 legal immigrants, only 160,916 came from Europe, with the former Soviet Union leading with 63,420, and Poland second with 28,048. Meanwhile there were 292,589 from Asia, and most of the rest of 350,000 from Mexico, the Caribbean, and Latin America.

The enormous change in immigration can be easily seen in the trends of the current century. Between 1901 and 1920, when entry into this country was at its peak, most of the immigration came from Italy, the Austro-Hungarian empire (including the present Austria, Hungary, Czechoslovakia, and Yugoslavia), Russia, Canada, and the United Kingdom.

From 1921 to 1940, the three leading nations of origin were Canada, Germany, and Italy, all now minor players.

And today? The leading nation is Mexico, with 111,000 legal immigrants, followed by the Philippines, then by China (both Mainland and Taiwan), Korea, and Vietnam. In fact, just those five nations account for half of all new Americans. *No European country is included in these top five.*

The Europeans are obviously outweighed four to one by other nations—just the inverse of the American population. But, you may ask, how can you say that they want to come here but are excluded?

What is the evidence?

It has existed in the Immigration and Naturalization Service statistics all along, but no one has noticed. I stumbled on it by asking questions about the "lottery"—the last chance ferry to America—that the young Frenchwoman spoke about.

Each year, a certain number of permanent resident visas is reserved for a postcard lottery open to all nations except those with the most current immigrants. It is done, the government says almost apologetically, as a way of compensating "countries that Congress determined to be adversely affected by the Immigration and Nationality Act Amendments of 1965," the law that destroyed America's successful immigration policy.

Fifty-five thousand spots are reserved, for which *7.6 million people* applied by postcard through the State Department offices around the world. But, as the INS assumes, there were probably few Europeans—who are ostensibly content to stay home— among them.

Nonsense. Quite the opposite is true. *Of the massive volume of postcards in the lottery, some 3.5 million actually came from Europeans,* not counting the United Kingdom, which with Canada, was not eligible. That outpouring of applications from Europe to come and live in America is so large that it represents the *total number of immigrants* we take in from all over the world in four years! In France, for example, some 70,000 people applied to become American immigrants, but we take in only 3,000 a year.

Obviously, if we were to return to the old system based on the ethnic makeup of the nation, we would have an immigration flood of Europeans that would almost match that of the turn of the century.

As many Americans worry about the future, the question of

immigration has become central to their concerns. Except for Native Americans, the United States is obviously a nation of immigrants, and any opposition to continued immigration is a thorny issue. But as the composition of the immigrant group changes dramatically, many worry about the future ethnic makeup of the nation. Is it swinging too drastically away from the European core that made it great? Can the new immigrants be as easily absorbed into our Anglo-American culture?

How much of the fear about the new immigration is well-founded and how much of it is the result of paranoia?

The trigger for the dissatisfaction is threefold:

1. That the ethnic mix of new immigrants has been heavily skewed away from Europeans toward Mexicans, Latin Americans, Asians, and those of Caribbean origin.

2. Of the legal immigrants who arrive here, too many are not an asset to the nation, but have instead become a financial burden to taxpayers.

3. That the invasion of *illegal* immigrants is costing us billions and bringing in too many people who are uneducated and find it difficult to assimilate.

In some regard, all three fears are reasonable.

The ethnic shift in immigration has been a dramatic one. During 1861 to 1880, over five million immigrants arrived here, most still from the three major sources: Great Britain, Germany, and Ireland. In just those two decades, as many new people arrived here as in the entire history of the Republic prior to the Civil War.

Before 1882, immigration to American shores was virtually wide open. People literally got off the boat and were "Americans," if not yet citizens. The first laws barred prostitutes. Then, the Immigrant Act of 1882 gave the Secretary of the Treasury further control, including restrictions against convicts, mental defectives, and paupers. A head tax of fifty cents per person was imposed on immigrants. That same year, Congress passed the Chinese Exclusion Act, which was not repealed until World War II.

Immigration reached 5,246,613 in the decade of 1881–1890, almost half of whom were still immigrants from Great Britain, Germany, and Ireland. But by the turn of the century, the mix had changed.

By the first decade of the twentieth century, 1901–1910, most immigrants came from Italy, Austro-Hungary, Poland, and Russia, including millions of Jews. That decade broke all records: 8,795,386 new Americans came to these shores, flocking to the cities and into the new factories as America became an industrial giant.

The doors were still relatively wide open, until February 5, 1917, when Congress passed the first significant restriction on immigration. It was a literacy test in the immigrant's own language, which had been passed by Congress several times but vetoed by Presidents Cleveland, Taft, and Wilson. But that February, a worried Congress overrode Wilson's veto by a large margin.

The next step was to put in numerical limitations, which was done in three stages, in 1921, 1924, and finally in 1929. Immigration from the Western Hemisphere—from Canada to Argentina—was unrestricted. But aside from that, the new laws set up quotas for each country based on the number of its former nationals then living in America. Statistically, that favored Europeans.

But immigration was tapering off by itself. The U.S. Depression discouraged migration from Europe, its major source. From over 4 million in the 1920s, immigration dropped to 528,000 in the 1930s, the lowest influx in our history since the 1820s.

The new exodus from the victims of Hitler would have been enormous, but Congress turned many away. Only 250,000 refugees of Nazism were permitted to enter the country. After World War II, we took in 400,000 "displaced persons," but total immigration in the 1940s was only 1 million.

In 1952, the immigration code was revised again, but it still basically maintained the "National Origins" quotas, which favored Europeans. It also allowed citizens and permanent resident aliens to bring in their close relatives. In that decade of the 1950s, immigration picked up with 2.5 million coming in.

In the 1950s, another category of legal immigration was enlarged—refugees from war-torn Europe and from the Cold War: those fleeing newly Communized countries in Eastern Europe, followed by refugees from the Hungarian uprising, then 700,000 refugees escaping from Castro's Cuba.

The great change in immigration took place in 1965 and was the father of the present push for Multiculturalism and Diversity. Just as the European integration into the Anglo ethic had been virtually completed, the rules were dramatically revised.

Europe, which had been favored under the quota system, was no longer favored. In fact, it was heavily discriminated against. Immigrants from Mexico, the Caribbean, Latin America, and Asia took their place instead.

The method was simple. The "national origin" system was totally abolished by the Immigration and Nationality Act of 1965, passed by the 89th Congress and signed into law by President Lyndon Johnson. The new method was termed "family unification," but the reality was that the new immigrants who arrived in America after that—and in the following thirty years—no longer looked like America.

It was a program that heavily discriminated against Europeans, and a significant early victory for the New Establishment.

As the INS itself says about the effect of that law, one that is still dramatically changing the American sociological landscape: "The major source of immigration to the United States has shifted since 1965 from Europe to Latin America and Asia, reversing the trend of nearly two centuries."

Let's take a look at the numbers in two periods, one prior to 1965—the swing year—and one after it. In the full decade of 1951–1960, there were only 2.5 million legal immigrants, of which 1.7 million were from Europe or Canada, or more than 70 percent, a solid reflection of the American population.

Since then America has been flooded with Third World immigrants. During the 1981–1990 decade, there were over seven million immigrants, the largest number since the turn of the century.

Equally dramatic has been the change in the nations of origin. The Europeans and Canadians suddenly became much less important feeders into the immigration stream. Of the 7.3 million immigrants in the 1980s, less than 1 million, or only 13 percent, came from those traditional areas—a drop from the 70 percent of thirty years before.

The INS adds:

"In fiscal year 1988, Asia was highest at 41 percent, followed by North America (mainly Mexico) at 39 percent, and Europe at 10 percent." The leading countries? Mexico, the Philippines, Haiti, Korea, India, Mainland China, the Dominican Republic, Vietnam, and Jamaica.

All in all, a fertile field for the advancement of the New Establishment's concept of a Multicultural America.

Protests against the 1965 policy flooded Congress as immigration reached new heights. FAIR, the Federation of Americans for Immigration Reform, states that at the present rate, immigration in the 1990s will reach some 13 million, surpassing even the giant migration at the turn of the century.

The reasons are twofold: The 1965 law, which instituted "family reunification," became the trigger for vastly increased immigration, especially of those with less education and fewer skills. And despite protests, the next law, the Immigration Act of 1990, actually resulted in an *increase* in the total number of immigrants by some 40 percent, most of them from Third World countries.

(Family reunification was of little value to most Americans of European origin. On average they have been here some eighty years and their families are long since reunified or dead.)

The increase of 1990 was created by expanding the number

of immediate family members allowed to join legal immigrants in this country. How many people per immigrant. Two? Five? No, the number is in fact *unlimited*. This has caused a deluge of immigration from Third World countries where large families are commonplace.

To respond to citizen protests, a Commission on Immigration Reform was named by the White House and chaired by former Congresswoman Barbara Jordan of Texas. It recommended that legal immigration be cut by one-third.

In the Congress, Senator Alan Simpson of Wyoming and Congressman Lamar Smith of Texas tried to implement the recommendation, but they were rebuffed. Their hope was that both the number of immigrants and the categories of family members who could automatically join them here would be reduced. But it never happened. In 1996, Congress and the President refused to act.

In our immigration law, the words *families* and *relatives* do not refer only to nuclear families. Instead, the law defines it in broad linguistic strokes. Today, all legal immigrants can automatically, without any limit on the number, bring in spouses and minor children, who are considered "immediate family."

But once immigrants becomes citizens, they can bring more distant relatives into the country as well. At that point, the "reunification" law permits them to bring in parents, adult children, and even brothers and sisters! In fact, in 1994, brothers and sisters of former immigrants accounted for 65,000 new Americans.

Thus for every immigrant, one can count perhaps six to ten, or more, new Americans in one generation, then considerably more in the next. It is an asinine, irrational, destructive immigration system with both expected and unexpected drawbacks.

One drawback is the cost of legal immigrants, something we didn't count on. Supposedly, immigrants are sponsored by citizens who swear to take care of them financially. But that turns out to be mainly a myth. Older parents who go on SSI Social Security and unwed mothers on AFDC and a host of other programs put legal immigrants on some variation of the dole that is currently burdening state and federal governments.

FAIR shows that immigrants actually receive far more government charity than citizens who pay the bill. While 14 percent of citizens are below the poverty line, immigrants have a 29 percent poverty level. If we take into account *all* welfare programs, from AFDC to SSI to Food Stamps to Housing and School Lunches, immigrants receive 47 percent more aid than citizens!

One report shows that one-fourth of all immigrants from Vietnam go on welfare, as do nearly one-half of those from Cambodia. This is considerably more than the 14 percent of African-American citizens on the welfare rolls.

Another drawback to excessive immigration was pointed out by the Presidential Commission headed by Barbara Jordan. It is that large-scale immigration is depressing the wages of American citizens.

We now have strong statistical proof of that theory—especially its negative effect on African-American workers who are being pushed out of the low-skilled jobs by immigrants.

Since the 1970s, the income gap between educated Americans and high school dropouts has risen by more than 50 percent. Part of the reason is the competition between native-born Americans and immigrants for unskilled jobs. According to economics professor George Borjas of the University of California, a third of the inequality is caused by the downward wage pressure on American workers from immigrants willing to work for less.

In Dallas, the Federal Reserve Bank concurs. The reason for unusually high unemployment in cities like Laredo and El Paso, they say, is the immigration to border cities of Texas from Mexico.

Another drawback is that the major abusers of welfare and other social services are the least deserving immigrants—*illegals* who sneak across the border or overstay their visitors' visa, then quickly latch onto federal and state social services, from welfare to hospitalization.

That has reached epidemic proportions in a dozen states, especially California, Florida, New York, Illinois, Texas, and nearby Arizona and New Mexico, a trend staunchly supported by the New Establishment.

Thirty percent of all students in the Los Angeles school system are now children of illegal immigrants. The welfare rolls and hospital use by immigrants has so skyrocketed that California estimates its own costs at $3 billion a year, with national estimates of up to $15 billion.

Crime by illegals is far out of proportion to the citizen population. In 1980, our prisons housed 9,000 criminal aliens. And today? Over 53,000, a 500 percent increase. In fact, there are 450,000 criminal aliens in prisons, on probation, or on parole nationwide. So rapid is their growth that criminal aliens now make up one-fourth of all federal prison inmates. After they complete their sentences, they're supposed to be deported. But that process has become a legal joke.

The INS gives criminal aliens 72 hours to surrender for deportation but New York City reports that 87 percent of criminal aliens just disappear into the countryside.

Illegal immigration continues to grow as economic conditions in Third World countries worsen, especially in Mexico right on our border, which has recently suffered a painful currency devaluation.

It is also rising because of several failures by the American government:

1. The permissive attitude of the New Establishment, which plays on the "guilt" of successful Americans to excuse illegal immigration.
2. The inability of the INS to stop illegals at the border.
3. The failure of outraged citizens to get any real relief from New Establishment–influenced courts, even when they pass legislation to remedy the situation.

Is it important? One would think so.

FAIR estimates that there are five million illegal immigrants now residing in the United States. To this five million, we must add three million more illegals (plus their expanded families) who came here illegally but were granted "amnesty" and permanent residence, then eventual citizenship, under the Immigration Act of 1986.

The "amnesty" concept for illegals only encourages Mexicans and others to gain entrance to America in any way possible, knowing that it will someday, somehow, pay off.

Each year, the INS figures show that over a million illegals crossing over from Mexico are apprehended and sent back. But the border is still hopelessly porous. Detentions of illegals rose some 50 percent in 1996, but the INS admits that for every illegal caught, at least another eventually makes it successfully into America.

The failure of the border patrol in stopping the mass migration of Mexicans has a few exceptions, particularly in El Paso, Texas. There, the border patrol chief, Silvestre Reyes, developed a new theory, one that reversed the INS technique of apprehension *after* the fact. Reyes decided to stop illegals *before* they got into America. By stationing 400 agents one hundred yards apart from one end of El Paso to the other, and beyond, he virtually dried up the traffic in illegals. Before the blockade, hundreds of Mexicans a day would wade across the Rio Grande, then melt into the city's Hispanic neighborhoods.

One would think his success would be heralded by Washington. Instead, they were confused, even angered. If other border areas stopped illegals before they entered the States, how could the INS show that they "detained" over a million a year? "We got caught behind the curve," an executive assistant commissioner of the INS confessed.

The INS was embarrassed by complaints from the Mexican government, from Mexican-American pressure groups, and even from officials in their own agency. Reyes showed that they had needlessly been (and still are) ineffective and the bureaucracy didn't like it.

"He showed Washington that you can control the border," said an INS official in Los Angeles. To this day, there is conflict within the government about stopping illegals before they get here, but Reyes' obvious answer to our sieve-like border is *beginning* to catch on.

One of the great rackets benefiting illegals, and a continuing magnet to inspire them to break through our borders, is a misinterpretation of the Constitution by the courts that is costing us billions of dollars each year. Its toll will be even greater in the future—in added crime, failure of assimilation, and in the strength added to the New Establishment's injurious dogma of Multiculturalism.

It is rather unthinkable but true. A child born to a pregnant illegal immigrant is not only not deported back to the country of origin with the mother, but the baby automatically becomes a citizen of the United States!

Is it a serious problem, perhaps involving as many as ten thousand new infant citizens a year?

Think again. Last year, in California alone, 100,000 children of illegal alien mothers became automatic citizens, and probably some 250,000 nationwide.

Mexicans may not be able to read English, but they understand that if they can manage to give birth on this side of the border, they will have hit the American welfare jackpot. The result? Three-fourths of all the children born in the San Diego County Hospital, and some two-thirds of all births in the public hospitals of Los Angeles County, are to mothers who are illegal immigrants, generally from Mexico.

When they are ready to give birth, these illegals present themselves at the hospital for delivery of the child. The next morning, the nurse brings the mother and the infant down to the social worker and testifies that the child was born at the hospital and is therefore automatically an American citizen. The social worker then declares the child eligible for AFDC welfare and arranges for benefits, which include a sizable monthly cash payment, plus food stamps for the new American.

For the once-impoverished mother, who is often unmarried, her baby is a no-lose lottery ticket that will pay off for years.

As the mother of a new American, she can also apply for housing aid, either in a "project," or with a cash voucher that she can exchange for rent. And she will receive WIC, extra nutrition for an infant child and mother in the form of vouchers, or even food baskets delivered to her home.

The hospital bill of $3,000 is automatically paid by taxpayers through Medi-Cal, the local version of Medicaid, with the cost being split between Californians and us all, from Bangor to Biloxi. Meanwhile the mother, who might otherwise be reported to the INS and deported as an illegal alien, is instead given permanent residency, since she is the mother of an American!

(In cases where the father is known, he too is generally given immigration protection.)

When the child grows up, he or she can use the citizenship granted at birth to "reunite" the family in America under the 1965 Immigration Act. They can bring in parents, adult children, brothers, and sisters and make the once "illegal" mother and father quite legal and future citizens. Then they can also bring in their extended family, what the INS refers to as "Chain Immigration" with no theoretical end point.

Bizarre? Absolutely. And all this because of a sexual encounter in Mexico some nine months before.

It is even worse than we believe, says Constitutional scholar Professor Peter Schuck of Yale University Law School, because none of it is necessary. He is convinced that it is all a legal mistake to begin with. Children born here of illegal immigrant parents *should not legally be automatic American citizens* no matter what our ignorant New Establishment courts may say.

Schuck, who lays out his opposition in his volume *Citizenship*

Without Consent: Illegal Aliens in American Polity, says that the present practice is a misinterpretation of the Constitution. The basis for the decision to grant citizenship to children born here to illegals is supposedly the Fourteenth Amendment, which was passed in 1868 in order to grant citizenship to freed slaves.

It says absolutely nothing about illegal immigrants. The amendment merely states that it applies to people "subject to the jurisdiction thereof of the United States." This could hardly apply to illegal immigrants for three reasons:

1. They are citizens of another country, subject to that nation's jurisdiction.
2. They were not invited into the United States and came here illegally.
3. There were no illegal immigrants in 1868, when the Fourteenth Amendment was passed and our borders were totally open. Therefore the Amendment could hardly apply to a nonexistent situation.

In addition, the Fourteenth Amendment has been declared by prior courts to be *exclusionary* rather than *inclusionary*. In fact, the Supreme Court ruled several times in the nineteenth century that Native Americans owed their allegiance to their tribal authorities, and were not "subject to the jurisdiction of the United States" and were not therefore citizens even if born on what is nominally American soil.

It wasn't until 1924, for instance, that Native Americans were given blanket citizenship by Congress.

Not surprisingly, America (except for Canada, which needs immigrants) is the only country in the world that has the irrational policy of granting citizenship to children of illegal immigrants born here. Citizenship in England, France, Germany, Japan, and Russia depends on the citizenship of the parents. Australia grants citizenship to the child of an immigrant born there but only when the entry is legal. Surely that is the correct policy and would conform to our Constitution.

In fact, just such a case was decided by the Supreme Court in *United States v. Wong Kim Ark.* Mr. Ark was born in San Francisco in 1873. His parents were *legal* immigrants from China and the court ruled in his favor. Since he was born here and his parents had entered within the law, the court decided he was a citizen.

Then why did the Supreme Court rule that *illegals* born here were also citizens?

They never did. Did Congress pass a law granting that right to illegals? No. Then who did?

All this misinformation is based on relatively recent decisions by lower courts, which have a habit of New Establishment activism, much of it blatantly unconstitutional. They have obviously stretched, twisted, and overinterpreted the Constitution to fit their own biases.

Professor Schuck believes the practice does not require a Constitutional amendment to be stopped, but that it can be eliminated with a simple act of Congress.

Several Congressmen agree and six bills were presented in the 104th Congress (January 1995–January 1997), but never became law. One was by Congressman Brian Bilray of California. His piece of legislation, HR 1363, simply states: "To amend the Immigration and Nationality Act to deny citizenship at birth to children born in the United States of parents who are not citizens or permanent resident aliens."

Like Professor Schuck, Bilray believes the courts were in error and that a Constitutional amendment is not needed. "It is my view that a Constitutional amendment would be superfluous," says Bilray, who is confident that the Supreme Court would uphold the Congress once they pass his, or a similar, bill.

For a long time, there was an unspoken conspiracy between the two major political parties that "winked" at illegal immigration. The Democrats countenanced it because once the immigrants became citizens (as happened after the amnesty of 1986), it meant more votes for their party. The Republicans looked the other way because they believed that the illegals were needed as cheap labor, in farms, gardening, construction, as maids, and even in factories.

In fact, in the 1996 bill designed to *cut down* illegal immigration, the House Agriculture Committee approved an amendment to allow as many as 250,000 farm workers, mainly from Mexico.

The American people have always disliked illegal immigration, but for most of the country it seemed like a faraway problem. Surely California was being overrun, as were some large cities. But to the typical American suburbanite, few immigrants—legal or illegal—marred the clean streets and lush lawns, or the feeling of peace for which they paid heavily and thoroughly enjoyed.

But that barrier between the suburbanite and the immigrants is starting to break down as Hispanic immigrants arrive to live among owners of Jeeps and BMWs in relatively high-income redoubts. One town under attack is Mount Kisco in Westchester County, an affluent New York suburb north of Manhattan. The village of nine thousand—home to many celebrities such as financier Carl Icahn and part of the Town of Bedford, where the ultrarich such as Ralph Lauren live—feels that their community's peaceful atmosphere is being destroyed.

What has happened is that Mount Kisco has suddenly become almost 15 percent Hispanic in population. Many of these new residents are illiterate immigrants, many illegal, from small towns in Guatemala and Honduras. They used to disrupt traffic as they sought work as day laborers each morning from passing trucks, but the town has now set aside a parking lot for such solicitations. To pay the house rentals, they pack themselves up to twenty-five at a time into a single house, which makes it possible for the men to send money back home to support their children while they gain a foothold in America.

According to townspeople, they have become a problem—urinating in public, becoming drunk, committing knifings and other crimes, even destroying town signs and generally disrupting the once-placid community. As one resident wrote to the local paper, "We want our town back."

For a while, it was a phenomenon that the community just observed, almost tolerantly. But it is now beginning to mar the town's image of itself, and people are angry. Three times in the fall of 1996, the police and the town's building inspectors raided the immigrant houses and arrested sixty-five people in all for violating the housing rules. Quickly, the Westchester Hispanic Council and the American Civil Liberties Union defended them in court.

"The police think we're trying to take their country away from them," said one of the laborers, "but we're not."

American citizens are not so sure, especially when the threat touches the heartland of suburbia. Citizen anger over the immigration situation has risen sufficiently in the past few years so that both political parties have decided that they had better obey the will of the people. Finally, California, which generally leads the nation because of its sophisticated citizen-initiative program, put Proposition 187 on the ballot to decide whether or not to cut off most social services to illegal immigrants.

"Prop 187," as it is called in shorthand, was put to a vote in November 1994. It proposed that most services now available to illegals be cut off, including public social services, public health care services (except in an emergency), and public schools, from elementary to college. At present, illegals can even attend the California State University system at the same low tuition as citizens, an expensive accommodation for people who have broken the law.

Perhaps most important, Prop 187 required state and local agencies, especially hospitals, to report illegal immigrants to the federal INS and to the California Attorney General, an obligation that they now refuse to carry out.

Thus armed with information, action could be taken for the speedy deportation of illegals, of whom there are over two million in California, with at least 300,000 more entering the state each year. The numbers are somewhat smaller in New York, but just

275

as damaging to the economy and the taxpayers—especially to African-Americans, who are losing jobs to Hispanic illegals.

The voters overwhelmingly approved Prop 187 by a vote of 59 percent. But the following day, the state was blocked from acting on the people's will. Once again, it was the federal court system that was to blame.

"Two groups—the American Civil Liberties Union and the Mexican-American Legal Defense and Education Fund—sued the state in federal court on November 9, 1994, the day after Prop 187 passed," relates a spokesman for the California Attorney General's Office. "The Judge, Marianne Pfaelzer, issued a temporary restraining order against the state, followed up by a preliminary injunction saying we couldn't enforce Prop 187. We also had to notify all local authorities about the court order. The judge has said that she intends to 'modify' her decision, but it's been two years and we're still waiting. Meanwhile, until she does, we can't even appeal to a higher court. It's a real case of Catch-Twenty-two, and Prop 187, which was voted by the people, is not being enforced."

According to California officials, Judge Pfaelzer has not given her reasons for holding up enforcement of Prop 187. But her motives are obvious. They are in line with the New Establishment's activist judicial behavior, which takes power away from the people and the legislators, often by inventing Constitutional law that doesn't exist.

If a case in federal court does not follow New Establishment "guidelines," it will generally lose, as we shall soon see. And conversely, if it fits cozily within the new dogma, the odds of a favorable decision are good.

Meanwhile, Congress is timidly becoming involved in the Great Multicultural Flap as it applies to immigration. It has even been forced to make minor reforms to fight the specter of massive illegal immigration, especially from Mexico.

The contest is a rough one. On the other side of the Mexican-American border there are some 115 million people who see America as the Promised Land. And facing them are a pitiful "army" of 5,000 guards patrolling some 2,000 miles of border, most of it unmarked and undefended against intruders.

The enticements for Mexicans are extraordinary. They can leave an impoverished, politically corrupt Third World nation to enter the United States, a country with the opportunity and means to enrich them, and with a welfare, health and education framework favorable to such uneducated people. And for those who want work (and many Mexicans do) it is available in abundance at anywhere from $4 to $10 an hour—up to ten times what they now earn—offering the *beginning* of a decent life.

And do not forget the enticement that a child born to illegals here automatically becomes an American citizen, with all that entails. It is surprising that the border patrol turns away only two million Mexicans each year!

So brazen and aggressive is the migration of Mexicans from their country into the United States that the President of Mexico, Ernesto Zedillo, has proposed dual nationality for Mexican immigrants. This would allow them to vote in both countries, further weakening the assimilation of Spanish-speakers into the Anglo-American culture. The same is true of immigrants from the Dominican Republic and Columbia, who are petitioning their countries to do the same—to permit them to become U.S. citizens without losing legal ties to the country of their birth.

This should not be permitted for immigrants from any nation. How can new citizens swear an oath of fidelity to America if they remain citizens of another country?

It is incumbent on the U.S. Congress to pass a law that denies American citizenship to immigrants with dual citizenship who do not permanently renounce their allegiance to, and citizenship in, a foreign nation.

With such an irresistible magnet as a First World nation alongside a Third World country, with a long common border—the only such situation in the world—one would need enormous defenses to stop illegals. These are defenses we do not have, nor are they contemplated by our politicians.

But pressured by voters, the Congress finally, in September 1996, passed what is called "The Illegal Immigration Reform and Immigrant Responsibility Act of 1996."

The bill attempts to make reforms in our childlike immigration policy as it mainly involves illegals. (Attempts to reform the permissive and damaging "Chain Immigration" of legal immigrants were turned down.)

Reforms are surely needed, but those passed are highly inadequate and do not address the question of benefits granted illegals. With the lure of America—and high rewards for breaking the law—one can safely state that unless drastic measures are put into place, not only will illegal immigration continue, it will increase severely over the years.

What is the government doing to fix things? The new legislation provides a few sops to public outrage:

1. Five thousand new Border Patrol agents (only a small percentage of the number needed).

2. The fingerprinting of illegal aliens apprehended anywhere. (Why wasn't this done before?)

3. Nine hundred INS investigators to enforce alien smuggling and three hundred to track down and apprehend visa overstayers. (It has been estimated that 200,000 visa "overstayers" continue to accept our hospitality once their time is up.)

4. A fourteen-mile triple fence from the Pacific Ocean inward to reduce entry from the San Diego–Tijuana area. (All that along a 2,000-mile border?)

5. Increases the ban on applying for legal entry from three to ten years for those who have already violated immigration laws. (Do they mean that prior to this would-be-illegals were soon allowed back in legally?)

6. Mandates detention of criminal aliens pending deportation. (Weren't they detained prior to this?)

7. Requires sponsors of an immigrant to sign a legally en-

forceable affidavit to provide financial support if needed. (Didn't they have to sign that before this?)

8. Streamlines procedures for removing ineligible aliens from taxpayer-subsidized housing. (How did they get in there in the first place?)

Some of these new conditions are valuable, but they only exist because of public pressure and not because of long-time government policy. But trying to stop illegal immigration with such legislation is reminiscent of King Canute attempting to hold back the ocean tide. There is only one way to block a massive discontented Third World people from exercising its self-interest by illegally trying to enter the United States.

That solution is to turn our borders over to the military— perhaps a job best done by the National Guard, which is usually composed of local troops. A reasonable estimate of manpower required is perhaps as many as fifty thousand.

To handle the whole complex immigration issue, many changes have to be made. (I hesitate to use the overworked word *reform,* which is generally a euphemism for maintaining the status quo). These include:

1. Change the present law back to the national origin quotas. This means much greater concentration on European immigration, which is now discriminated against, and which contrary to myth—as we have seen—is readily available.

2. Allow only minor children and spouses to join legal immigrants already here. No entry should be provided parents of adults, or brothers or sisters, or other relatives. Stop "Chain Immigration" cold.

3. Make illegal entry a criminal offense and handle it that way, with detention jailing, then deportation, with permanent exclusion from ever legally immigrating to America.

4. Eliminate citizenship rights for children born here of illlegals.

5. Pass federal legislation cutting out social welfare benefits for illegals throughout the nation, except in medical emergencies. Eliminate their ability to attend taxpayer-supported colleges.
6. Pass federal legislation making it a crime of collusion for anyone, whether doctor, nurse, employer, or social worker, to harbor illegals or to fail to report their whereabouts to federal authorities for deportation.
7. Deport criminal aliens back to their countries of origin for incarceration there.
8. Turn over control of the borders to the military with the Border Patrol playing a supporting role.

And what if we do not have the determination to enact such a forceful plan to protect our culture? Then we should understand that present "reforms" will do little to stop the inexorable drive to enter America illegally.

America has many decisions to make to preserve the Anglo-American Judeo-Christian culture that has made us both different and great. One is to disregard the New Establishment appeals for continued large-scale immigration from the Third World countries to the near-exclusion of new citizens from Europe. Another is to consider cutting back on immigration *drastically* for a decade or more.

Americans must eliminate any feelings of guilt in regard to immigration. As the seven million strong lottery shows, a vast proportion of the planet, especially the poor of the Third World, would overwhelm this nation if they were permitted.

Controlling immigration so that it benefits America and its own citizens (the duty of every sovereign country) and not the interests of the dispossessed around the globe, must be the first consideration in shaping the future of the nation.

CHAPTER NINE

OUR IRRESPONSIBLE, IRREPRESSIBLE COURTS

The Enforcement Wing of the New Establishment

ON NOVEMBER 5, 1996, PROPOSITION 209, WHICH HAD been placed on the California ballot by citizen petition, was passed by a vote of 54 percent and fixed in state law.

Not even the governor or the state legislature could amend or eliminate it. Through the initiative, one of the superior examples of democracy in action (available in only twenty-four states), the people had spoken. For Californians, it was the law of the land. Or at least they thought so.

The proposition was a simple one, which did not take away anyone's rights, but merely eliminated *extra privileges* for certain groups of people. As we have seen, it declared that state-run programs involving public employment, contracting, and college admission could not grant special preference to anyone because of race, gender, or national origin.

Was it rational to cut off those privileges? Of course. In fact, the Supreme Court, just months before, had held that any such program was itself probably unconstitutional, except within certain narrow limits.

Proposition 209 seemed secure against judicial tampering. But the people of California had not counted on the new *activist* court, the enforcement wing of the New Establishment. On November 6, the day after its passage, the Southern California branch of the American Civil Liberties Union (which supports affirmative action even though that program curbs civil rights for others), joined with minority groups. At Federal District Court in San Francisco it sued the state to stop the enforcement of Prop 209.

The judge, Thelton E. Henderson, a former Justice Department civil rights prosecutor, decided that even though the people had passed the proposition, it was "probably unconstitutional."

Why? Because it singled out minorities and women. His opinion strained reality. The women and minorities had already been singled out for favorable treatment. Prop 209 was merely trying to remove that unconstitutional preference.

Nevertheless, District Court Judge Henderson held up enforcement of 209 for several months.

The entire federal judiciary is prone to act unethically—to use their personal biases instead of the law or the Constitution in making decisions. But perhaps the federal district courts are the gravest offenders. Occasionally, they are called to task by higher courts, the first line before the Supreme Court being the Circuit Court of Appeals.

That is what happened with California's Proposition 209 when the lower court used the favorite trick of questioning its constitutionality to keep it from being enforced. By issuing an injunction, the vote of the citizens became meaningless.

The Proposition 209 case went to the Ninth Circuit Court of Appeals in San Francisco, which after a hearing, ruled against the lower court and for the people of California. They demanded that the injunction be lifted and 209 be enforced. On April 8, 1997, in a 3 to 0 decision, the court decided that Proposition 209 does not discriminate (which was already obvious to all intelligent laymen), but instead "addresses in neutral fashion race-related and gender-related matters."

Encouraged by the decision announced by Judge Diarmuid O'Scannlain, Congressman Charles T. Canady said he plans to reintroduce his Equal Opportunity Act of 1997, which would prohibit the use of race or gender preferences in the entire federal government, an enormous step forward in blocking unfair and intentional New Establishment dogma.

The first part of this scenario was a replay of what happened to Proposition 187, voted into law in 1994 by 59 percent of Californians, which cut off most social services to illegal immigrants. In the first step of that judicial battle, Federal District Court Judge William Matthew Byrne, Jr. said he believed it was unconstitutional because in the tussle between taxpayer-citizens and illegals, "there was a balance of hardship" in favor of the illegals!

Thus, in perfect Freudian–New Establishment code, the illegals who had crashed our borders became the "victims" and the American citizens the "oppressors," a turnabout that gives this rogue philosophy immense power among the uneducated and/or the fashionable among us.

Not every judge is involved in such speculative theory, but increasingly members of the federal judiciary (and state judges as well) have created a world of their own in which they are not just jurists, but legislators, even would-be philosophers, willfully crossing over into everyone's legal bailiwick to seize power.

The significance of this trend is enormous. The modern judiciary's decisions touch every aspect of our lives, from childbearing to finance to crime to race relations to education, marriage, welfare, divorce, civil liability, and even future involvements such as the Internet and genetics that we cannot yet imagine.

By and large, Americans are a law-abiding people who look to their institutions, especially the courts, to be fair and to regulate society for the greater good of the nation. Knowing this, the New Establishment uses the public's respect for the courts as a lever to achieve its goals. Unfortunately, that coincides with the judiciary's relatively new desire for increased power, which permits judges to exercise their personal biases, all the while disguising them as judicial decisions based on law.

This is not transient power. Federal judges are named for life, as are certain state magistrates, a situation that is rightfully now under attack.

The Constitution set up three branches of government, each as a check and balance on the others. The federal judiciary—at least the Supreme Court portion of it—was established by Article III in 1789. It grew in power after Chief Justice John Marshall established that institution's jurisdiction in determining what is and what is not Constitutional. In doing so, the Court took certain powers away from Congress, the federal legislative branch, a move that angered President Thomas Jefferson, who was a firm believer in the direct will of the people.

But over the years, the public accepted that restraint on Congress as a right of the Court, as long as its rulings were truly based on the Constitution and not on the latest cultural fad or personal bias.

Today, that hoped-for objectivity is disappearing as many judges go far afield from the text of the Constitution. That august document and the law itself are more likely to be used as a Rorschach test in which judges call on their social and political biases to interpret legislation and executive decisions.

This new activism is becoming epidemic at every level of the judiciary. As we have seen, it was used in Kansas City to *raise taxes,* which is a purely legislative function and absolutely outside the jurisdiction of courts. By forcing a consent decree on the school district, the federal district judiciary seized control of the desegregation process, then authorized the spending of $1 billion of taxpayer money over seven years for a racial integration plan that involved a magnet school with swimming pools and even a planetarium. Yet at the end, there was no improvement in educational quality.

Finally, in 1995, after years of ineffectual intervention by the lower court, the Supreme Court, by a narrow 5–4 decision in the case of *Missouri v. Jenkins,* ended this meddling in the affairs of the state legislature.

This one usurpation was finally stopped, but the danger to the nation is that there is no general way to control this anti-democratic oligarchy—a judiciary imbued with power that it has granted to itself, without any effective outside check or balance.

Judicial bias ranges from the mundane to the awesome, much of it based on New Establishment theory that the rights of certain individuals and groups, no matter how outlandish, are more important than the rights of the majority.

In New York City, the homeless had found a haven in Pennsylvania Station, with warmth, public bathrooms, and unlimited space in which to set up "home." But it was also a public nuisance for travelers, especially when the homeless monopolized benches and spaces. Trying to protect the public, Amtrak decided to evict the homeless, knowing that New York City has a network of free shelters.

When Penn Station was sued by an advocacy group, the case came before the federal district court in Manhattan. It was heard by Judge Constance Baker Motley, who delivered a thirty-three-page ruling that Amtrak's behavior was "unconstitutional," a fanciful but increasingly common ruling used when jurists want to defy community standards.

The squatters, she said in effect, had the right to settle down wherever they wanted as long as it was a "public" space. Apparently this meant that virtually any place—a street, a sidewalk, even the recently declared public space of shopping malls—was as good a bedroom as anywhere, and just as "constitutional."

In a typical New Establishment display of "victim" sensibility,

Judge Motley said that the ejections were akin to "labeling the homeless as a criminal class."

Traditionally, the courts have balanced the rights of the community with those of the individual, including those of the accused. But in advancing the exaggerated "rights" of *certain* individuals over those of others and the community, the courts are overstepping their power. They have yielded to New Establishment blandishments of "social individualization"—that individual desires, no matter how bizarre, are more important than those of the community—as the prime criterion of the law.

Today, it is increasingly the *Federal Courts v. American People,* a contest that is escalating, and that the people are losing.

In Middletown, New Jersey, an unbathed homeless man spent a great deal of time in the local library. His body odor made it difficult for people to sit within a broad radius of him, undermining the value of the public library. He followed library workers around, making negative comments, often shouting and disrupting the library's decorum. Many complaints about his noxious presence were made to library officials by angered citizens.

Here was a classic case of the community trying to protect itself against exaggerated "social individualization."

The library finally evicted him. But soon after, the American Civil Liberties Union sued in court. Judge H. Lee Sarokin of the Federal District Court in Philadelphia, who handled the case, ruled against the library, saying it had violated the homeless man's constitutional rights. The Middletown Library had to accept him back, smelly or otherwise.

(That same judge, it is worth noting, had overturned the triple murder conviction of Rubin "Hurricane" Carter, saying prosecutors had violated his constitutional rights, and he had also released a man convicted of murdering a policeman, claiming that the prosecutors had withheld evidence. Despite that, Judge Sarokin was elevated to the U.S. Court of Appeals. He has since resigned.)

State courts suffer from the same debilitating nonjudicial behavior, exercising what appears to be a bias against a decent and orderly society. In New York City, a state appeals court even ruled in favor of a fifteen-year-old who took a loaded weapon into his school, Howard Taft High School in the Bronx.

An astute security guard spotted the handle of a gun peeking out of the student's jacket, pulling down its left side. He grabbed the boy, who broke and ran. The guard called "code red," the signal that a gun was involved, into his walkie-talkie. Another security man captured the youth, and a police officer who was summoned searched the boy and found the gun, which was loaded.

But it turned out to be a futile arrest. In Family Court, where the teenager was charged with delinquency, the judge threw the case out. He freed the gun-toting youth, saying that "the outline of the gun was not visible . . . and was not remotely suspicious." The school and the police, the court held, had violated the teenager's Fourth Amendment rights against search and seizure. All criminal charges were dropped and he was released.

The Board of Education held its own hearings, and although it couldn't criminally prosecute the youth, he was suspended for a year for bringing a loaded gun into his school—a fact no one disputed.

The young man sued the Board to remove his suspension, but lost. Then, represented by the Legal Aid Society, he appealed to the state court of appeals. There, Justices Ernst Rosenberger, Joseph Sullivan, Betty Weinberg Ellerin, and Angela Mazzarelli ruled unanimously in his favor, revoking the suspension and sending him back to school. (We hope without the loaded gun.) All mention of the incident was removed from his school records. In a New Establishment wave of a judicial hand, nothing had really happened.

An official of the Board of Education put the court's ridiculous attitude into perspective: "How is this any different from the same type of situation in an airport? If you're suspected of carrying a gun, you're searched and it's not illegal."

(In a surprise verdict in 1997, a higher state court upheld the boy's suspension from school, but he had still escaped all criminal charges.)

The Board official might have also mentioned that 130 guns are seized from students each year in New York schools, several of which were used to kill fellow students. He might also have revealed that several schools in New York have metal detectors, which could also be viewed as part of an illegal search and seizure.

The disorderly society, which seems to be the goal of much of the New Establishment–influenced judiciary, has both its frivolous and serious sides.

On the painfully humorous front, the 10th Circuit Court of Appeals in Oklahoma heard the case of a male criminal who sued the prison because he wanted to become a female but had been refused free hormone injections. The court ruled that he could not get the injections under the Fourteenth Amendment, which only gave him "equal protection under the law." But he might be entitled to the injections, it said, under the Eighth Amendment of the Bill of Rights.

Why that? Because that amendment bans "cruel and unusual punishment," which the court interpreted as the withholding of free hormone therapy!

One of the more serious side effects of permissive New Establishment courts was seen in Florida, as reported in *USA Today*. "Florida prison doors will swing wide open for 445 murderers, sex offenders, kidnappers, and child abusers beginning today," they reported on November 6, 1996.

Release of the dangerous prisoners generated large-scale protests from the public, but a Corrections Department spokesman said: "We've done everything we can to keep them locked up, but we don't have any choice. Our hands are tied."

The release program was born in the early 1980s when a

federal judge ruled that Florida prisons were overcrowded, and placed a ceiling on the number who could be incarcerated. To meet the court order, the state started awarding "gain time" for good behavior in order to empty the cells early. After a number of dangerous felons were released, the state attorney general decided to revoke automatic gain time for violent inmates. The prisoners complained that their early release had been promised and sued.

On March 11, 1997, the U.S. Supreme Court heard the case and ruled for the Florida felons—that it was too late to revoke the early release privilege.

Among the 300 additional felons released that March were murderers and rapists, including one man who stabbed his father then hung his body from an exercise bike. Another murderer led a teenage gang which beat a homeless man to death with baseball bats. The mass releases will continue, up to an additional 2,200 felons.

"A hell of a lot of innocent people are going to be robbed, raped and murdered," says Lee County (Florida) Sheriff John McDougal. "How many people are going to have to die to pay for this blunder?"

When faced with an autocratic federal court system that is sympathetic to criminals, the public can feel a sense of powerlessness. That has happened in Philadelphia, where an order by Federal District Court Judge Norma Shapiro has kept the city hostage to its criminals for over a decade.

In the 1980s, ten prisoners in a city jail—later joined by the *entire* inmate population of Philadelphia—sued in federal court protesting overcrowding and other poor conditions of the jails. Their claim was that it was an unconstitutional violation of Article VIII, and therefore a federal matter.

District Court Judge Norma Shapiro heard the case and decided for the prisoners. She forced a "consent decree" on the city, which required that it release a number of supposedly nonviolent prisoners, including carjackers and drug dealers and thieves, until the 5,000 inmate population came down to a cap of 3,750. In addition, the district attorney's office was kept from jailing new felons, who after their conviction were immediately let out onto the street.

"Many, many criminals were let out of jail and many new ones never went in. Together, they committed many, many crimes," says Bill Davol, a spokesman for the office of Lynne Abraham, the Philadelphia District Attorney. Ms. Abraham, in fact, has compiled a list of those crimes, which is a frightening inventory of mayhem—whose responsibility rests on the head of the permissive federal judiciary.

In 1996, the cap was lifted by Judge Shapiro to give Philadelphia a chance to rectify prison overcrowding on its own, but the same situation of unjailed felons still dogs the City of Brotherly Love.

The technicalities used to free the undeserving are growing as the judiciary increasingly sees the criminal as the "victim" of society, rather than the other way around.

One recent case showed the dire effects of such an attitude. A federal judge in New York, Harold Baer, heard the case of a woman who had been arrested in a car loaded with narcotics. In a videotaped forty-five-minute interview with the police, she confessed to receiving $20,000 for transporting the drugs, and to making twenty such large drops in Manhattan over the last four years. But despite the clear evidence, Judge Baer ruled against the prosecution, threw the case out of court, and freed the woman.

Why? Because he claimed that the evidence was unfairly obtained.

It seems that at 5:00 A.M., police noticed a car with out-of-state plates moving slowly, then stopping. A woman got out, opened the trunk, at which point four men dropped two large duffel bags inside. As the police approached, the woman drove off and the men moved away quickly. The police finally stopped the car. Inside the trunk, they found seventy-four pounds of cocaine and five pounds of heroin, with a street value of $4 million. But Judge Baer ruled that the search, like that of the school-boy with the gun, was illegal. Since the search was not valid, the confession was invalid as well, as was the evidence of the enormous cache of narcotics. He freed the woman of all charges. But what about the suspicious men who ran when police approached? Wasn't that a sign that something illegal might be going on, and a search justified?

No, said Judge Baer, it was quite normal for them to run away from the police, who are viewed in that community, he said, as "corrupt, abusive, and violent." Their flight, he ruled, was "hard to characterize as evasive conduct." If the men had "not run when the cops began to stare at them," the judge wrote, "it would have been unusual." In that part of town, he said, the people are afraid of the cops!

Judge Baer concluded: "I find that even collectively, these facts fail to meet the requisite standards of reasonable, articulate suspicion that any criminal activity was afoot."

(Finally, when press pressure bore down on Judge Baer, he reversed his own decision.)

In a similar case in North Carolina, Federal District Court Judge James Beaty heard the case of a man who had been convicted of the shotgun killing of his parents. The man's fingerprints were on the murder weapon, and other evidence pointed toward a conviction, which the prosecutor obtained. But Judge Beaty overturned it. Why? Because a juror had looked at the tree where the shotgun was hidden after the crime.

This type of judicial behavior not only violates reasonability, but often opposes the will of the people, as in the two California initiative propositions turned down by the courts. Unfortunately, such arrogant seizure of power is becoming more prevalent in the New Establishment–influenced judiciary, some of it quite blatant.

In Arizona, the state constitution was amended by voters to

require that all official state business be conducted solely in English. The state was sued by Hispanic groups, and the case finally reached the U.S. Circuit Court of Appeals of the Ninth District. Did they decide to support the majority of the people?

Quite the contrary. The jurists ruled that the Arizona law making English official was "unconstitutional," the favorite gambit of judicial license. Why? They claimed that language "diversity" (that word again), adds to the "multicultural character of our society." If the law were to stand, the jurists warned, there would be "no encouragement" for the blessings of multiculturalism, only "coercion" for English.

The federal court's insistence that it knows best, even when it is patently ignorant, is plaguing the nation's legislative environment. By a narrow 5–4 decision, the Supreme Court has struck down the rights of states to limit the term of office of Congressmen, even though most states had passed such legislation through voter initiatives.

The court's majority argument was that qualifications for federal elected officers cannot be controlled by states—which is a blatant fallacy. Our electoral college system, for example, is entirely state based. A plurality of one vote within almost every state is sufficient to throw *all* its electoral votes to a particular presidential candidate. In addition, if no one receives a majority of the electoral college vote, the House of Representatives chooses the President by state vote—one vote per state regardless of its population.

As Supreme Court Justice Sandra Day O'Connor once reminded her colleagues: States are *not* administrative subdivisions of the federal government but retain substantial sovereignty for themselves.

Now, the New Establishment-influenced federal court is trying to tell states that they *cannot even limit the terms of state legislators,* a theory with no precedent or basis in law. In April 1997, Judge Claudia Wilken, a federal district court judge in Oakland, ruled that California's lifetime term limits of six years for State Assembly legislators and eight years for state Senators, passed as part of Proposition 140, are unconstitutionally broad—even though they have been upheld by the California Supreme Court.

Twenty states have some form of term limit on state legislators, and are waiting for the Supreme Court to make a final decision. In interfering with the wishes of state voters, says Dan Lundgren, California's Attorney General, Judge Wilken "fuels the frustration citizens harbor toward a judiciary that too often extinguishes their mandates."

Some judicial decisions are so bizarre that they seem fictional, as if the system was creatively engaged in protecting criminals rather than innocent citizens.

That happened in the 4th Circuit Court of Appeals, which covers five eastern states and is headquartered in Richmond, Virginia. The criminal involved was Rodney Hamrick of Wheeling, West Virginia, who was serving time in the federal pen for threatening the life of President Reagan.

In jail, he built five crude bombs and threatened to blow up several targets including the courthouse. He didn't carry out that threat, but did actually mail one of his bombs to the U.S. Attorney who had prosecuted him. The bomb fizzled, burning the envelope, but did not go off.

Hamrick was convicted on a bomb count by a federal district court, but the decision was overruled by a three-judge panel of the 4th District Court of Appeals. Why? Because in a unique decision, the court ruled that since the bomb was so crudely constructed, it was not a dangerous weapon! Poor workmanship was suddenly confused with innocence.

The ridiculous decision of the three-man panel embarrassed the full contingent of fourteen 4th District judges. They met, *en banc* as it is called, and narrowly (eight to six) overturned the decision of their peers and convicted Hamrick.

Judges today try to exercise power even where there is no

conflict in law to decide, which is their original duty. Instead, many judges see their mission as an opportunity to influence society, with or without the benefit of law. As I've already mentioned, Federal District Court Judge Robert P. Patterson, Jr., former president of the New York State Bar Association, issued an injunction against the New York transit system to stop a twenty-five cent subway fare increase.

The decision was not based on matters of law. Rather, he had labeled the fare rise a matter of "racial discrimination" because so many riders were black or Hispanic.

Governor Pataki correctly pointed out that the fare rise had nothing to do with race. *But the governor was apparently unaware that the dominant New Establishment culture believes virtually everything has everything to do with race or sex or ethnicity, especially when discord can be manipulated for its own purposes.*

The judicial system of America is often at odds with the needs and visions of the people. Both political parties, for instance, seem united on the importance of what are called "Family Values," the maintenance of traditional families and morality.

But too often the courts have their own definitions of what constitutes a family, or values. In New York, the Court of Appeals, the state's highest court, heard a case in which marriage was once again demeaned.

In New York, the state law does not permit unmarried couples to jointly adopt a child. When two unmarried couples, including a lesbian pair, tried to do just that, they were blocked. The lower courts turned them down because it was both against the law and obviously demeaning to the institution of marriage. But the New York State Court of Appeals, headed by Judge Judith S. Kaye, in an unprecedented opinion, overruled the lower court and allowed each of the couples—one heterosexual and one lesbian but without benefit of marriage—to jointly adopt a child.

The lesbian mother, who had delivered a child after artificial insemination, suddenly had a co-parent, her female lover. And the child, by court fiat, had become a real-life ringer for the heroine of a former New York City textbook entitled *Heather Has Two Mommies.*

New York's Governor opposed the ruling, saying that such decisions "should be made by the elected officials of the people, namely the Legislature and the Governor, and not by an appointed judiciary."

But his protest, like that of other citizens, was futile against an entrenched oligarchic judiciary that has no effective opposition from a confused public and cowed elected officials.

The New Establishment concept that "someone kept me from achieving," or conversely, that "someone or something made me do it," has infiltrated the judiciary and led to widespread abuse of the insanity defense. Regularly, we see courts countenancing verdicts that the lay public simply does not accept as reasonable.

In a small town near Allentown, Pennsylvania, a seventeen-year-old boy admitted to killing both his parents—his forty-six-year-old father and his forty-eight-year-old mother. He shot them, then locked the house and drove away in his mother's car. When the car ran out of gas, he was arrested.

At the trial, it was revealed that just four days before, two brothers in a nearby town had been accused of killing their parents and the seventeen-year-old had talked about it with his parents. The young killer seemed like a typical youngster with no apparent aberrations. He had been a Boy Scout, was on the swimming team, and regularly attended church.

The two sides provided their own psychiatrists, who offered the court contradictory testimony about the defendant's mental state, which is usual in such subjective psychological contests.

There were six possible verdicts, including the obvious one of murder, which could have meant life imprisonment. As the foreman read the verdict, the shocked prosecutor looked straight ahead with no comment. The public defender wept with joy as did several jurors.

The teenage killer had been declared *not guilty* by reason of insanity, the same neo-Freudian verdict that has kept John Hinckley, the frustrated assassin of President Reagan, out of jail, and held in an institution which he can leave anytime psychiatrists decide that he is no longer mentally ill.

Despite their fascination with psychology, such verdicts upset most Americans, who cannot fully accept the concept that people are not responsible for their acts. In fact, if one were to look at murder solely from the psychological viewpoint, it might always seem psychotic, and therefore not punishable. It even seems that the more heinous the crime, the more open to false psychological analysis it becomes.

In Lebanon, Ohio, a twenty-five-year-old man was accused of burglarizing a home, then beating the sixty-five-year-old male occupant over the head eight times with a rolling pin. After that he stabbed him four times with a butcher knife so that the victim required 100 stitches. The burglar also attempted to choke the man's eighty-four-year-old mother.

At the trial, in his defense, the accused stated that he had been a sleepwalker for years and had no memory of the attack. He testified that he had "night terrors" since childhood and often woke up in places other than where he had originally gone to sleep.

The verdict was predictable. He was declared not guilty by reason of insanity, which places him in a mental institution until he "recovers" from his murderous "illness."

Certain judges are more prone to New Establishment social insanity than others. Florida Supreme Court Judge Rosemary Barkett, who has since been named to the U.S. Court of Appeals, has voted to spare the killer of an eight-year-old girl because he had "learning problems" as a child. She also argued that a man who shotgunned his former lover could not have acted with premeditation because he was "emotionally charged."

The disparity between the values of the court and those of the public is becoming more manifest each day. In the case of homosexuals in the military, an angered Pentagon blocked the President's plan to have them serve as everyone else does.

Instead, the compromise "Don't Ask, Don't Tell," was instituted, which in many ways is similar to the old program of exclusion, one heavily supported by Americans, especially by the 28 million veterans. There have always been homosexuals in the military, but if they were silent about their sexuality, no one knew, or really cared.

But this traditional attitude was not enough for New Establishment afficionados. When a homosexual was dismissed from service, the case was taken by the ACLU to Federal District Court Judge Eugene Nickerson on Long Island, who ordered the serviceman be reinstated.

The reason? The Pentagon regulation of "Don't Tell" was an infringement of the man's rights, the judge said. Merely admitting that he was a homosexual was not sufficient grounds for action by the military because the statement, or admission, was, he ruled, "free speech," protected by the First Amendment.

Whether one believes homosexuals should, or should not, be admitted to the military, that jurist's argument surely deserves a New Establishment award for originality.

Of course, it is hard to see how the military's policy is unconstitutional. The courts have ruled that military service is not a right, but a privilege. At present, the services have a legal right to bar people for considerably less, including flat feet, punctured eardrums, or excessive anxiety. Nor is the military required to be tolerant of such usual behavior as drinking alcohol in living quarters, a right civilians have but which is prohibited to enlisted service personnel.

This conflict over values between the judiciary and the average American was highlighted at the end of 1996, when the question of homosexual marriage came up in a district court in Hawaii. Same-sex marriages are overwhelmingly disapproved of by Americans, as all polls show.

In fact, politicians steer as far away as they can from supporting it. Congress passed a law—the "Defense of Marriage Act"—in 1996 that prevents such marriages, if permitted by one state, from being universally accepted throughout the nation. The President eagerly signed it.

But that has not deterred individual judges from converting their bias in favor of same-sex marriages into judicial decisions. That happened in Hawaii in December 1996, when state Circuit Court Judge Kevin S. C. Chang ruled that Hawaii *must* grant marriage licenses to three complaining couples even though they are not heterosexual, but gay and lesbian.

He made that decision, he said, because the state had failed to convince him that children adopted by such parents would be worse off than the natural child of a normal couple. Thus, there was no reason why homosexuals should not be married. Besides, it was up to the state to show a "compelling interest" why it should continue to ban same-sex marriages.

Of course, that was not the point at all. If jurists do not uphold the public voice as evidenced by the acts of their legislatures, they will—except in obvious cases of unconstitutional deprivation of rights granted under the Bill of Rights—be creating their own insular culture based on personal, not legal or communal, concepts.

Western society has sanctified marriage as both a civil and religious institution based on the hope that such unions will produce children to be raised as part of a nuclear family. Homosexual couples, of course, cannot procreate together. Thus their supposed nuclear family through adoption may elicit curiosity, but will eventually detract from the strength of the heterosexual married family, the basic unit of civilization.

Judge Chang's decision was greeted with such outrage that he put his order on hold until it is reviewed by the Hawaii Supreme Court.

The power of the American judiciary stems from the Constitution's setting up of the Supreme Court in 1787. It did not specify its size, or the terms of office, except to say that Justices "shall hold their offices during good behavior," which has been interpreted (rightly or wrongly) to mean for life.

The Constitution set up only the Supreme Court, but in Article III, Section 1, it allowed for "such inferior courts as the Congress may from time to time ordain and establish." In 1789, Congress established the U.S. Court of Appeals, followed by the federal district courts, all of whose judges were to serve that same term "during good behavior."

In Article II, Section 2, the U.S. Senate is granted the power to confirm or reject the President's nominations for the federal bench. This vital power is then shared between the executive and the legislative branches, although as we shall see, the Senate is usually lax in investigating and confirming the judges of the "inferior courts," who are the base of the whole federal judiciary.

The original size of the Supreme Court, which included the Chief Justice and five Associate Justices, was established as six members by the Judiciary Act of 1789. In 1807, one additional seat was added by Congress, making a total of seven. In 1837, the Court was enlarged to eight members, but then reduced again to seven in 1840. In 1863, during the Civil War, it was increased to eight, then to its present nine in 1869.

It has remained at that size despite an attempt by President Franklin D. Roosevelt to increase it to twelve, a move that was called "packing the Court." Because many of FDR's New Deal programs were being ruled unconstitutional by a conservative Supreme Court, he tried to push Congress to enlarge its size. Then he could name three additional Justices sympathetic to the New

Deal. But though Congress was generally allied with Roosevelt, it refused this request as being anti-traditional.

Unlike the Supreme Court, or the House and Senate, the rest of the federal judiciary expands regularly. The last time was in 1990, when eighty-five new federal judgeships were created by Congress. As of 1997, there were 846 federal judges, including nine on the Supreme Court, 179 in the Court of Appeals in thirteen Districts, divided geographically, and the rest in the Federal District Courts, of which there are ninety-four districts and 658 judges. And all appointed by the President.

There is great turnover—some three to four judges each month—which gives Presidents power lasting far beyond their four or eight years in office. This makes the confirmation process by the Senate invaluable. But the reality is that it is mainly perfunctory, with little investigation of the nominee's prior judicial record. For instance, of the most recent 183 nominees for the federal bench, 181 were confirmed without any hearings.

At the state and local level, the situation is quite similar, with thousands of judges in an enormous judicial system.

What then can be done to make the judiciary as *impartial* and bound by the law and the Constitution as it should be?

Something *must* be done. Partisan politics, personal bias, and misinterpretations of the Constitution are rampant in the New Establishment–influenced judiciary.

• The first remedy is for Presidents to select those federal judges who have a reputation for impartiality, and who are reluctant to be led by their personal biases, whether conservative or liberal, traditional or activist. This is especially important in nominations for the U.S. Court of Appeals, most of whose nominees come from the Federal District benches and who already have a judicial record that can be studied.

• The U.S. Senate must become more vigilant and active in examining the nominees for the federal bench, especially in marking up the judicial record of all candidates for review by Senate members on both sides of the aisle.

• The President and the Senate should ignore the outside recommendations of groups such as the American Bar Association, which have become increasingly politicized and have an agenda that is not necessarily impartial.

• Presidents should try not to yield to such contemporary ideas as affirmative action in making judicial selections. For example, some 60 percent of all appointments to the federal bench from 1993 to 1997 were either women or minorities, recipients of social advantage that may well be declared unconstitutional in the future.

• On the state level, these same precautions should be taken by governors and members of the state senates who are involved in appointing and confirming major jurists.

Bias is the enemy from whatever quarter it comes, whether liberal or conservative. Today, we are seeing a growing sense of polarization and enmity between opposing ideological camps, and between traditionalists and those who seek rapid change. Inventive new concepts in social action and law regularly pummel our culture, and too many jurists take advantage of that lack of stability to intrude their personal biases—rather than the law or the Constitution—into the equation.

Over the last thirty years, the activist federal judiciary has virtually destroyed the authority of the Tenth Amendment to the Constitution, which is quite specific in what the federal government may do, and what is left to the states.

The simple amendment, the last one in the Bill of Rights, reads, in full:

"The powers not delegated to the United States by the Constitution, nor prohibited by it to the States, are reserved for the States respectively, or the people."

Instead of amending the Constitution when it was required,

the federal government has for decades illegally pressed its power—uninhibited by the judiciary, the supposed guardians of the august document. In fact, the courts, including the Supreme Court, have virtually ignored Washington's waiving of the Tenth Amendment, preferring to interpret a permissive, free-wheeling Constitution that exists mainly in their imaginations, rather than follow the actual document.

That is why it is considered such a novelty that in 1992, in a majority decision written by Justice Sandra Day O'Connor, the long-neglected Tenth Amendment was suddenly called into play. In that case, *New York v. United States of America,* the court upheld a complaint by Governor Mario Cuomo of New York that the EPA was requiring the state to "take title" to some radioactive waste and assume all liability for cleaning it up.

Calling on the forgotten Tenth Amendment, Justice O'Connor ruled in favor of New York State. She reminded Washington that "States are not mere political subdivisions of the United States," but have certain sovereign powers granted them by the Constitution.

But such traditional interpretations are noteworthy in their very rarity. Since the environment surrounding the judiciary is changing rapidly, I believe it is essential to change the judiciary with it. Otherwise we shall end up with fashionable concepts of the moment, at either end of the polarization, made permanent because of the permanence of the judges involved.

To handle that situation, there is only one remedy. We must end the practice of naming federal judges for life.

Though it had been valuable in the past, when it insulated jurists from the passions of the moment, it is no longer viable. The court, from the lowly district ones to the Supreme Court itself, insists on *injecting* itself into those very passions, making their tenure a danger to democracy rather than an asset.

Where once the courts codified and protected democracy— the rule of the people—they now too often seek to outflank it, to *unilaterally* decide whether laws passed by Congress, the state legislatures, or by voter initiatives should actually be enforced or just shelved. Their true mandate is to use the Constitution as their guide, but that is currently considered an unsophisticated approach by many jurists, who more often look to their own biases—and those of their peers—for edification. As observers have commented, this is the courts' "Post-Constitutional" phase, one in which jurists attempt to *write* the law instead of interpreting it.

This phase is one we should meet head on. The need for reform of judicial tenure calls out.

There are several possible ways to shape such a reform. The most efficient one is to limit the term of office for federal judges. I would suggest a five-year term for "inferior" judgeships such as those in the federal district court system, and a seven-year term for judges on the U.S. Court of Appeals. Most judges nominated to that higher office already have a judicial record that can be examined before they are appointed and confirmed.

In the case of the Supreme Court, a reasonable term of office is ten years instead of the present lifetime tenure.

With such a turnover, the people will be better served. The political and personal biases of high court justices are increasingly predictable, as are their decisions. With only ten years on the bench, no biased Justice will be able to permanently misread the Constitution or distort the common law.

Changing the length of tenure of federal judges can be accomplished in several ways. One is for Congress to challenge the vague wording of the Constitution, which says that Supreme Court judges shall serve "during good behavior," which has been interpreted as a lifetime appointment.

But Congress was given the right not only to choose the number of Supreme Court Justices (originally six) but to create "inferior" courts. Who is to say they cannot pass a law limiting the term of office of these federal judges?

The problem, of course, is that the High Court would finally decide if such a law was unconstitutional. Considering its vested interest, the Court could knock it down. A more pragmatic way to limit the terms of office for all federal judges would be a constitutional amendment, which bypasses both the President and the high court.

There have been suggestions that Congress be empowered by a super-majority to overrule Supreme Court decisions with which its disagrees. This is not a sound idea. This would deprive the judiciary of its independence as the third stanchion of democracy. Instead the reform should limit any one federal jurist (or any one President who appoints them) to "load" the judiciary long-term with biased decisions contrary to the Constitution, whether they come from the left or right, the New or Old Establishment.

By limiting the term of office (including those of the High Court) we will create a *fluid* situation in which no one point of view will any longer be able to control our judiciary.

Is it a sound idea? Definitely yes, if only because judicial behavior is changing rapidly, generally for the worse. Only the intervention of the people will be able to balance the power of the courts as the enforcer of the New Establishment or any other dogma that may threaten us in the future.

CHAPTER TEN

DOGMA IN THE
DOMINANT CULTURE

The Selling of the
New Society

AN ENTERTAINER APPLIED FOR A JOB ON A CRUISE line and was accepted. But there was one obstacle he first had to hurdle.

In the close, confined quarters of a cruise ship—where entertainers often double as ship's crew—the line's policy was not to hire anyone who was HIV positive. Science now knows that the virus can be spread not just by sexual contact, but by blood transmitted through a scratch, or perhaps even saliva. For most of the millions who take cruises, the company's precaution made sense.

The applicant was tested, and the results came back: He was HIV positive. Quickly the cruise line recalled their offer of employment. Just as quickly, the entertainer filed a complaint with the Miami office of the EEOC, claiming he was a victim of discrimination.

The federal agency sided with him, even went to court on his behalf, pointing out that being HIV positive is now considered a "disability," and that he was therefore a "protected" person under the Americans With Disabilities Act.

The cruise line countered that he could be a threat to the lives of hundreds of passengers, but nevertheless they lost. The man was awarded $15,000 in back pay and $75,000 in compensatory damages. Most important, Federal District Judge Wilkie D. Ferguson, Jr. ruled that the cruise line was now prohibited by law from *ever* testing other applicants or crewmembers for being HIV positive.

"This is wonderful for us," said a spokesperson of the EEOC.

Perhaps, but it might be less wonderful for the American public, which normally looks to the courts to protect them from societal and physical danger.

Public opinion, which strongly backs HIV testing, is part of the *Majority Culture*, one made up of the traditional values to which most Americans adhere, even cherish. But in the universe of the New Establishment, that has less currency than the *Dominant Culture*, one perhaps thirty years in the making that applauds not only the court's move on HIV, but agrees with virtually every other infringement on the community's rights in favor of *social individualism*, a perversion of traditional freedom and individuality.

This new Dominant Culture has abrogated the rights of society and the Majority Culture to define what is reasonable in both thought and action. The two cultures, which exist side by side, are in daily conflict. But the *Dominant* one, though divorced from the feeling and opinions of most Americans, is winning out in the public arena.

This New Establishment doctrine seeks to remake American culture—and by extrapolation the world's—in its own image. Unfortunately, it is not isolated in academe or the government but is being brilliantly marketed systematically through every possible outlet, from newspapers to films, from Broadway to television.

It bombards our psyches with millions of images that confuse us and that many find hard to resist. This selling of the Dominant Culture, even when its tenets are patently absurd, has been so successful that the New Establishment has cleverly managed to dictate to Americans how they should perceive themselves and their fellow citizens.

The Dominant Culture hopes to generate a mind-set that will make it acceptable, even psychologically rewarding, to continue to grant enormous privileges to those people on the fringes of the mainstream, while penalizing the mainstream itself.

That mainstream—the great army of the ignored middle class—has in fact become the beast of burden for the new coalition of the elite and the so-called victim class, those who are sensitive to supposed exploitation and those who are supposedly exploited. The middle class who pays for it all, in both money and lost equanimity, are the true victims of this Dominant Culture.

What exactly is the Dominant Culture?

Basically, it encompasses virtually everything Americans think about, believe in, and discuss publicly. It determines which plays, movies, books and television shows will be produced and how they will be received by the media. It even decides what is and what is not news, and how it will be presented. It also determines what is chic and what is old-fashioned or boring.

It sets style, fads and fashions in manners and mores, even in the realm of politics and ideas. It determines what Americans are *supposed* to think. It sets up the sense of right and wrong in societal matters, and what actions should be approved or disapproved. Thus it has enormous power.

What it does not include, fortunately, is the almost suppressed Majority Culture, the thoughts reserved for the privacy of one's mind or discourse with family and friends. Those values and opinions either ignore or are often in stark opposition to those of the Dominant Culture. But though that latter culture may often be totally askew from the needs and values of the people, it generally reigns supreme because of its command of the messengers.

Despite a reasonable economy, the nation finds itself in a deep psychological malaise, an ailment that can be traced almost entirely to the Dominant Culture. Some Americans, particularly those who rely on it as a secular substitute for religion, admire and embrace it. But many Americans do not, seeing it as injuring the national psyche and accelerating the decline of the civilization. Others fear it and follow the conformity of thought that it demands, thereby increasing its power.

One daily, grinding factor is that the Dominant Culture—unlike any in the past—has little interest in the truth. For example, in all the discussion of sexual harassment in the armed forces, the reality of common fornication between male and female soldiers has been hidden as inconvenient. And as we have seen, several other truths, from the deterioration of college education to the affirmative action for women to the rank bias of many courts to the numerous aberrations of the New Establishment, have been similarly played down by the Dominant Culture.

But the astute among the public are not fooled. They know that the Dominant Culture no longer represents them as the prevalent culture once did thirty years ago.

Youngsters can hardly remember that era, but they do hear of a better day from their parents and grandparents. What they glean about the former America from periodicals, old movies, and intergenerational scuttlebutt rings true. It's not just that those were simpler times, but that the psychological needs of the community were sounder and were being met. People were not merely a collection of vying, whining, hyphenated, gender-split, litigious groups as they are today.

It was before people were sacrificed to a dogma that insists that one "victim" is worth a thousand of the hard-working bourgeoisie.

The Dominant Culture forgets that it is the sweat and creativity of the middle class that provides the surplus, in money, energy, and concern, that makes their obsessive interest in "victims" possible.

In the 1940s, 1950s, and through most of the 1960s, the community was key. Through free speech and social criticism, people expressed their opposition to conformity, which provided a natural balance in a democracy. The outsider had to fight for space in the consciousness of the nation. This is as it should be.

Today, it is quite the opposite. The outsider-victim is at the helm, in charge of what people are supposed to think and do. In today's Dominant Culture, it is the everyday American and his spokespeople who have to fight for space in the collective psyche. This is not as it should be.

From conformity to the majority, we now have conformity to the minority, which in democratic terms is rank totalitarianism.

It is not nostalgia that makes the prior culture look better than the present one. It *was* better in the pre–New Establishment days when the current pomposity, the posturing of moral superiority, the sexism and racial bigotry, the distortion of the truth, and manufactured, forced equalities would never have been tolerated.

Today's Dominant Culture seeks to make New Establishment dogma into fact, even when the "facts" strain credibility. One such fallacy is its bias against *nature* in favor of *nurture,* or the effect of environment on human beings. We saw this at work for fifty years in the case of Freudian psychology, which preached the family causation of mental illness. Finally—through the efforts of such scientists as Dr. Solomon Snyder of Johns Hopkins—we learned that most of these diseases were organically, not environmentally, caused.

Today, we see that same bias working in disputes over excellence and failure, as in the weaker female skill in mathematics and science, and thus in high technology, the lifeblood of the economy. Traditionally, that was seen as a case of "nature"—that males had a better grasp of abstractions, thus mathematics. In brain science research, it has been shown that males have superior three-dimensional visio-spatial skills on which much of this difference is based. This research is confirmed by standardized test scores of math and science, in which men as a group always excel.

But this flies in the face of New Establishment dogma that honors *nurture* and decries *nature.* It states, for example, that social bias is the main reason for comparative female failure in math and science.

The media often pick up that Dominant Culture theme. In a recent article on women in chess, published in a major periodical, the writer explored the phenomenon of female weakness at the classic game. The piece decries the fact that women have so little impact in chess, pointing out that of the top 100 players in the world, only one is a woman, a Hungarian named Polgar.

The cause of such failure? The article examines the phenomenon and concludes that it is a matter of lack of interest in chess by women, and perhaps that, at least temporarily, they are not aggressive enough for a game that some call mentally "violent."

But not a word about the probable reality, which is *nature.* Men excel in math and three-dimensional thinking, which are the basic ingredients in chess playing. But the New Establishment dogma of "What if?"—in this case women as chessmasters—is more important than the truth, which can sometimes be unpleasant.

The only saving grace of the article is that the author did not advocate including chess as a part of Title IX of the Gender Equity Act of 1993, which makes it a possible violation of the law if women do not achieve as well as men in scoring—a policy that, as we have seen, has already been enforced in the National Merit Scholarship case.

Perhaps the government might soon, by fiat, decide to establish an equal number of female chessmasters. It doesn't sound probable, but in the Dominant Culture of today, you never know.

One strong indication of the health, or sickness, of any culture is the state of the arts. Today, to the New Establishment sin of anti-intellectualism must be added the Dominant Culture's worship of anti-art.

The most glaring example of that philistinism was the "socialist realism" of the Soviet Union, which suffocated art in that once-cultured nation for half a century by politicizing all creative expression.

The same phenomenon is taking place in America today under the aegis of the New Establishment. In the language of health, today's art is not only sick, but the patient's expression is mindless.

In the theater, the politicization of themes is as much a sign of bad art as it is in Mainland China. At home, on Broadway, a vital part of the Dominant Culture, two tendencies are obvious: revivals and plays that reflect the current obsession with victimization—tales of homosexuality, racial and ethnic minorities, and feminism.

Broadway's only interest in the Majority (not Dominant) Culture is through revivals that make the box office phone ring because they are reminiscent of a healthier era. Of the plays on Broadway, no less than ten were recent revivals, including *The King and I; Grease; Showboat; Chicago; A Funny Thing Happened on the Way to the Forum; Once Upon a Mattress; A Doll's House; Annie; Candide; The Gin Game; 1776;* and *The Little Foxes.* Added to those are several British imports, including two by Andrew Lloyd Webber.

But where is the once-vaunted American creativity that filled Broadway with drama and music that expressed the essence of the people? It has fallen to low New Establishment levels with its Politically Correct obsession with victimization. Even the opera *La Boheme* has been transformed into the Tony winner *Rent,* in which the traditional heroine Mimi, who died of tuberculosis in the original, is now HIV positive and dying, while a transvestite supporting character does die of AIDS. (Puccini, beware.)

Angels in America, the supposed masterpiece of a recent Broadway season—capturing both a Tony and a Pulitzer Prize—not only focused on AIDS but added a little male frontal nudity for cheap titillation to round out the victimization.

Variety reports that producers are actively seeking out these niche victim audiences for commercial reasons. The publication describes how the producers of a Terrence McNally play, *Love! Valour! Compassion!*—about eight gay men weekending on Fire Island—sought to market the work to homosexuals.

Similarly, there are increasing numbers of plays and films with black casts, black authors, and black directors, from Spike Lee to August Wilson, with an implied message of "separatism." One such recent Broadway hit, *Bring in 'Da Noise, Bring in 'Da Funk,* won a Tony.

Seven Guitars by Wilson was an expression of his theory of black plays by black authors for black audiences, which was criticized by a dean of drama criticism, Robert Brustein, and resulted in a face-to-face debate by them at Town Hall sponsored by *American Theatre* magazine.

The two men see theater differently. For Wilson, it is an opportunity to explain the black experience, mainly as a victim. To him, "color blind" casting is an "aberrant idea," while Brustein questions whether there shouldn't be "some kind of statute of limitations on white guilt and white reparations" and its emphasis on "separatism."

The same narrowness of the Dominant Culture holds true for the feminist theme. Off Broadway, we are treated to the *Vagina Monologues,* a one-woman show about you-know-what. Introducing the phrase "Victim Art," Arlene Croce of *The New Yorker* wrote an article about her refusal to review a dance-theater piece that plays off these New Establishment absurdities.

What about theater that concerns itself with the aspirations and struggles of the great segment of the population, which is neither African-American, Hispanic, feminist, homosexual, or lesbian?

Broadway caters to them mainly through revivals, a sad confession that the Dominant Culture is too vapid to illuminate the life of the broad mass of people. Little in current musicals or dramas concerns itself with society at large, and it is mostly content to concentrate on its fringes. One major exception, *Sunset Boulevard*—written by an Englishman—is a remake of an old Hollywood film, and is no longer on Broadway.

Drama seems to be dying, or is already dead, as the Dominant Culture fails to produce any new talent to rival the likes of Eugene O'Neill or Arthur Miller or Tennessee Williams or William Inge.

Instead, "identity politics," which is beloved by the new culture, forces writers to narrow their vision to appease certain groups, and in the process, ignore the mass of the people. Arthur Miller sees the failure of drama today based on the narrowness of its vision.

Playwrights "would get more size and scope if they felt they had an audience that represented the American people," he says. "We had the illusion . . . that we were addressing America."

Critic Robert Brustein, who is also director of the American Reportory Theatre, in a *Times* Op-Ed piece, laments that there is no longer an audience on Broadway for real drama. But the reason may be hidden: Politicized victim art has replaced true drama, and hungry playwrights are moving where the producers are.

Any culture whose art is not only narrow, but stagnant and deteriorating (as it is today), soon finds that it has become part of a faded, short-lived civilization.

Painting, sculpture, photography, performance art, even the new video art that is so representative of the Dominant Culture has become an outsider's joke. Sensible nonartists laugh at the pretentious failures of those who strive mightily to gain approval from the overserious, self-conscious New Establishment. Traditionally, secular religions, whether Fascism, Communism, or Freudianism, and especially the New Establishment, have little interest in, or understanding of, art—except for its political value.

The current Dominant Culture, though repeating the Soviet Union's politicizing of art, is doing it in a much less realistic mold. A woman has created a "living sculpture" by covering her body in chocolate; In "Piss Christ," urine has been used as a medium of artistic conveyance along with the head of Jesus. A giant sculpture appropriately entitled "Sexual Politics" is made up of numerous casts of various shapes of vaginas.

At the Venice Biennale, forty-one national pavilions exhibited

313

the works of their best artists, including "Crushed Vehicles," a small mountain of pressed cars. Among the American representation was a new form of "painting," video works by Bill Viola. In one piece, as *The New York Times* described it: "In 'Hall of Whispers,' blurred and gagged faces struggle to speak from five television screens placed on the walls of a dark passage."

In some ways, the Dominant Culture of today is attempting to re-create the early days of Freudian analysis, when middle-class existence was considered an immaterial joke. The mentality of the elite who frequented the couch thought they were sophisticated enough to assume that apparent reality was meaningless. Only the "inner mind," which could be driven to the surface by analysis, was "real."

Today, a similar attack on reality is in many ways being organized by the New Establishment. It strives to create its own world and then force the rest of us to live in it. The tenets of this secular pseudo-religion: "What if," "Victimization," "Underrepresentation," "Group Identity," "Political Correctness," "Sexual Harassment," "Affirmative Action," "Bilingualism," "Gender Equity," "Multiculturalism and Diversity," among others, strive to shape a new society on the basis of the denial of the truth and decency embodied in Judeo-Christian society.

There is no doubt that we are witnessing a ferocious clash between the Majority and Dominant Cultures.

It is not a spectator sport that we can afford to stand by and merely observe. It is a to-the-end struggle that will determine the shape of Western society for the next century and beyond, if that historic culture still exists when the battle has finally played itself out.

Recapturing the high ground against a most inventive and devious foe will not be easy. But there is little choice if one values the accumulated achievements of Western civilization—with all its blemishes and unprecedented freedom and magnificence.

ENDNOTES

Chapter One *The New Establishment*
Material from the opening survey chapter is mainly covered in the notes for the chapters that follow.

Chapter Two *Gods of the New Establishment*
Background material on Sigmund Freud from the following sources:
Jones, Ernest. *The Life and Work of Sigmund Freud.* New York: Basic Books, 1953.

Freud, Sigmund. *Collected Papers.* New York: Basic Books, 1959.

Breuer, Josef, and Sigmund Freud. *Studies on Hysteria.* New York: W.W. Norton, 1963.

Freud, Sigmund. *An Outline of Psychoanalysis.* New York: W.W. Norton, 1963.

———. *An Autobiographic Study.* New York: W.W. Norton, 1963.

———. *The Origins of Psychoanalysis.* New York: W.W. Norton, 1962.

———. *The Id and the Ego: Letters, Drafts and Notes to Wilhelm Fliess.* New York: Anchor Books, 1957.

Gross, Martin L. *The Psychological Society.* New York: Random House, 1978.

Material on the Oedipus complex from Chess, Stella. *Origins and Evolution of Behavior Disorders from Infancy to Early Adulthood.* Cambridge, Mass.: Harvard University Press, 1995.

Material on Karl Marx from Marx, Karl. *Capital* [*Das Kapital* in the original German]. New York: Oxford University Press, 1995.
———. *The Communist Manifesto.* Oakland, Calif.: Gateway Edition, 1985.

Chapter Three *American Women*

Statistics on the number of female medical students at Harvard, Yale, and University of California obtained from the schools.

Flexner report from Flexner, Abraham. *Medical Education in the United States and Canada.* Bulletin No. 4. New York: Carnegie Foundation for the Advancement of Teaching, 1910. Reprinted by Science and Health Publications, 1960.

Growth in number of female doctors from "Projected and Actual Physician Population, 1994–2010," Center for Health Policy Research, American Medical Association, 1994, Chicago.

Number of female physicians in the United States from Lillian Randolf, "Physician Characteristics and Distribution in the U.S." and "Federal and Non-federal Physicians by Age and Sex for Selected Years, 1970–1994," American Medical Association, 1995, Chicago.

Gross, Martin L. *The Doctors.* New York: Random House, 1967.

Material on medicine and science from Shapiro, Arthur K., M.D., and Elaine, M.D. *The Powerful Placebo: From Ancient Priest to Modern Physician.* Baltimore: Johns Hopkins University Press, 1997.

Quotes and statistics on female medical students and faculty from Janet Bickel, Association of American Medical Colleges. "Women in U.S. Academic Medicine, Statistics, 1996." 1996, Washington, D.C.

Figures on MCAT performances of men and women applicants from Association of American Medical Colleges. "Characteristics of MCAT Examinees, 1994–1995." 1995, Washington, D.C.

Material on Stuyvesant High School and Bronx High School of Science from admissions office of Stuyvesant and from the Westinghouse Science Talent Search.

Statistics on medical student academic failure from Barzansky, B., et al., "Educational Programs in U.S. Medical Schools," *JAMA*, vol. 274 (6 September 1995): 716.

Figures on acceptance of women medical school applicants, 1960 and 1995, from the Association of American Medical Colleges.

Statistics in AMA study of residents from Lillian Randolf, "Appendix II, Graduate Medical Education," *JAMA*, vol. 274 (6 September 1995): 755.

Number of female doctors in surgery from "Physician Characteristics and Distribution in the U.S.," American Medical Association 1995, Chicago.

SAT scores by gender from College Entrance Examination Board and Educational Testing Service, "1995 Profiles of SAT Program Test Takers," Princeton, N.J. 1995.

————, "Mean SAT/SAT I Scores for College-Bound Seniors, 1972–1996 (Recentered Scale)," Princeton, N.J. from "1996 College-Bound Seniors, A Profile of SAT Program Test-Takers," College Board, New York, 1996.

Figures on PSAT from the Educational Testing Service, Princeton, N.J.

Gender equity complaint against ETS, "ACLU Claims Test for Merit Scholars Is Unfair to Girls," William H. Buckley, *Wall Street Journal*, February 16, 1996, and interviews with organizations involved, including FairTest.

Shaywitz, Bennett A., and Sally E. Shaywitz, "Sex Differences in the Functional Organization of the Brain for Language," *Nature*, 16 February 1995.

Number of female members of the bar from American Bar Association, Washington, D.C.

Statistics on female law students from ————, "Legal Education and Bar Admissions Statistics, 1963–1996," American Bar Association, Washington, D.C.

Report on attitude toward women lawyers from ————, "Fair Measures Toward Effective Attorney Evaluation," American Bar Association, April 1997, Chicago.

●　　●　　●

Information on IQ scores from several sources including:

Eysenck, Hans J., and Leon Kamin. *The Intelligence Controversy.* New York: John Wiley & Sons, 1981.

Jensen, Arthur R. *Bias in Mental Testing.* New York: Free Press, 1980.

Matarazzo, Joseph D. *Wechsler's Measurement and Appraisal of Adult Intelligence.* New York: Oxford University Press, 1972.

Block, N. J., and Gerald Dworkin. *The IQ Controversy.* New York: Pantheon Books, 1976.

Eysenck, Hans J. *The Structure and Measurement of Intelligence.* Berlin, New York: Springer-Verlag, 1979.

Hernstein, R. J. *IQ in the Meritocracy.* Boston: Atlantic Monthly Press, 1973.

Moir, Anne, and David Jessel. *Brain Sex.* Secaucus, N.J.: Lyle Stuart, 1989.

Some material on women law students from Mansnerus, Laurie, "Men Found to Do Better in Law School," *New York Times,* 10 February 1995.

Female protest against law school teaching from "Law School Women Question Teaching Method," Emily H. Bernstein, *New York Times,* 5 June 1996.

LSAT scores from Law School Admissions Council, Newtown, PA.

Graduate Record Exam results from *Trends and Profiles: Statistics about General Test Examinees by Sex and Ethnicity,* Merilee Grandy, *RR-94-1 and 2.* Princeton, N.J.: Educational Testing Service, 1994.

Greer, Germaine. *The Obstacle Race: The Fortunes of Women Painters and Their Work.* New York: Farrar, Straus and Giroux, 1979.

"Female Science," *Insight,* 20 February 1995.

Material on Colonel Hallums at West Point from Thomas E. Ricks, "Army at Odds: West Point Posting Becomes Minefield for Senior Officers," *Wall Street Journal,* 13 March 1997.

Donnelly, Elaine, "Will Combat Roles for Women Downgrade Military Readiness?" *Insight,* 8 May 1995.

Chapter Four *Colleges in the New Establishment*

de Tocqueville, Alexis. *Democracy in America,* Vol. I. Trans. Henry Reeves, rev. Frances Bowen. New York: Knopf, 1966.

Report on required college subjects from *The Dissolution of General Education: 1914–1993*. Princeton, N.J.: National Association of Scholars, 1996.

Material on Yale sophomore courses from *Light and Truth*, a student publication, New Haven, Winter 1995.

Harvard requirements from *Introduction to the Core Curriculum: A Guide for Freshmen*. Cambridge, Mass.: Harvard University, 1996.

Material on Shakespeare from Innerst, Carol, "Colleges: Dost Thou Thumb Thine Nose at Shakespeare?" *Washington Times*, 29 December 1996.

Additional material, Honan, William H., "At Colleges, Sun Is Setting on Shakespeare," *New York Times*, 29 December 1996.

Statement on Columbia curriculum from Carbranes, Jose A., "Our Common Ground," *Wall Street Journal*, 9 June 1995, Op Ed.

Grade inflation background from Goldin, Davidson, "In Charge of Policy, and Heart, Colleges Join Against Inflated Grades," *New York Times*, 4 July 1995.

New SAT scoring system from *More Students Getting Top Scores on SAT I*. New York: The College Board, March 1995.

Material on electives from Honan, William H., "The Dry Yields to the Droll, the Prosaic to the Provocative in College Offerings," *New York Times*, 3 July 1996.

Stanford University course list from Sacks, David O., and Peter A. Thiel. *The Diversity Myth: "Multiculturalism" and the Policies of Intolerance at Stanford*. Oakland, Calif.: Independent Institute, 1995.

Controversy over Professor Bird from Mahler, Jonathan, "Jewish Studies: Part of the Canon," *New York Times*, 17 July 1996, Op Ed.

Comments by Professor Rita Simon from "The Consequences of Diversity," *Academic Questions,* Fall 1996. Vol. 9, no, 4, p 20.

Critique of Ivy League schools from Neusner, Jacob, "Cheers for No-Name U," *The American Enterprise*, September 1996.

Material on Williams College from Shalit, Wendy, "A Ladies Room of One's Own," *Commentary*, August 1995.

Racial and ethnic housing at Cornell from Hill, Mary Jo, "Do Theme Dorms Sanction Self-Segregation?" *Christian Science Monitor*, 15 July 1996.

Material on Michael Meyers from personal interview and ibid.

Curriculum statistics at State University of New York from *SUNY's Core Curriculum: The Failure to Set Consistent and High Academic Standards*, New York Association of Scholars and the Empire Foundation for Policy Research, July 1996.

Arthur Schlesinger quoted from Schlesinger, Arthur M. *The Disunity of America: Reflections on a Multicultural Society*. New York: W.W. Norton, 1992.

Quote by Michelle Easton from Easton, Michelle, "The Finishing School of the 90s," *Wall Street Journal*, 28 March 1996, Op Ed.

Comment on Hampshire College and Eurocentrism from Taylor, John, "Are You Politically Correct?" *New York*, 22 January 1991.

Material on Cynthia Wolf from Butterfield, Fox, "Suit Depicts Fight on MIT Faculty," *New York Times*, 5 May 1992.

Controversy over Judith Kleinfeld, University of Alaska, from Wulf, Steven, "Federal Guidelines for Censorship," *Academic Questions*, Spring 1995. Vol. 8, no. 2, p 58.

Comment by Robert Cole, quoted in Lubman, Sarah, "Campus Speech Codes," *Wall Street Journal*, 22 December 1993.

Material on *Vassar Spectator* and other college papers from Sowell, Thomas, "Unsung Heroes," *Forbes*, 6 January 1992.

Maryland law and theft of college paper from Garneau, George, "Censorship by Theft," *Editor and Publisher*, 24 December 1994.

Decision in Stanford "free speech" case from Superior Court, State of California, County of Santa Clara, Case No. 740309, *Robert J. Corry v. The Leland Stanford Junior University, et al.*

Anthony Lewis comment on free speech on campus from "Living in a Cocoon," *New York Times*, 27 November 1995, Op Ed.

University of California, Riverside, free speech case from Lubman, Sarah, "Campus Speech Codes," *Wall Street Journal*, 22 December 1993.

Chapter Five *Diversity, Multiculturalism, Bilingualism, and Other Myths*

Material on Yonkers schools from Berger, Joseph, "A Shared Victory," *New York Times*, 26 September 1996.

Statistics on earnings of African-American married couples from Holmes, Steven A., "Quality of Life Is Up for Many Blacks, Data Says," *New York Times*, 18 November 1996.

Failure of Chapter I program from personal interview with Department of Education personnel.

Ebonics background from Manning, Anita, "Schools to Recognize Black 'Ebonics,' " *USA Today*, 20 December 1996.

Further background from Holmes, Steven A., "Black Voice of the Streets Is Defended, and Criticized," *New York Times*, 30 December 1996.

Statistics on bilingual education from National Clearinghouse for Bilingual Education, Washington, D.C.

Background on New York bilingual program from "New York's Bilingual Bureaucracy Assailed as School Program Grows," *New York Times*, 4 January 1993.

New York City Board of Education, *Educational Progress of Students in Bilingual and ESL Programs: A Longitudinal Study, 1990–1994*, October 1994.

Spanish surname background: Newman, Maria, "Schools Are Likely to Stop Automatic English Testing," *New York Times*, 27 February 1996, and personal interview with bilingual officials at New York City Board of Education.

Proposed Action Plan for Bilingual Education in New York State, New York State Education Department, Office of Bilingual Education, September 1989, Albany, NY.

Details on lawsuit by Chinese community in San Francisco from personal interviews with school officials and the legal opinion of the Supreme Court, with references 414 U.S. 563 1974.

Additional material on Chinese class action suit from personal interviews with San Francisco city attorney and former bilingual official of the city.

Comment by Chief Justice on bilingual education from Supreme Court decision.

Background on "Lau Remedies" from *Ask NCBE*, no. 3, National Clearinghouse for Bilingual Education, Washington, D.C.

Information on use of foreign languages in civic affairs and schooling from U.S. English, Inc., Washington, D.C.

Chapter Six *Sexual Harassment*

Material on W. R. Grace from Henrique, Diana B., "Sexual Harassment and a Chief Executive," *New York Times*, 30 March 1995.

Background on IBM case from Holden, Benjamin, "IBM Set Back in Sexual Harassment Case," *Wall Street Journal*, 18 July 1995.

EEOC definitions from U.S. Equal Opportunity Employment Commission (EEOC), "Facts About Sexual Harassment," EEOC-FS/E-4 (Washington, D.C.: GPO, January 1994).

Sexual harassment statement from "Gruntal & Co. Incorporated Non-Harassment Policy," 1 November 1996.

Harris v. Forklift case: Greenhouse, Linda, "Court 9–0 Makes Sexual Harassment Easier to Prove," *New York Times*, 10 November 1993.

Also EEOC notice, EEOC, "Enforcement Guidelines on *Harris v. Forklift*," no. 92-1168 (Washington, D.C.: GPO, 8 March 1994).

Statement by R. Gaull Silberman from "After Harris, More Questions on Harassment," *Wall Street Journal*, 17 November 1993, Op Ed.

Material on man who sued female public official from several sources, including personal interview with attorney.

Domino Pizza case background from Associated Press, "Chain Must Pay Male Sex Harassment Victim," *New York Times*, 24 November 1995.

Jenny Craig counselors case from Colson, Margaret, "Female Chauvinist Pigs?" *Time*, 12 December 1994, and Peterson, Karen S., "Some Hope Move Will Sensitize Men," *USA Today*, 16 December 1994.

Talmud case from Hentoff, Nat, "Assaulted by the Talmud," *The Progressive*, August 1994.

Background on Professor Silva from various sources including Bernstein, Richard, "Harassed by Sexual Harassment," *New York Review of Books*, 13 January 1994.

Antioch sex code from Wolff, Jennifer, "Sex by the Rules," *Glamour*, May 1994.

Report on case of Allan Mandelstamm from Bauer, Henry H., "The Trivialization of Sexual Harassment," *Academic Questions*, Spring 1992. Vol. 2, no. 5, p 55.

Harvard University sexual harassment guidelines: "Memorandum to: Members of Harvard Law School Community. From: Dean Robert C. Clark," 25 October 1995.

University of Minnesota case reported in Gross, Barry R., "Salem in Minnesota," *Academic Questions*, Spring 1992. Vol 5, no 2, p 67.

Comment by Meg Greenfield from "Sexual Harasser?" *Newsweek*, 7 October 1996.

Quote by Anthony Lewis from "Time to Grow Up," *New York Times*, 14 October 1994.

Several background sources of sexual harassment involving children and students from Henry, Tamara, "More Kids Sue School over Peer Sex Harassment," *USA Today*, 1 October 1995; Savage, Daniel G., "School Officials Face Lawsuits If They Ignore Sex Harassment of Students," *Los Angeles Times*, 2 September 1996.

Information on mixing of sexes and sexual practice in the Army from personal interview with Pentagon spokesman.

Background on countersuits by men from Murraya, Kathleen, "A Backlash on Harassment Cases," *New York Times*, 18 September 1994.

Chapter Seven *Affirmative Action: The New Racism and Sexism*
Background on SBA affirmative action programs from Barrett, Paul A., "Legal Beat," *Wall Street Journal*, 13 June 1995.

Arnold O'Donnell Washington, D.C., case from Barrett, Paul A., "A White Man Is Ruled Eligible for Set-Asides," *Wall Street Journal*, 13 June 1995.

Figures on SBA "set-asides" from Holmes, Steven A., "U.S. Issues New Strict Tests for Affirmative Action Plans," *New York Times*, 29 June 1995.

Lynn Abernathy quote from "Between the Ideal and Reality," *US News & World Report*, 31 July 1995.

Author interview with Fire Chief Bob Grate of California on Forest Service affirmative action.

"Keeping Up" column by Seligman, Daniel, *Fortune*, 12 June 1995.

Material on Kingston, New York, student discipline from Rabkin, Jeremy, "Reagan's Secret Quotas," *New Republic*, 5 August 1985.

Conflict between minorities on affirmative action from Kirkpatrick, Melanie, "Not Black Enough for This Law School," *Wall Street Journal*, 11 January 1995, Op Ed.

Business Week quote, editorial, "Affirmative Action, Negative Outcome," 4 July 1994.

Pentagon affirmative action policy from Barrett, Paul M., "Foes of Affirmative Action Target Pentagon's Budget," *Wall Street Journal*, 2 May 1995.

Pentagon policy also from Holmes, Steven A., "Pentagon Seeks to End Preference Program," *New York Times*, 1 May 1995.

Comment by Mortimer B. Zuckerman from an editorial, "Remember the Real Victims," *US News & World Report*, 26 June 1995.

Statement by California State Senator Tom Campbell from Hanson, Gayle M. B., "Color Blind Initiative Makes Foes See Red," *Insight*, 20 February 1995.

Memphis Fire Department case from "A Right Turn on Race?" *Newsweek*, 25 June 1984.

Also, Drinan, Robert F., "Another Look at Affirmative Action," *America*, 9 February 1985.

Adarand decision from Greenhouse, Linda, "Justices, 5 to 4, Cast Doubt on U.S. Programs That Gave Preferences Based on Race," *New York Times*, 13 June 1995.

Adarand decision: "Affirmative Action—II," editorial in *Wall Street Journal*, 13 June 1995.

Comments by Justices O'Connor and Scalia on Adarand from National Weekly Edition, *Washington Times*, 19–25 June 1995.

Simon, Richard, "MTA Policy on Women, Minority Contracts Struck Down," *Los Angeles Times*, 2 August 1995.

Material on minority firms failing in California: Torres, Vicki, "A Door Slams," *Los Angeles Times*, 4 January 1996.

Dellinger, Walter, Assistant Attorney General, Office of Legal Counsel, U.S. Department of Justice, "Memorandum to the General Counsel, Re: Adarand," 28 June 1995.

Aftermath of Adarand from Holmes, Steven A., "Government Acts to Set Up Its Policy on Race Programs," *New York Times*, 29 June 1995.

Affirmative action points at the University of California from, "Black U.C. Regent Scores Liberal Racism," *Human Events*, 4 August 1995.

Material on admissions policies at the University of California from University of California, Office of the President, "Guidelines for Implementation of University Policy on Undergraduate Admission," 13 November 1996.

Minority medical students statistics from Association of American Medical Colleges, Division of Community and Minority Progress, *Minority Students in Medical Education: Facts and Figures IX*, Winter 1996. Washington, D.C.

Hopwood case from Phillipos, Jim, "Court Lets Hopwood Ruling Stand," *Austin American Statesman*, 2 July 1996; press releases, University of Texas, 19 March and 21 April 1996.

Byron Wiley quote from Honan, William H., "Organized Efforts Grow Nationally to End Affirmative Action," *New York Times*, 31 March 1996.

Department of Education warning from Applebome, Peter, "Texas Is Told to Keep Affirmative Action in Universities or Risk Losing Federal Aid," *New York Times*, 26 March 1997.

Chapter Eight *The New Immigration*
Statistic on immigration from various nations over several periods supplied by the Immigration and Naturalization Service (INS), Washington, D.C.

Postcard "lottery" information from INS.

Effect of illegal immigration on Texas employment, quoted in Lind, Michael, "Liberals Duck Immigration Debate," *New York Times*, 7 September 1995, Op Ed.

Downward pressure on wages from illegals from editorial, "Common Sense on Immigration," *New York Times*, 11 June 1995.

Citizenship of children born here of illegals from various sources, including: Schuck, Peter H., and Rogers M. Smith, *Citizenship Without Consent: Illegal Aliens in the American Polity*. New Haven: Yale University Press, 1985.

Text of HR 1363 regarding children of illegals from Representative Brian Bilray, and Lewis, Neil A., "Bill to End Automatic Citizenship for All Born in the U.S.," *New York Times*, 14 December 1995.

El Paso story: Brinkley, Joel, "A Rare Success at the Border Brought Scant Official Praise," *New York Times*, 14 September 1994.

Mount Kisko situation from Dugger, Celia W., "Immigrants and Suburbia Square Off," *New York Times*, 1 December 1996.

Information on federal court decision on Proposition 187 from personal interview with California Attorney General's Office.

Chapter Nine *Our Irresponsible, Irrepressible Courts*
Material on court intervention against Proposition 209 from various sources, including: Koch, Ed, "Judge's CCRI Ruling Was Wrong, But . . . ," *New York Post*, 3 January 1997.

Missouri v. Jenkins, "Farewell to the Old Order in the Supreme Court," *New York Times*, 2 July 1995.

Homeless court decision from "Removal of Homeless at Penn Station Is Halted," *New York Times*, 22 February 1995.

Judge Sarokin background from various sources, including: MacFarquhar, Neil, "Federal Judge to Resign, Citing Political Attacks," *New York Times*, 5 June 1996.

Material on gun-carrying student from Associated Press, "Court Overturns Suspension of Bronx Student with Gun," *New York Times*, 18 September 1996; and *New York Post*, 18 September 1996.

Comment on release of prisoners in Florida from Bacon, John, "Freedom Awaits Killers" *USA Today*, 26 November 1996.

Material on Judge Shapiro and Philadelphia situation from personal interviews with officials in Philadelphia District Attorney's office, and legal background from *Harris v. Reeves* 946 F. 2d 214 Third Circuit 1991.

Background on Judge Baer from Gest, Ted, "Disorder in the Courts?" *US News & World Report*, 12 February 1996.

Also, Van Natta Jr., Don, "Judge Finds Wit Tested by Criticism," *New York Times*, 7 February 1996.

Shotgun killing of parents in North Carolina from lead editorial, *Wall Street Journal*, 15 February 1996.

Rodney Hamrick from Leo, John, "Stupid Court Tricks," *US News & World Report*, 18 March 1996.

Judge and subway fare rise from Perez-Pina, Richard, "U.S. Judge Blocks 25¢ Fare Increase; Sees Possible Bias," *New York Times*, 9 September 1995.

Dao, James, "New York's Highest Court Rules Unmarried Couples Can Adopt," *New York Times*, 3 November 1995.

"Jury Finds Teen-Ager Insane in Killing of Parents," *New York Times*, 22 October 1995.

"Sleepwalk Defense Results in Acquittal," *New York Times*, 28 February 1995.

Material on Judge Barkett from Lipping, Thomas J., and Marianne E. Lombardi, "The Judicial Activism of Rosemary Barkett," *Washington Times*, 17 March 1994.

Same-sex marriage decision from Goldbert, Cary, "Gain for Same-Sex Parents," *New York Times*, 5 December 1996.

Tenth Amendment background from Greenhouse, Linda, "Blowing the Dust Off the Constitution that Was," *New York Times*, 28 May 1995.

Chapter Ten *Dogma in the Dominant Culture*

Wilson, August, "The Ground on Which I Stand," *American Theatre*, September 1996.

Lack of dramatic material on Broadway from Brustein, Robert, "End of Broadway's Run," *New York Times*, 8 April 1996, Op Ed.

Video art form from "Past Upstage Present at Venice Bienial," *New York Times*, 10 June 1996.

INDEX

Adarand case, 240–43
Affirmative action, 30–34, 65–66,
    214–15
    African-Americans and, 250–51
    arguments against, 251–52
    becoming legitimate, 220–28
    colleges and, 244–46
    Disadvantaged Business
        Enterprises and, 215–16
    ending, 252–53
    Federal Bureau of Investigation
        and, 226
    Federal Communications
        Commission and, 213
    federal government and, 216–28
    futuristic scenario concerning,
        232–33
    at Harvard Medical School, 73
    Hispanics and, 250–51
    judicial system on, 237–44,
        248–50
    law schools and, 247–50
    mentally disabled and, 236
    minority population and, 229–30
    past discrimination myths, 233–35
    Pentagon and, 230–31
    professional schools and, 246–50
    quotas, 216–28
    reforming, 252
    replacing, 253
    women and, 33–34, 250
African-Americans, 31–33, 152–56,
    254
    affirmative action's impact on,
        235, 250–51
    northern, 153–54
    southern, 154
Age Discrimination in Employment
    Act, 221
Air Force, women in, 103
American Civil Liberties Union, 276
American Cultural Revolution
    (1960s), 48–49
Americans With Disabilities Act of
    1990, 236
Anglo-American culture, 145–52
Artists, male vs. female, 95–96
Arts, state of, 310–14

Assimilation, 157–64
Association of American Medical
    Colleges (AAMC), 69,
    72–74, 246–47
    bulletin, 72

Bakke, Allan, affirmative action
    lawsuit, 238–39
Bilingual education, 29–30, 160–73
    reality of, 164
    solution to, 172–73
    see also English language
Bilray, Brian, citizenship legislation,
    273
Black English, 158–60
Brains, biological differences in male
    and female, 86–87
Bronx High School of Science,
    standardized tests, 74–75
Brown University:
    academic curriculum, 110
    grade inflation, 120

California, affirmative action's
    impact on, 228–29
Canady, Charles T., Equal
    Opportunity Act of 1997, 283
Carbranes, Jose A., on Western
    civilization education, 117–18
Cash and Non-Cash Benefits for People
    of Limited Income, 55–56
Chinese community, bilingual
    education and, 166–69
Chinese Cultural Revolution
    (1960s), 126
Citizenship, dual, 277
Citizenship Without Consent: Illegal
    Aliens in American Polity
    (Schuck), 271–72
City College of New York, 255
City University of New York
    (CUNY), 169
Civil Rights Act of 1964, Title VII,
    220–21, 222–23
    concerning sexual harassment,
    188
Civil Rights Act of 1991, 189, 221

Civil service grades, 220
Civil Service Reform Act, 220
Colleges:
    academic curriculum, 108–18,
    122–26
    affirmative action's impact on,
    244–46
    all-female, 98
    all-male, 98
    anti-Political Correctness at,
    135–43
    bilingual, 169
    elective courses, 122
    free community, 255–57
    free speech and, 140–41
    grade inflation, 118–21
    multiculturalism's impact on,
    133–36
    new segregation policies, 131–33
    Political Correctness' impact on,
    20–23, 122–23, 127–43
    sexual harassment in, 195–202
    special studies, 123–24
    Western culture prejudice in,
    124–26
    see also Professional schools;
    individual names
Columbia College, academic
    curriculum, 116–18
Compassion, 59–61
Congressional Research Service, on
    welfare, 55–56
Constitution of the United States:
    Fourteenth Amendment, 223, 272
    Tenth Amendment, 301–302
Conversion hysteria, 40–41
Cornell University:
    grade inflation, 119
    new segregation policies, 131–32
Court of Appeals, 299, 300
Cuadrado, Mary, on bilingual
    education, 160

Das Kapital (Marx), 54
Deconstruction, 25
Dellinger, Walter, on affirmative
    action programs, 243

Department of Education:
National History Standards, 36
Office of Civil Rights, 224
Department of Housing and Urban
Affairs (HUD), 23
Disadvantaged Business
Enterprises, 215–16
"The Dissolution of General
Education: 1914 to 1993,"
108–109
Diversity, 144–56
The Doctors (Gross), 71
Dominant Culture, 306–14
definition of, 307
media and, 310
Donnelly, Elaine, on women in
military, 104

Ebonics. *See* Black English
Education, 157–58, 253–57
Education Act, Title IX, 202
Educational system:
affirmative action's impact on, 224
developmental psychology training
in, 52
social control of children in,
202–205
standardized tests, 73–75, 81–87,
89–90, 94–95, 121–22
see also Colleges; Professional
schools
Educational Testing Service, 84–85
SATs gender-neutral questions,
82
Egalitarianism, 63–66
English Empowerment Act of 1996,
171
English language, 158–64
judicial decisions concerning, 292
movement concerning, 169–73
Political Correctness' impact on,
24–25
English Only movement, 169–73
Equal Employment Opportunity
Commission (EEOC),
184–87, 221–23, 225–26,
235–37

Equal Opportunity Act of 1997, 283
Equal Opportunity/Affirmative
Action (EO/AA), 198–202

FAIR (Federation of Americans for
Immigration Reform), 265
FairTest, 84–85
Family values, 294–95
Federal Aviation Administration,
diversity training, 194
Federal Bureau of Investigation,
affirmative action's impact
on, 226
Federal Communications
Commission, affirmative
action's impact on, 212–13
Federal district courts, 300
Federal government:
Adarand decision and, 243–44
involvement in campus Political
Correctness, 136–37
Political Correctness' impact on,
23
quota system, 217–28
social control of schoolchildren,
202–205
*Firefighters Local Union No. 1784 v.
Carl W. Stotts*, 237–38
Flexner Report, 70
Fourteenth Amendment, 223, 272
Free speech, in colleges, 140
Freud, Sigmund, 40–47
Freudian psychology, 309
Freudian theory, 40–53
denial of personal responsibility,
49–50
victimization, 49–50
Fronting, 231

Gender Equity Act of 1993, 83–84
Georgetown University, academic
curriculum, 116
Good Society, 62, 63
Goodman, Mark, on freedom of the
press, 139–40

Graduate Record Examination
organization (GRE), study,
94–95
Greer, Germaine, on artists, 95–96
Gregor, William J., on women in
military, 104
Gruntal & Company, 186–88
Guilt, 60–61

Hallums, James, at West Point, 102
Harris v. Forklift, 189–90
Harvard Law School, "Sexual
Harassment Guidelines"
document, 199–200
Harvard Medical School, affirmative
action's impact on, 73
Harvard University:
academic curriculum, 113–15
grade inflation, 119–20
Henderson, Thelton E., Proposition
209 and, 282
Hispanics, 155–56, 164–65, 254
affirmative action's impact on,
250–51
statistics concerning, 165
Hopwood Case, 248–50
Hostos Community College, 169

The Id and the Ego (Freud), 45
The Illegal Immigration Reform &
Immigrant Responsibility Act
of 1996, 278–79
Immigrants, illegal:
children of, 270–74
crime and, 268
Mexican, 276–77
reasons for rise in, 268
social services and, 267–68
solutions concerning, 278–80
Immigration:
drawbacks concerning excessive,
266–68
ethnic shift in, 262–66
European, 146–49, 258–61
fears concerning, 262
illegal, 267–80
Irish, 148–49

Italian, 150
Jewish, 149–50
lottery, 261
past discrimination myths
concerning, 234–35
statistics concerning, 260
Third World, 260
Immigration Act of 1990, 265–66
Immigration and Nationality Act of
1965, 261, 264–65
Infantile sexuality, 42–44
IQ tests, 86–87, 95

Jesus, as prophet, 59
John F. Kennedy High School,
Bronx, New York, 256
Judicial system, 16–18
on affirmative action, 237–43,
249–50
Court of Appeals, 299–300
on English as official language,
292
family values and, 294–95
Federal district courts, 300
federal judges' length of tenure,
302–304
federal level of, 284–86, 299–301
on homosexuals in military, 297
insanity defense and, 296
power of, 299
prison release programs, 288–90
reform, 300–304
ridiculous decisions made by, 293
on same-sex marriages, 298–99
social individualization and, 286
state and local levels of, 287–89,
300
Supreme Court, 299–300
technicalities used by, 290–91
on term limits, 292–93

Kleinfeld, Judith, on Native
American students, 136–37

Lau v. Nichols, 166–69
Law School Admission Council, 90

Law School Admission Test
(LSAT), 89–90
Law schools:
affirmative action's impact on,
247–50
Socratic method of instruction,
91–92, 93
Legal profession, women in, 89–93
Lentz, Thomas, on academic
failure, 77
Levitoff v. Secretary of Agriculture,
219
Light and Truth (Yale student
publication), academic
curriculum article, 112

Majority Culture, 306, 307
Marriage:
assault on, 157
same-sex, 298
Marx, Karl, 53–54
Marxism, 54–59
middle-class and, 57–59
the poor and, 55–57
Math, male superiority in, 94,
309–10
MCAT scores, 72–74
Media:
Dominant Culture and, 310
English language and, 25
Political Correctness and, 24
Medical profession:
fields most women doctors enter,
79–81
surgery, 80–81
women in, 68–81
Medical schools:
academic failure in, 77–78
affirmative action's impact on,
246–47
Men:
superiority in math and science,
94, 309–10
white, 26–27
Meritor Savings Bank v. Vinson, 189
Metropolitan Transportation
Authority, 242

Mexican-American Legal Defense
and Education Fund, 276
Middle class, 307, 308
Marxism and, 57–59
Military, 308
homosexuals in, 297
pregnancy in, 207–208
sexual harassment in, 205–10
women in, 5–8, 98–105
Minorities, 25–29
discrimination against, 28–29
Missouri v. Jenkins, 285
Mount Kisco, New York, Hispanic
immigrants in, 274–75
Multiculturalism, 37, 144–56
impact on colleges, 133–35

National Association for Law
Placement, 90
National Association of Scholars
(NAS), study, 108–109
National Merit Scholarship exam,
84–85
Native Americans, 272
Navy, women in, 103
Neusner, Jacob, on Ivy League
schools, 127
New Establishment, 1–3
affirmative action programs,
30–34
African-Americans and, 31–33
bias against Western civilization,
36–37
bilingualism concepts, 29–30
colleges and, 107–43
as cult, 18–19
Freudian theory and, 40–53
impact on male-female relations,
34
judicial system, 16–18
Marxism and, 54–59
membership, 13
military and, 5–8
minorities and, 25–29
multibillion-dollar foundations
support of, 37
Political Correctness, 20–25

New Establishment (*cont.*)
power of, 16
prophet Jesus and, 59
public school system and, 52
racial discord and, 31
revisionism and, 35–37
sexism and, 31
sexual harassment and, 34
social and cultural impact of, 8–11
social individualization, 15–16
spiritual base, 39–67
theory that sustains, 14–15
"What if?" game, 66–67
white males and, 26–27
women and, 26, 33–34, 68–106
New McCarthyism, 135
New York University Law School, 92
New York v. United States of America, 302
North Carolina Corrections Department, affirmative action's impact on, 225–26

The Obstacle Race: The Fortunes of Women Painters and Their Work (Greer), 96
O'Connor, Sandra Day:
on quotas, 239–40
on racial politics, 241
on states' powers, 292, 302
O'Donnell, Arnold, on SBA set-aside program, 217
Oedipus complex, 46
Office of Civil Rights of the Department of Education, 224
Official Scrabble Player's Dictionary, 24–25
Old Establishment, 11–13

Peay, J. H. Binford, III, on women in military, 104
Pentagon, affirmative action's impact on, 230–31
Perfect Society, 62–63

Pfaelzer, Marianne, on Proposition 187, 276
Political Correctness, 2, 20–25
fight against campus, 135–43
impact on colleges, 20–23, 122–23, 127–43
impact on English language, 24–25
thesis, 20
Powell, Lewis, on affirmative action, 224–25
Preliminary Scholastic Assessment Tests. *See* PSATs
Princeton University:
academic curriculum, 115
grade inflation, 119
Prison release programs, 288–90
Professional schools, affirmative action's impact on, 246–50
Proportionalism. *See* Quotas
Proposition 140, 293
Proposition 187, 275–76, 283
Proposition 209, 240, 281–83
PSATs, 83
Psychoanalysis, 40–41

Quotas, 216–28

Racism, 31
Reverse discrimination, 214, 224–25
Revisionism, 35–37
Reyes, Silvestre, border patrol technique, 269–70

Sarokin, H. Lee, on social individualization, 286
SATs, 81–83, 121–22
gender-neutral questions, 82
Schizophrenia, 47
Scholastic Assessment Tests. *See* SATs
Schroeder, Pat, on women in military, 99–100
Schuck, Peter, on children of illegal immigrants, 271–72
Science, male superiority in, 94, 309–10

Scientists, women, 96–97
Segregation, college, 131–33
Seligman, Daniel, on affirmative
    action, 227–28
Sexism, 31
Sexual harassment, 34
    in colleges, 195–202
    definition of, 176–77
    EEOC and, 184–87
    grade school, 202
    law, 177–79, 188–95
    media headlines concerning,
        182–84
    men vs. women, 193–94
    in military, 205–10
    regulating, 210–11
    same-sex, 191–93, 195
Shalit, Wendy, *Commentary* article,
    127–29
Shaywitz, Sally and Bennett, on
    male and female brains, 87
Simon, Rita J., on diversity, 125–26
Slavery, 60–61
Small Business Administration set-
    aside program, 215–17
Smithsonian Institution, revisionism
    and, 35–36
Social individualization, 286
    system of, 15–16
Social Text, 25
Socratic method of instruction, law
    school, 91–92, 93
Standardized tests, 74–75
    IQ, 86–87
    Law School Admission Test
        (LSAT), 89–90
    male vs. female scores on, 94–95
    MCATs, 72–74
    National Merit Scholarship exam,
        84–85
    PSATs, 83
    SATs, 81–83, 121–22
Stanford University:
    fight against Political Correctness
        at, 142–43
    grade inflation, 119
    new segregation policies, 132

Western Culture course, 124–25
State University of New York
    (SUNY), multiculturalism's
    impact on, 133–35
Studies of Hysteria (Freud), 41
Stuyvesant High School,
    standardized tests, 74–75
Supreme Court, 299–300

Tenth Amendment, 301–302
Theater, 311–13
Therapeutic Society, 51–53

Under-representation, 64–65
U.S. English, Inc., 170–71
U.S. Forest Service, affirmative
    action's impact on, 218–19
U.S. Labor Department, 219
United States Medical Licensing
    Examination (USLME),
    77–78
United States v. Wong Kim Ark,
    273
Universities. *See* Colleges;
    individual names
University of California system,
    affirmative minority
    admissions systems, 245–46
University of Pennsylvania, new
    segregation policies, 132–33
University of Texas Law School,
    affirmative action's impact
    on, 247–50
URM (Under-Represented Minority
    students), 247

Victimization, 49–50

Wechsler, James, Freudian theory
    experience, 47
Welfare, 55–57, 157
    illegal immigrants and, 267–68
West Point, 98–103
Western civilization, bias against,
    36–37, 124–26
"What if?" game, 66–67

Women:
affirmative action's impact on,
33–34, 250
artists, 95–96
brains of, 86–87
equal achievement of, 88–89
failing in math and science,
309–10
in legal profession, 89–93
in medical profession, 68–81
in the military, 98–105
as minority, 26
New Establishment and, 68–106

past discrimination myths
concerning, 233–34
scientists, 96–97
"Women in U.S. Academic
Medicine, Statistics, 1995"
bulletin, 72
Women's revolution, 233–34
Works Progress Administration, 56

Yale University, academic
curriculum, 110, 111–13

Zuckerman, Mortimer B., editorial,
234–35

ABOUT THE AUTHOR

THE END OF SANITY is the ninth work of social criticism by author, editor, and educator Martin L. Gross.

Five of his books have been trenchant studies of government waste, corruption, and inefficiency. The first of these, *The Government Racket: Washington Waste from A to Z,* published in 1992, triggered a widespread debate on government spending and the need to reform. Mr. Gross has testified five times before the U.S. Congress, which has adopted many of his suggestions. His books have received widespread praise from both sides of the aisle and from the White House.

Three works in this series were *New York Times* bestsellers, including *The Government Racket,* which reached number three on the list; *A Call for Revolution;* and *The Tax Racket.*

His other nonfiction works include *The Brain Watchers, The Doctors,* and *The Psychological Society,* critiques of personality testing, medical care, and psychology and psychiatry, all of which aroused considerable controversy within the professions. Backed by academics in each field, these books resulted in considerable reform in training and practice.

He is the author of *Man of Destiny*, a work of political fiction also published by Avon Books.

Mr. Gross has appeared on numerous national television programs including "Larry King Live," "20/20," "Good Morning America," "Prime Time Live," and "CBS This Morning," as well as on the Fox News Network, CNN, PBS, and C-Span.

The former editor-in-chief of *Book Digest* magazine, he is an experienced Washington reporter and commentator, whose syndicated column, "The Social Critic," appeared in newspapers throughout the nation, from the *Los Angeles Times*, to the *Chicago Sun-Times* to *Newsday*.

Mr. Gross has served on the faculty of the New School for Social Research and was Adjunct Associate Professor of Social Science at New York University. He lives and works in Connecticut.